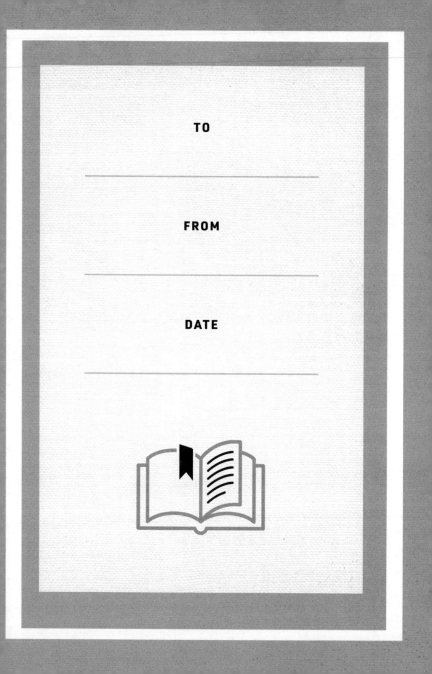

TO

_____

FROM

_____

DATE

_____

KNOW YOUR BIBLE

DEVOTIONS
FOR MEN

365
DAILY READINGS

INSPIRED BY THE 3-MILLION-COPY BESTSELLER

KNOW YOUR BIBLE

DEVOTIONS FOR MEN

TRACY M. SUMNER

BARBOUR
PUBLISHING

© 2022 by Barbour Publishing, Inc.

ISBN 978-1-63609-206-5

Adobe Digital Edition (.epub) 978-1-63609-403-8

Unless otherwise noted, scripture quotations are taken from the King James Version of the Bible.

Scripture quotations marked NIV are taken from the Holy Bible, New International Version®. NIV®. Copyright © 1973, 1978, 1984, 2011 by Biblica, Inc.™ Used by permission. All rights reserved worldwide.

Published by Barbour Publishing, Inc., 1810 Barbour Drive, Uhrichsville, Ohio 44683, www.barbourbooks.com

Our mission is to inspire the world with the life-changing message of the Bible.

ecpa Member of the Evangelical Christian Publishers Association

Printed in China.

KNOW YOUR BIBLE

DEVOTIONS FOR MEN

Through sixty-six separate books, 1,189 chapters, and hundreds of thousands of words, the Bible shares one extraordinary message: God loves you.

From the first chapter of Genesis, where God creates human beings, through the last chapter of Revelation, where God welcomes anyone to "take the water of life freely," the Bible proves God is intimately involved in, familiar with, and concerned about the lives of people. His amazing love is shown in the death of His Son, Jesus Christ, on the cross. That sacrifice for sin allows anyone to be right with God through simple faith in Jesus' work.

These truths are found in the pages of scripture. But sometimes, they can be obscured by the vast amount of information the Bible contains. That's why *Know Your Bible* was written. More than three million copies of that little book have been sold, and many readers have said how helpful they found its simple survey of God's Word.

Now, *Know Your Bible* has inspired this one-year devotional, a collection of 365 daily readings that focus on key scriptures in biblical order—from Genesis 1:1 to Revelation 22:21. Over the course of twelve months, you'll get a clearer perspective on what the Bible's big picture means to you. And if you're feeling ambitious, there's even a built-in reading plan to help you read through the Bible itself.

Every page of scripture contributes to the overall message of God's love and concern for people. . .for *you*. Your Bible is certainly worth knowing! We hope that, as you read your Bible and this devotional, you'll find that God's Word is truly life-changing.

~ The Editors

WHAT IS GENESIS ALL ABOUT?

The Bible's first book never explains God; it simply assumes His existence: "In the beginning, God created the heaven and the earth" (1:1). Chapters 1 and 2 describe how God created the universe and everything in it just by speaking: "God said. . .and it was so" (1:6–7, 9, 11, 14–15). Humans, however, received special handling, as "God formed man of the dust of the ground, and breathed into his nostrils the breath of life" (2:7), and woman was crafted from a rib of man.

Those first two people, Adam and Eve, lived in perfection until they ruined paradise by disobeying God at the urging of a "subtil" (crafty, 3:1) serpent. Sin threw humans into a moral freefall as the world's first child—Cain—murdered his brother Abel. People became so bad that God decided to flood the entire planet, saving only the righteous Noah, his family, and an ark (a large boat) full of animals. After the earth repopulated, God chose a man named Abram as patriarch of a specially blessed people, later called "Israel" after an alternative name of Abram's grandson Jacob. Genesis ends with Jacob's son Joseph, by a miraculous chain of events, ruling in Egypt. . .setting up the events of the following book of Exodus.

Genesis answers the greatest question we all have: "Where did I come from?" Knowing the answer—*God*—can give us meaning in a world that's otherwise hard to figure out.

Reading Plan: Genesis 1–3

HOW BAD IS SIN?

The LORD said unto Cain, Why art thou wroth? and why is thy countenance fallen? If thou doest well, shalt thou not be accepted? and if thou doest not well, sin lieth at the door.

GENESIS 4:6–7

To answer today's question, skim Genesis 4–6 and see how Adam and Eve's disobedience spun everything out of control. The Bible's early chapters show God ejecting the first couple from their garden paradise and warning their first son about his jealousy and anger. Cain was miffed that his younger brother Abel's animal offerings pleased God more than Cain's own fruits.

Cain ignored God. . .and killed his brother. It's worth noting that by humanity's second generation, sin had led to murder; only ten generations later, God flooded the earth because "the wickedness of man was great in the earth, and. . .every imagination of the thoughts of his heart was only evil continually" (6:5).

Sin—rebellion against God—has been humanity's dominant trait since the Fall. It's terribly destructive, both in this life and beyond, as it causes eternal separation from God.

However, a hint of good news appears in Genesis 3:15. As God condemned Satan for tempting Adam and Eve, God said a descendant of the woman would "bruise" (or crush) Satan's head, but Satan would bruise his opponent's heel. Eve's descendant is Jesus, who died on a cross to pay for sin—hers, yours, and everyone's—then rose again to defeat death for all time.

Sin is bad. But God is very, very good.

Reading Plan: Genesis 4:1–7:9

WHAT DID NOAH DO AFTER THE FLOOD?

And Noah builded an altar unto the Lord; and took of every clean beast,
and of every clean fowl, and offered burnt offerings on the altar.

GENESIS 8:20

Put yourself in Noah's place. You've been floating around in a huge wooden boat on what was probably very rough water. You've been cooped up with thousands of animals, and the air on the boat is anything but sweet. But now, after hundreds of days at sea, God brings the boat to land.

What would be the first thing you'd do once you step back onto dry ground? Build shelter for yourself and your family? Get busy planting crops? Build fences for your livestock? All are practical options, but Noah chose none of them. Instead, he began to worship God, building an altar and sacrificing to the Lord.

Genesis 6:9 (NIV) introduces Noah as "a righteous man, blameless among the people of his time, and he walked faithfully with God." And according to today's scripture verse, he was a man willing to express his gratitude for God's greatness and goodness to him.

Noah's sacrifice pleased God, as do the sacrifices we offer to Him today. But while Noah sacrificed animals, we can please God by offering ourselves: "Therefore, I urge you, brothers and sisters, in view of God's mercy, to offer your bodies as a living sacrifice, holy and pleasing to God—this is your true and proper worship" (Romans 12:1 NIV).

Reading Plan: Genesis 7:10–10:32

WHAT MAKES ABRAHAM SO IMPORTANT?

*Now the L*ORD *had said unto Abram, Get thee out of thy country,
and from thy kindred, and from thy father's house, unto a
land that I will shew thee. . . . So Abram departed, as the Lord
had spoken unto him; and Lot went with him: and Abram was
seventy and five years old when he departed out of Haran.*

GENESIS 12:1, 4

Christians hold up the patriarch Abraham (originally called Abram) as
a great of example of faith and obedience. . .and as the man God used
to establish the Hebrew nation and set in motion His plan to bring the
Messiah into the world. Abraham didn't fully understand it at the time,
but that's what God meant when He promised, "All peoples on earth will
be blessed through you" (Genesis 12:3 NIV).

Hebrews 11:8 (NIV) makes an interesting statement about Abraham's
obedience: "By faith Abraham, when called to go to a place he would
later receive as his inheritance, obeyed and went, even though he did
not know where he was going."

Abraham obeyed, *though he did not know where he was going.* What
an incredible demonstration of faith! He followed—not blindly but out
of complete faith in the God who called him. And because he obeyed,
he became one of the most important men in the Bible—an example
well worth following.

Reading Plan: Genesis 11–14

HOW DID ABRAM WAIT ON GOD?

*And Abram said, Lᴏʀᴅ God, what wilt thou give me, seeing I
go childless, and the steward of my house is this Eliezer of
Damascus? And Abram said, Behold, to me thou hast given
no seed: and, lo, one born in my house is mine heir.*

GENESIS 15:2–3

Abram remembered the promise God had made him before he'd departed
his homeland and begun his journey of faith: "I will make you into a
great nation, and I will bless you; I will make your name great, and you
will be a blessing" (Genesis 12:2 ɴɪᴠ).

Abram understood—or at least *thought* he understood—that this
promise meant God would give him children and descendants. Later,
however, he found himself asking God, "Where are the descendants you
promised me? Am I supposed to treat my servant Eliezer as my heir?
This isn't what You promised me, Lord!"

Abram had a passion for God's promise—and for the God who made
it. Now, having waited so long for the promise to become reality, Abram
complained to God and asked Him to renew and strengthen his faith.

If you have waited and waited for God to keep a specific promise, follow
Abram's example and express your frustration, your lack of patience, and
even your inward twinges of unbelief. Bring all those things to Him with
an honest heart, remembering that God still cares about your struggles
and will always keep His promises.

Reading Plan: Genesis 15–18

WHY DID GOD BLESS SARAH?

And the LORD visited Sarah as he had said, and the LORD did unto Sarah as he had spoken. For Sarah conceived, and bare Abraham a son in his old age, at the set time of which God had spoken to him.

GENESIS 21:1–2

Sarah, the wife of the patriarch Abraham, was hardly a picture of unshakable faith in God. In fact, when she heard that God had promised her and Abraham a son, she laughed. *That's preposterous!* she probably thought. *How can an eighty-nine-year-old woman and a ninety-nine-year-old man possibly have a baby?* (see Genesis 18:10–12).

Sarah doubted God because she focused on her circumstances. But that didn't stop God from keeping His promise. When Sarah gave birth to Isaac, she said, "God has brought me laughter, and everyone who hears about this will laugh with me" (21:6 NIV).

Despite Sarah's lack of faith, God kept His promise to make Abraham's descendants a blessing to the whole world. God may wait years to fulfill His promises, but His timing is always flawless. Although Abraham and Sarah were not perfect in their obedience or faith, God was perfectly faithful to His own word.

He still is today, even when we doubt.

Reading Plan: Genesis 19–21

WHY WOULD GOD COMMAND ABRAHAM TO KILL ISAAC?

And [God] said, Take now thy son, thine only son Isaac, whom thou lovest, and get thee into the land of Moriah; and offer him there for a burnt offering upon one of the mountains which I will tell thee of.

GENESIS 22:2

One day, God—the same God who had miraculously given Abraham a son and promised to bless the whole world through him—commanded Abraham to do the unthinkable: sacrifice his beloved Isaac on an altar.

Abraham had no way of knowing that God was testing his faith, but he obeyed anyway. He took Isaac to a place called Moriah, where he built an altar and prepared to take his son's life. But before Abraham could finish the sacrifice, an angel of the Lord stopped him. God then told Abraham:

> *"Because you have done this and have not withheld your son, your only son, I will surely bless you and make your descendants as numerous as the stars in the sky and as the sand on the seashore. . . . And through your offspring all nations on earth will be blessed, because you have obeyed me."* Genesis 22:16–18 NIV

Abraham knew that his son was a gift from God. He also believed God and trusted Him to keep His promises. At the last second, God came through.

In a most powerful way, Abraham set for us an example of obedience to God, even when His will doesn't seem to make sense. There will be many times when other options seem better. Obey God anyway.

Reading Plan: Genesis 22–24

DAY 8

WHY WOULD GOD BLESS A TERRIBLE PERSON LIKE JACOB?

*And Jacob said, Swear to me this day; and he sware unto him:
and he sold his birthright unto Jacob. Then Jacob gave Esau
bread and pottage of lentiles; and he did eat and drink, and rose
up, and went his way: thus Esau despised his birthright.*

GENESIS 25:33–34

Jacob, the son of Isaac and grandson of Abraham, wasn't a nice person—especially in his early years. His name means "deceiver," and it fits. He was a cheat and a liar who wronged Esau, his older brother, and his father by stealing his brother's birthright, effectively making himself—not Esau—the forefather of the nation of Israel (Genesis 27).

Jacob had some strengths, but his knack for dishonesty to get what he wanted was certainly not exemplary. Yet somehow, God blessed Jacob and made him a huge part of His plans to establish the nation of Israel and bless the entire world through his family and nation.

How can that be? we might wonder. *How could God use a terrible person for such important purposes?* God didn't bless Jacob because he deserved it: He blessed him because he was part of His plan. Later, Jacob acknowledged, "I am unworthy of all the kindness and faithfulness you have shown your servant" (32:10 NIV).

God doesn't bless or use any of us because of our own goodness. He uses us because we fit into His plans for His own glory and the good of others.

Reading Plan: Genesis 25–27

WHAT DOES "YOU REAP WHAT YOU SOW" MEAN?

And it came to pass, that in the morning, behold, it was Leah: and he said to Laban, What is this thou hast done unto me? did not I serve with thee for Rachel? wherefore then hast thou beguiled me?

GENESIS 29:25

After reading about how Jacob selfishly cheated his brother and deceived his father (Genesis 25–27), you might not feel much sympathy for him when you read how a man named Laban deceived him and practically stole seven years of his life.

Here's the story in a nutshell: Jacob had agreed to work seven years for Laban in exchange for the privilege of marrying Laban's daughter Rachel. But after the time was up, Laban deceived Jacob into taking Leah, Laban's other daughter.

Jacob the deceiver had been deceived. . .and he wasn't happy about it.

Jacob became a living example of this New Testament warning from the apostle Paul: "Do not be deceived: God cannot be mocked. A man reaps what he sows" (Galatians 6:7 NIV).

Jacob was wrong in deceiving his brother and father, but that didn't change God's plans for him or the nation of Israel. But it changed Jacob's path and brought God's hand of discipline upon him.

Our disobedient words and actions may not alter God's ultimate plan for us as His beloved children, but they lead us down paths He never intended.

Reading Plan: Genesis 28–29

HOW DID GOD RESPOND TO JACOB AND RACHEL'S FAITHLESSNESS?

And God remembered Rachel, and God hearkened to her, and opened her womb. And she conceived, and bare a son; and said, God hath taken away my reproach: and she called his name Joseph; and said, The Lord shall add to me another son.

GENESIS 30:22–24

One part of fallen human nature we Christian men often battle is the tendency to run ahead of God and try to fulfill His promises for Him.

Case in point: In the first half of Genesis 30, Jacob and Rachel refused to prayerfully and faithfully wait on God; instead, they essentially took His place and did what He had promised to do. . .but in their own way. After a heated exchange with her husband (verses 1–2), Rachel hatched a plan to have Jacob sleep with her servant and produce a "surrogate" child.

Despite Jacob and Rachel's faithlessness, God remained faithful and eventually gave them a son, Joseph. He did this not because of their goodness but because He still had a plan to work out.

The apostle Paul wrote, "If we are faithless, he remains faithful, for he cannot disown himself" (2 Timothy 2:13 NIV). Jacob and Rachel were indeed faithless when they went ahead of God. But God remained faithful in fulfilling the promise He'd made to Abraham many years before.

Just as God was faithful to them, He is faithful to us. When we are faithless, God keeps loving us and working to bring us back to Him and to His plans.

Reading Plan: Genesis 30–31

WHAT DOES JACOB'S CONTEST TEACH US ABOUT PRAYER?

And when he saw that he prevailed not against him, he touched the hollow of his thigh; and the hollow of Jacob's thigh was out of joint, as he wrestled with him. And he said, Let me go, for the day breaketh. And he said, I will not let thee go, except thou bless me.

GENESIS 32:25–26

Genesis 32 includes a strange but telling account of a painful wrestling match between Jacob. . .and God! It's odd (to say the least) to think of a mere man wrestling with God. Certainly, the almighty Creator of the universe could end the struggle in an instant. But our heavenly Father had a lesson to teach Jacob—and us.

God wanted to humble and bless Jacob, which is why He dislocated his hip. God also wanted Jacob to understand that prayer isn't always easy—that it involves persistent, sometimes painful, pleading with God until He answers.

If you've ever suffered a dislocated joint, you might partially understand what Jacob experienced that night. A dislocated toe or finger can be agonizing, but imagine the pain Jacob felt when God dislocated his hip!

Though nearly incapacitated, Jacob stubbornly held on to his God, setting an example for us all. Prayer hurts sometimes, but in the midst of our pain, we should keep praying and clinging to our God with everything we have.

Reading Plan: Genesis 32–34

WHY DID GOD GIVE JACOB A NEW NAME?

And God said unto him, Thy name is Jacob: thy name
shall not be called any more Jacob, but Israel shall
be thy name: and he called his name Israel.

GENESIS 35:10

When Jacob met alone with God in a place called Bethel, God blessed him (Genesis 35:9). But not only did God bless Jacob, He gave him a new name: Israel, which means "one who struggles with God." This wasn't the first time God told Jacob that his new name would be Israel. But this time, God not only gave Jacob his new name but made the same covenant He had made with Abraham (see Genesis 35:9–12).

Jacob's birth name means "deceiver," or "supplanter"—and he certainly lived up (or *down*) to it at times. He was a liar and deceiver who did his brother and father wrong. But now, after Jacob had confessed to God, "I am unworthy of all the kindness and faithfulness you have shown your servant" (32:10 NIV), God set him on a new path—with a new identity.

When you are saved through the work of Jesus, God gives you a new identity and calls you by new names. While you retain your given name, He also calls you beloved, blessed of the Lord, His child, a child of His kingdom, and many other descriptors of who you are in Jesus Christ. Each one expresses just how much He loves and values you.

Reading Plan: Genesis 35–36

HOW SHOULD WE RESPOND TO UNJUST TREATMENT?

*And his master saw that the L*ORD *was with him, and that the L*ORD *made all that he did to prosper in his hand. And Joseph found grace in his sight, and he served him: and he made him overseer over his house, and all that he had he put into his hand.*

GENESIS 39:3–4

Joseph was a man who endured the kind of mistreatment that would make most of us shout *Injustice!* at the top of our lungs. Yet Joseph— whose brothers sold him into slavery, who was falsely accused of rape and imprisoned in Egypt—never complained but instead continued to honor, serve, and obey God in word and deed. Not only that but he humbly served others through it all.

Joseph set an example of how to respond when we're treated wrongly. So did many of the Old Testament prophets, who were imprisoned, abused, and sometimes murdered for speaking the words God had given them to speak. And, of course, so did Jesus, who was beaten, humiliated, and killed horrifically—simply because He was fully committed to doing His Father's will.

So let's follow the example of Joseph and the prophets. Even better, let's follow the example of Jesus, who willingly suffered at the hands of men so that we could be made right with God.

Reading Plan: Genesis 37–39

HOW DID JOSEPH RISE ABOVE HIS TRIALS?

And Pharaoh said unto Joseph, I have dreamed a dream, and there is none that can interpret it: and I have heard say of thee, that thou canst understand a dream to interpret it. And Joseph answered Pharaoh, saying, It is not in me: God shall give Pharaoh an answer of peace.

GENESIS 41:15–16

When Joseph began his career as an important leader in Egypt, Pharoah (who many scholars believe was Sesostris III) showed great humility and wisdom by reaching out to Joseph for help no one else could provide.

The king of Egypt had had a strange and troubling dream that none of his men could explain. So he sent for Joseph, who had earned a reputation for interpreting dreams. Joseph told Pharaoh that his dream was God's warning about a coming famine. There would be seven years of abundant crops, followed by seven years of nearly none. But they could head off mass starvation, he said, by storing away one-fifth of their crops during the time of plenty so that they could feed the people during the time of famine.

Pharaoh was so impressed with Joseph's wisdom that he put him in charge over all the land of Egypt.

At this pivotal point in history, God used two men to save both the Egyptians and the Israelites: Joseph, to whom He had given understanding of Pharaoh's dream, and Pharaoh, to whom He had given the wisdom and humility to listen to a foreigner.

Reading Plan: Genesis 40–41

WHAT DO JOSEPH'S BROTHERS TEACH US ABOUT UNCONFESSED SIN?

And they said one to another, We are verily guilty concerning our brother, in that we saw the anguish of his soul, when he besought us, and we would not hear; therefore is this distress come upon us.

GENESIS 42:21

Around twenty years had passed between the day Joseph's brothers had sold him into slavery and the day ten of them traveled to Egypt to buy food during a harsh famine in Canaan. When they arrived, they met with Joseph, who by then was a high-ranking official in Egypt. Joseph's brothers didn't recognize him. . .but he recognized them. He had the authority to do to them whatever he pleased—including putting them to death.

Joseph spoke harshly to his brothers and imprisoned them for three days. Soon, they concluded that this mess was a punishment for what they had done to their brother.

There was no logical connection between their current situation and their action against Joseph, but a guilty conscience sees every trouble as sin's penalty. Reuben, who had opposed his brothers' treatment of Joseph, told them, "Didn't I tell you not to sin against the boy? But you wouldn't listen! Now we must give an accounting for his blood" (Genesis 42:22 NIV).

The story of Joseph's brothers shows that no matter how hard we may try to bury our sin in the back of our minds, we'll never truly remove our wrongdoing until we confess—to God and to those we've hurt—and seek forgiveness.

Reading Plan: Genesis 42–43

WHAT IMPORTANT EXAMPLE DID JOSEPH SET?

And Joseph said unto his brethren, Come near to me, I pray you. And they came near. And he said, I am Joseph your brother, whom ye sold into Egypt. Now therefore be not grieved, nor angry with yourselves, that ye sold me hither: for God did send me before you to preserve life.

GENESIS 45:4–5

When other people bring unfair personal loss or conflict upon you, it can be difficult—maybe impossible—to see the purpose and forgive them. These kinds of situations may leave you asking, *How can I move on?*

Joseph suffered extraordinarily unjust treatment at the hands of his brothers. But his final response can provide helpful wisdom for when we're mistreated. Instead of berating his brothers or holding his misery against them, he looked past his suffering and saw God working behind the scenes to save the lives of millions, including his own family.

Romans 8:28 (NIV) says, "And we know that in all things God works for the good of those who love him, who have been called according to his purpose." God did that in Joseph's life, and He can do it in yours.

Reading Plan: Genesis 44–45

WHAT IMPORTANT EXAMPLE DID THE ELDERLY JACOB SET?

And he said, I am God, the God of thy father: fear not to go down into Egypt; for I will there make of thee a great nation: I will go down with thee into Egypt; and I will also surely bring thee up again: and Joseph shall put his hand upon thine eyes.

GENESIS 46:3–4

As a terrible famine ravaged the land, Israel (formerly Jacob) left Canaan, the promised land, to escape certain starvation. Today's passage suggests that he felt fear and trepidation about going to Egypt. *What about the promises God made about the promised land?* he may have wondered.

But God did what He always does for His committed followers: He reassured Jacob, telling him that He would still make Israel a great nation—it would just be in the land of Egypt for now. Even better, God promised that He would—in the fairly distant future—bring His people back.

What would you do if you started pursuing a life path you *knew* was God's will, but then circumstances forced you onto a different one? Would you respond in fear and doubt, or would you go straight to your loving heavenly Father for encouragement and reassurance?

Jacob chose the latter option. . .and so should you.

Reading Plan: Genesis 46–48

WHY DO BAD THINGS HAPPEN TO GOOD PEOPLE?

But as for you, ye thought evil against me; but God meant it unto good, to bring to pass, as it is this day, to save much people alive. Now therefore fear ye not: I will nourish you, and your little ones. And he comforted them, and spake kindly unto them.

GENESIS 50:20–21

The levels of injustice that Joseph endured would break most men. First, his brothers tossed him into a dry well and sold him into slavery in Egypt. Then, while serving as Potiphar's servant, he was imprisoned under the false accusation of attempting to rape Potiphar's wife.

Though he was treated wrongly, Joseph remained faithful to God. Eventually, these events led to an opportunity to save his own family from starvation—and to keep Jesus' family tree growing.

Joseph's story illustrates a crucial truth for Christians today: God sometimes allows His people to suffer trials and unfair treatment as part of His plan to achieve great things in their lives.

Jesus endured that same kind of treatment when He was arrested, unjustly tried, beaten nearly to death, and then crucified. He did nothing to deserve such horrible abuse, but He did it to save us all from eternal death.

Reading Plan: Genesis 49–50

WHAT IS EXODUS ALL ABOUT?

The Israelites prospered in Egypt, having settled there at the invitation of Abraham's great-grandson Joseph, who entered the country as a slave and rose to second in command. But after Joseph died, a new pharaoh saw the burgeoning family as a threat—and made the people his slaves. God heard the Israelites' groaning, remembering "his covenant with Abraham, with Isaac, and with Jacob" (2:24) and raising up Moses as their deliverer. God spoke through a burning bush, and Moses reluctantly agreed to demand the Israelites' release from Pharaoh.

To break Pharaoh's will, God sent ten plagues on Egypt, ending with the death of every firstborn child—except those of the Israelites. They put sacrificial blood on their doorposts, causing the Lord to "pass over" (12:13) their homes. Pharaoh finally allowed the Israelites to leave the country (the "Exodus"), and God parted the Red Sea for the people, who were being pursued by Egyptian soldiers after Pharaoh's change of mind.

At Mount Sinai, God delivered the Ten Commandments, rules for worship, and laws to change the family into a nation. When Moses delayed on the mountain, the people began worshipping a golden calf, bringing a plague on themselves. Moses returned to restore order, and Exodus ends with the people continuing their journey to the "promised land" of Canaan, following God's "pillar of cloud" by day and "pillar of fire" by night.

The story of redemption is on clear display in Exodus as God rescues His people from their life of slavery. In the same way, Jesus breaks our bonds of sin (Hebrews 2:14–15).

Reading Plan: Exodus 1–3

WHAT SHOULD I DO WHEN I DON'T FEEL QUALIFIED?

*And Moses said unto the L*ORD*, O my L*ORD*, I am not eloquent,
neither heretofore, nor since thou hast spoken unto thy
servant: but I am slow of speech, and of a slow tongue.*

EXODUS 4:10

Moses clearly heard God's call for him to lead the Israelites out of Egyptian slavery, but he didn't believe he was the right man for the job. Moses offered five reasons (excuses, actually) for why he couldn't follow God's order:

I'm not good enough (Exodus 3:11)
I don't know who to say sent me (Exodus 3:13)
The people won't believe me (Exodus 4:1)
I'm not a good public speaker (Exodus 4:10)
Someone else must be more qualified (Exodus 4:13)

God became angry with Moses for all his excuses. But He wasn't about to let Moses off the hook. So God told him to take Aaron, his brother, with him to Egypt to help with the talking (Exodus 4:10–17).

When God calls you to do something, you may find yourself questioning your qualifications like Moses did. If so, be honest with the Lord about your concerns, but don't make excuses. Just keep listening and following wherever He leads.

Reading Plan: Exodus 4–6

WHAT SHOULD I DO WHEN I NEED HELP?

And the L<small>ORD</small> said unto Moses, See, I have made thee a god to Pharaoh: and Aaron thy brother shall be thy prophet. Thou shalt speak all that I command thee: and Aaron thy brother shall speak unto Pharaoh, that he send the children of Israel out of his land.

EXODUS 7:1–2

Imagine how Moses must have felt as he prepared to confront Pharoah, the king of Egypt and perhaps the most powerful man in the world. If we were in Moses' place, most of us would find our hearts pounding and our hands shaking. Following such a call would require every ounce of courage we could muster—and that probably still wouldn't be enough.

Moses felt inadequate for the job (to put it mildly), and he confessed his insecurities to God. So the Lord gave him his brother Aaron as his spokesman (or "prophet"). Over time, Moses assembled a whole group of men who shared a passion for his calling.

Do you feel like you need encouragement or assistance from a fellow Christian who shares your passion for a task God has called you to do? Maybe you need a whole *team* of encouragers and helpers to help you overcome your feelings of inadequacy.

Whatever you need, tell God about it and ask Him to send the right people to help you make your calling a reality. He will be happy to answer such a prayer.

Reading Plan: Exodus 7–9

WHY IS BLOOD SO IMPORTANT IN THE BIBLE?

And the blood shall be to you for a token upon the houses where ye are: and when I see the blood, I will pass over you, and the plague shall not be upon you to destroy you, when I smite the land of Egypt.

EXODUS 12:13

The Bible says a lot about the red stuff flowing through our bodies. In today's scripture, God prepared His people for the tenth and final plague on Egypt—the deaths of all firstborn children. All the Hebrew children whose parents had smeared blood atop their doors, God promised to spare and "pass over."

In the Old Testament, people had to shed the blood of a perfect animal as a sacrifice to God for their sins. Why is blood so important in the Bible? Hebrews 9:22 (NIV) gives a simple explanation: "Without the shedding of blood there is no forgiveness."

That was God's truth in Old Testament times, and it's true in New Testament times as well. The difference is that we no longer have to sacrifice animals to obtain God's forgiveness. Jesus shed His own blood, making the old sacrificial system obsolete. Now, as the apostle Paul wrote, "we have now been justified by his blood" (Romans 5:9 NIV).

God wants so much to forgive our sins that He gave His one and only Son as the perfect blood sacrifice. Be sure you accept that gift by simple faith.

Reading Plan: Exodus 10–12

HOW COULD ISRAEL ESCAPE THE POWERFUL EGYPTIANS?

Moses said unto the people, Fear ye not, stand still, and see the salvation of the Lord, which he will shew to you to day: for the Egyptians whom ye have seen to day, ye shall see them again no more for ever.

EXODUS 14:13

The Hebrews left Egypt at Pharaoh's orders—God's tenth plague, the killing of the firstborn, finally convinced him to let the people go. But as they started their journey to the promised land, they suddenly found themselves facing another threat. The Bible says that after the Hebrews left Egypt, "The Lord hardened the heart of Pharaoh king of Egypt, so that he pursued the Israelites, who were marching out boldly" (Exodus 14:8 NIV). With all of Pharaoh's forces closing in, the Israelites became very frightened.

But God Himself stopped the threat. The Lord divided the waters of the Red Sea so that the Israelites could pass through. With all the Hebrews safe on dry ground, God caused the waters to rush back into place, drowning all of Pharaoh's men as they pursued the Israelites through the sea.

This account offers two important lessons about our God: First, He will never allow human opposition to thwart His plans. Second, God defends what's His, including His beloved people. We can take great comfort in both these truths.

Reading Plan: Exodus 13–15

WHAT CAN I LEARN FROM MOSES?

*And the people thirsted there for water; and the people murmured
against Moses, and said, Wherefore is this that thou hast brought us
up out of Egypt, to kill us and our children and our cattle with thirst?*

EXODUS 17:3

The people of Israel had traveled from the wilderness of Sin, and now
they were camped in a place called Rephidim. There, they realized they
had a serious problem: they had no water. Before long, their thirst led
to surliness, and they started to wonder if they, their children, and their
livestock would die of thirst in the wilderness.

The Israelites saw Moses as their undisputed leader, so they took
their needs to him. God—who had brought them out of Egypt, cleared a
path through the Red Sea, eliminated the Egyptian army, and provided
manna and quail for the Israelites to eat—had secured Moses' trust.
Now, he came to God with another need: water.

One of the keys to Moses' greatness as a leader is the fact that he
"cried out to the Lord" (Exodus 17:4 NIV). Moses—and God—knew that
the Israelites desperately needed divine aid. So Moses cried out to God,
who was ready and willing to miraculously meet His people's need that
day. Thousands of years later, God is ready and willing to meet your
needs too. Just cry out.

Reading Plan: Exodus 16–18

WHAT DO THE TEN COMMANDMENTS SAY TO US TODAY?

Honour thy father and thy mother: that thy days may be long upon the land which the Lord thy God giveth thee. Thou shalt not kill. Thou shalt not commit adultery. Thou shalt not steal. Thou shalt not bear false witness against thy neighbour. Thou shalt not covet.

EXODUS 20:12–17

God gave Moses the Ten Commandments on Mount Sinai while the Hebrews were in the Wilderness of Sinai. These commandments (Exodus 20:1–17) are ten laws for living.

While the first four commandments relate to people's relationship with God ("You shall have no other gods before me" and so on), the final six involve people's treatment of one another.

The fifth commandment tells God's people to honor and respect their parents, and the sixth tells us not to murder. The seventh warns against having sexual relations with people other than our own spouses, the eighth forbids taking things that don't belong to us, the ninth says not to lie about another person, and the tenth orders us not to covetously desire the possessions of others.

The final six of the Ten Commandments—as well as many other rules listed in the books of the law—show us how much God wants us to treat one another with love and respect. That's why the apostle Paul wrote, "For the entire law is fulfilled in keeping this one command: 'Love your neighbor as yourself'" (Galatians 5:14 NIV).

Reading Plan: Exodus 19–20

HOW DOES GOD WANT ME TO TREAT STRANGERS?

Thou shalt neither vex a stranger, nor oppress him:
for ye were strangers in the land of Egypt.

EXODUS 22:21

It's been suggested that the way a man treats a stranger tells a lot about his character. Most men treat their family and friends relatively well, but when it comes to those we don't know, many of us do well just to maintain a neutral attitude.

In today's scripture, God commanded the Israelites—and, by extension, us—to treat strangers with sympathy and compassion. Further, He reminded His people of their own centuries-long sojourn as strangers in Egypt. For that reason, God's command to "love your neighbor as yourself" (Leviticus 19:18 NIV) extended beyond Israel's borders.

Today's verse recalls Jesus' words to His followers: "So in everything, do to others what you would have them do to you, for this sums up the Law and the Prophets" (Matthew 7:12 NIV).

So, basically, always treat strangers the way *you* would want to be treated.

But how might you put the message of today's scripture into practice? The opportunities are endless: speak kind words to a stranger, stop and help someone who is broken down on the roadside, leave an extra-big tip to a waitperson. Ask God to show you ways to help a stranger today. He'll provide both ideas and opportunities.

Reading Plan: Exodus 21–23

WHY WERE GOD'S INSTRUCTIONS FOR THE TABERNACLE SO DETAILED?

And let them make me a sanctuary; that I may dwell among them.

EXODUS 25:8

In Exodus 25–31, God provided the Israelites with amazingly detailed instructions for the tabernacle—a temporary, portable place of worship that would one day be replaced by the temple in Jerusalem. The word *tabernacle* comes from a Hebrew word that means "dwelling place," and God intended for it to be a center of worship for the Israelites wherever they went.

God's instructions concerning the tabernacle were very thorough— even including the type of metal (bronze) that was to be used for the tent pegs!

While God's concern about such details might seem strange, Bible experts tell us that God wanted the Hebrews to understand how seriously He took worship. The people needed to worship God in the way *He* expected.

God still takes worship very seriously, but He no longer dwells in manmade buildings. Now, God lives inside His people in the person of the Holy Spirit. The apostle Paul put it this way:

Do you not know that your bodies are temples of the Holy Spirit, who is in you, whom you have received from God? You are not your own; you were bought at a price. Therefore honor God with your bodies.

1 CORINTHIANS 6:19–20 NIV

What an amazing privilege it is to have the one true God dwelling within us!

Reading Plan: Exodus 24–27

HOW DID GOD CHOOSE THE PRIESTS?

*And take thou unto thee Aaron thy brother, and his sons
with him, from among the children of Israel, that he may
minister unto me in the priest's office, even Aaron, Nadab
and Abihu, Eleazar and Ithamar, Aaron's sons.*

EXODUS 28:1

Today's scripture marks the official beginning of Israel's priesthood. It began with Aaron, Moses' older brother, and his sons. Aaron's descendants served as priests, working in the tabernacle during the Israelites' wilderness sojourn and in the temple after it was built in Jerusalem.

Aaron and his sons were the first priests for one reason: God chose them. Just as He chose Abraham and his descendants to establish the nation of Israel, and just as He chose Moses to lead the Israelites out of Egyptian captivity, He chose Aaron and his sons to serve as His priests. He didn't pick them by hosting a popularity contest or even by assessing their qualifications. He picked them simply because they were the men He wanted for the job.

Just as God chose Aaron, He has also chosen *you* to serve Him today. That is what the apostle Paul meant when he wrote, "For we are God's handiwork, created in Christ Jesus to do good works, which God prepared in advance for us to do" (Ephesians 2:10 NIV).

It's all right if you're unsure what you should be doing for God. Just spend some time with Him and ask what He's chosen you to do. Through scripture, Christian friends, your own feelings, or some other method, He will answer.

Reading Plan: Exodus 28–29

DAY 29

HOW SHOULD WE VIEW THE SABBATH TODAY?

*And the LORD spake unto Moses, saying, Speak thou also unto
the children of Israel, saying, Verily my sabbaths ye shall keep:
for it is a sign between me and you throughout your generations;
that ye may know that I am the LORD that doth sanctify you.*

EXODUS 31:12–13

When God revealed the Ten Commandments to the Israelites at Mount
Sinai, He told them, "Remember the Sabbath day by keeping it holy"
(Exodus 20:8 NIV). In today's passage, God reminded Moses to make sure
the Israelites kept the Sabbath by refraining from work on that day.

Because we as Christians live under the new covenant, we are not
restricted by the Sabbath laws. Paul affirmed this truth when the Holy
Spirit inspired him to write, "Therefore do not let anyone judge you by
what you eat or drink, or with regard to a religious festival, a New Moon
celebration or a Sabbath day. These are a shadow of the things that were
to come; the reality, however, is found in Christ" (Colossians 2:16–17 NIV).

Jesus once said, "The Sabbath was made for man, not man for the
Sabbath" (Mark 2:27 NIV). Clearly, there is still value in rest for God's
people. He doesn't want us working so hard and long that we become
burned out and useless.

So work—in your job and in your ministry—but don't forget to
rest regularly. And, by all means, spend some quiet time with your
heavenly Father.

Reading Plan: Exodus 30–31

WHY WOULD THE ISRAELITES REBEL AGAINST GOD?

And it came to pass, as soon as he came nigh unto the camp, that he saw the calf, and the dancing: and Moses' anger waxed hot, and he cast the tables out of his hands, and brake them beneath the mount. And he took the calf which they had made, and burnt it in the fire, and ground it to powder, and strawed it upon the water, and made the children of Israel drink of it.

EXODUS 32:19–20

God had miraculously brought the Israelites—His beloved, chosen people—out of slavery in Egypt and then performed countless miracles to meet their needs on the way to the promised land.

But then the people grew impatient—and they sinned terribly against their God.

As Moses spent weeks on Mount Sinai receiving God's laws, the people grew tired of waiting for their leader to return. So in a flagrant disregard for the first three commandments, they asked Aaron, Moses' brother, to build them a golden idol—just like ones they'd seen in Egypt. Aaron made the idol and an altar to place in front of it, and the Israelites made sacrifices (Exodus 32:1–6).

When Moses saw what was happening, he was furious with the people and his own brother. He prayed for the Israelites, but God still sent a deadly plague on them.

The Bible instructs God's people many times to "wait upon the Lord." The Israelites failed to do that, and it cost them dearly. May we never be like the Israelites at the foot of Mount Sinai.

Reading Plan: Exodus 32–33

WHY DID MOSES' FACE SHINE?

*And it came to pass, when Moses came down from mount
Sinai with the two tables of testimony in Moses' hand, when
he came down from the mount, that Moses wist not that
the skin of his face shone while he talked with him.*

EXODUS 34:29

When Moses discovered that the Israelites had been worshipping a pagan idol—one made by his own brother—he became so enraged that he threw down the tablets on which the Ten Commandments had been inscribed. They shattered. But God still wanted His people to have His commandments, so He instructed Moses to ascend Mount Sinai again, bringing along some replacement tablets.

Moses didn't realize it, but as he re-entered the camp, new tablets in hand, his face shone with God's glory. The brightness was so intense that Moses had to wear a veil because the people were afraid to come near him.

Moses had spent time alone with God, and the Lord's nature and character had noticeably rubbed off on him. The same thing happens to us when we prioritize building an intimate relationship with the Lord.

Spending regular time with God won't make your face shine like the sun. But it will change you. Your expression, your bearing, and your words will be different for the whole world to see. And don't you think this world could use some positive change?

Reading Plan: Exodus 34–35

WHAT DID THE ISRAELITES DO RIGHT?

*And they spake unto Moses, saying, The people bring much
more than enough for the service of the work, which the L*ORD
*commanded to make. And Moses gave commandment, and they
caused it to be proclaimed throughout the camp, saying, Let
neither man nor woman make any more work for the offering of
the sanctuary. So the people were restrained from bringing.*

EXODUS 36:5–6

Exodus 36–37 tells how the Israelites built the interior of the tabernacle,
the place where God's people would meet with God and worship Him until
the temple was later built in Jerusalem.

Moses had asked the people to contribute whatever they could to the
project. And they did—big time. In fact, they gave so much that the builders had to tell Moses, "The people bring much more than enough for the
service of the work, which the LORD commanded to make" (Exodus 36:5).

Picture the smile that must have crept over Moses' face! The tabernacle was apparently so important to the people that they had gone far
beyond their regular tithes, giving so much that Moses had to tell them
to stop. Can you imagine what God could do with the money if that same
spirit of generosity suddenly swept over Christian men today?

This sensation might start with you. Start by thinking about a
cause or a ministry that God has revealed to you. Then give. . .willingly
and generously.

Reading Plan: Exodus 36–38

HOW DOES GOD LEAD US TODAY?

For the cloud of the Lord was upon the tabernacle
by day, and fire was on it by night, in the sight of
all the house of Israel, throughout all their journeys.

EXODUS 40:38

Exodus 13:21–22 (NIV) gives us an extraordinary account of how God miraculously guided His people, the Israelites, after they had exited the land of Egypt: "By day the Lord went ahead of them in a pillar of cloud to guide them on their way and by night in a pillar of fire to give them light, so that they could travel by day or night. Neither the pillar of cloud by day nor the pillar of fire by night left its place in front of the people."

God's use of cloud and fire, which is also mentioned in today's scripture, was a visible sign of His dynamic, divine leadership. When the pillar of fire or cloud moved, the Israelites knew to follow; when it stopped, it was time for them to rest.

Today, God doesn't typically use pillars of fire or cloud. He has a much better way of leading His people: His written Word, the Bible, which He brings to life in us through His Holy Spirit.

To receive His guidance, just "trust in the Lord with all your heart and lean not on your own understanding; in all your ways submit to him, and he will make your paths straight" (Proverbs 3:5–6 NIV).

Reading Plan: Exodus 39–40

WHAT IS LEVITICUS ALL ABOUT?

Leviticus, meaning "about the Levites," describes how that family line should lead the Israelites in worship. The book provides ceremonial laws as opposed to the moral laws of Exodus, describing offerings to God, dietary restrictions, and purification rites. Special holy days—including the Sabbath, Passover, and Day of Atonement (Yom Kippur)—are commanded, so the people can be set apart (the meaning of the word *holy*) from the surrounding pagan nations. God commanded the Israelites, "Ye shall be holy; for I am holy" (11:44).

The family of Aaron, Moses' brother, was ordained as Israel's formal priesthood. They would oversee blood sacrifices for the people's sin; God told the Israelites, "The life of the flesh is in the blood. . .it is the blood that maketh an atonement for the soul" (17:11). The sacrifices described in this book are contrasted with Jesus' death on the cross by the writer of Hebrews: "Who needeth not daily, as those high priests, to offer up sacrifice. . .for this he did once, when he offered up himself" (7:27).

Leviticus lists several blessings for obedience and many more punishments for disobedience. Though we as Christians don't live under the rules of Leviticus, we still serve a holy God—and should treat Him as such.

Reading Plan: Leviticus 1–4

WHAT IS A SACRIFICE OF THANKSGIVING?

*And this is the law of the sacrifice of peace offerings, which he
shall offer unto the LORD. If he offer it for a thanksgiving, then
he shall offer with the sacrifice of thanksgiving unleavened
cakes mingled with oil, and unleavened wafers anointed
with oil, and cakes mingled with oil, of fine flour, fried.*

LEVITICUS 7:11–12

When we think of the Old Testament sacrificial system, our minds probably go first to the sacrifices priests made to atone for the people's sins. But today's passage describes a different kind—a sacrifice of thanksgiving.

The Israelites had many reasons to be thankful—their miraculous deliverance from Egyptian captivity, God's provision of food and water, safety in the wilderness, forgiveness for their sins, and many other examples of God's grace—so God wanted them to express gratitude.

As New Testament-era believers, we also have much to be thankful for, which is why the author of Hebrews wrote, "Through Jesus, therefore, let us continually offer to God a sacrifice of praise—the fruit of lips that openly profess his name" (13:15 NIV).

If we're not careful, God's continuous provision for us can start losing its wonder. When that happens, we might forget to be grateful for all He has done for us, most importantly providing salvation.

So today, why not jot down a list of things you are grateful for? Then tell God how thankful you are. Add to your list every day—and soon, voicing your gratitude will become second nature.

Reading Plan: Leviticus 5–7

HOW IMPORTANT WAS AARON'S CALL?

*And the Lord spake unto Moses, saying, Take Aaron and his
sons with him, and the garments, and the anointing oil, and
a bullock for the sin offering, and two rams, and a basket
of unleavened bread; and gather thou all the congregation
together unto the door of the tabernacle of the congregation.*

LEVITICUS 8:1–3

Like his brother Moses, Aaron received a very high calling from the Lord.
God chose Moses to lead His chosen people out of Egyptian bondage. The
Lord selected Aaron and his sons to serve as His priests over Israel—
with Aaron himself serving as high priest. This family was charged with
performing rituals and sacrifices on behalf of all Israelites.

Several passages in Leviticus specifically spell out the high priest's
solemn responsibilities. For instance, Aaron was the only one allowed to
enter the Most Holy Place and appear before the presence of God, who
had set Aaron apart for this holy calling.

The New Testament teaches that the church—all those people around
the world who truly follow Jesus Christ—is now God's "holy priesthood,
offering spiritual sacrifices acceptable to God through Jesus Christ"
(1 Peter 2:5 NIV) and His "chosen people, a royal priesthood, a holy nation,
God's special possession" (verse 9 NIV).

Like He did with Aaron, God has set you apart for His purpose and
will. This calling comes with amazing privileges. . .and responsibilities.

Reading Plan: Leviticus 8–10

WHY DID GOD GIVE SUCH SPECIFIC DIETARY LAWS?

This is the law of the beasts, and of the fowl, and of every living creature that moveth in the waters, and of every creature that creepeth upon the earth: To make a difference between the unclean and the clean, and between the beast that may be eaten and the beast that may not be eaten.

LEVITICUS 11:46–47

A lot of guys enjoy a good "surf and turf" meal—one that includes a well-prepared steak and a lobster.

For the Israelites living in Old Testament times, the "turf" part would have been fine, but the "surf" was forbidden. Why? He never explained, but in Leviticus 11, God told the Israelites which animals they could eat (clean) and which animals they could not (unclean). Crustaceans did not make the approved list.

Some believe that God enforced these dietary laws out of concern for His people's physical health. There may be some truth in this perspective, but in Leviticus 11:44 (NIV), God told the Israelites, "I am the LORD your God; consecrate yourselves and be holy, because I am holy." In other words, God gave His people laws about food (and other parts of life) because He wanted them to be different from the surrounding nations.

Today, God still calls on Christians to be "different," but that no longer pertains to the foods we eat. (When Jesus was on earth, He declared all foods "clean"—see Mark 7:19.) The Lord wants us to be different from the world in our speech, thoughts, and actions. In short, He wants us to be like Jesus!

Reading Plan: Leviticus 11–12

WHY WAS LEPROSY SO TROUBLING?

*And the LORD spake unto Moses and Aaron, saying, When a man shall
have in the skin of his flesh a rising, a scab, or bright spot, and it
be in the skin of his flesh like the plague of leprosy; then he shall be
brought unto Aaron the priest, or unto one of his sons the priests.*

LEVITICUS 13:1–2

Leviticus 13–14 deals with a terrible disease that affects the nerves, skin, eyes, and lining of the nose but has been virtually eradicated from the modern western world: leprosy.

In Old Testament times, Hebrews with leprosy had to follow very specific rules to be healed and cleansed—until then, they had to live apart from other Israelites.

Even in Jesus' day, people feared lepers. And Jewish religious leaders, who believed that leprosy was God's judgment on a person's sins, often went much further in their distance (and disdain) than the law of Moses required.

But Jesus, God's one and only Son, saw lepers much differently. To Him, they were among those people who desperately needed His healing touch—and needed to hear the Good News He came to deliver (see Matthew 8:1–4; Luke 17:11–19).

It's unlikely that we'll ever encounter a leper, but we'll certainly encounter people the rest of the world would rather avoid. When we do, let's love them the way Jesus loved when He healed those seemingly hopeless causes. Remember, *you* were hopeless before Jesus reached out to you.

Reading Plan: Leviticus 13:1–14:32

WHY DID GOD HAVE SO MANY RULES?

Thus shall ye separate the children of Israel from their uncleanness; that they die not in their uncleanness, when they defile my tabernacle that is among them.

LEVITICUS 15:31

If you're like most Bible-reading men, you probably look at some of rules God instituted in the law of Moses and wonder, *Why?*

Sometimes, God gave specific reasons for His laws. For example, near the end of Leviticus 15, God told the people that these ceremonial laws were to "separate the children of Israel from their uncleanness; that they die not in their uncleanness, when they defile my tabernacle that is among them."

If you ever find yourself wondering why God was so concerned with the Israelites' hygiene, consider this: God knows everything, and you don't. It's quite possible He has reasons for His commandments you're never going to understand. . .at least not on this side of heaven.

The entire Bible is permeated with encouragements for God's people to obey Him, even when we don't understand why.

God *always* knows what is best for us and for His kingdom. When we disobey, we set ourselves up for trouble because we don't understand God's reasons. But when we trust Him enough to obey His commands, even when they defy our understanding, we put ourselves in position to receive His best.

Reading Plan: Leviticus 14:33–15:33

WHAT IS THE DAY OF ATONEMENT?

And this shall be an everlasting statute unto you, to make
an atonement for the children of Israel for all their sins once
a year. And he did as the Lord commanded Moses.

LEVITICUS 16:34

The Day of Atonement (Yom Kippur), is the most important and serious of all the yearly Jewish feasts and festivals. The Israelites observed the Day of Atonement once a year. On that day, the high priest performed complicated rituals to *atone* (settle the differences between God and humans) for the people's sins.

Leviticus 16:1–34 describes the atonement ceremony. It involved two kid goats: one was sacrificed and the other was released into the wilderness, symbolically taking with it all the people's sins and impurities.

The New Testament teaches that the Day of Atonement's sacrifices—as well as all the other ones—were made obsolete under "a new covenant" between God and His people. This new covenant is God's promise and agreement with His people through Jesus, who "has died as a ransom to set them free from the sins committed under the first covenant" (Hebrews 9:15 NIV).

Today, we Christians can be grateful for a sacrifice far superior to any Old Testament offering or scapegoat. God Himself made that perfect sacrifice for us when He sent Jesus to the cross to die for our sins once and for all.

Reading Plan: Leviticus 16–17

IS "THE GOLDEN RULE" IN THE OLD TESTAMENT?

Thou shalt not hate thy brother in thine heart: thou shalt in any wise rebuke thy neighbour, and not suffer sin upon him. Thou shalt not avenge, nor bear any grudge against the children of thy people, but thou shalt love thy neighbour as thyself: I am the LORD.

LEVITICUS 19:17–18

Jesus put a New Testament spin on an Old Testament concept when He said, "So in everything, do to others what you would have them do to you, for this sums up the Law and the Prophets" (Matthew 7:12 NIV). You probably know this command by its famous nickname: the "Golden Rule."

Compare Jesus' words to today's scripture reading. Do you see how similar they are? God the Father wanted His people to love one another, and Jesus the Son wants us to do the same thing—by treating others as we would like to be treated.

Actions are important, but God also wanted His people to love others from their *hearts*, just as He wants today.

You don't have to spend a lot of time in this world to know that some people are just plain unlovable. That's why we must ask God to give us hearts that completely and unconditionally love all people. Never forget that our God is in the miracle business.

> **Reading Plan: Leviticus 18–20**

WHY DID SACRIFICIAL ANIMALS NEED TO BE PERFECT?

*Ye shall offer at your own will a male without blemish, of the beeves,
of the sheep, or of the goats. But whatsoever hath a blemish,
that shall ye not offer: for it shall not be acceptable for you.*

LEVITICUS 22:19–20

In Old Testament times, God required His people to sacrifice animals to "pay" for their sins. That's because "without the shedding of blood there is no forgiveness" (Hebrews 9:22 NIV). In today's scripture, God commanded His priests to sacrifice only flawless animals—the Lord deserved perfection, not just good or adequate things.

The Israelites had to repeat these animal sacrifices annually because the people kept sinning. But that all changed when Jesus—the totally innocent Lamb of God who was tempted like us but never sinned (Hebrews 4:15)—willingly gave up His life on a cross. As the apostle Paul said, "God made him who had no sin to be sin for us, so that in him we might become the righteousness of God" (2 Corinthians 5:21 NIV).

Jesus was God's perfect sacrificial lamb—He was perfect in His sinlessness, perfect in His mission and purpose, perfect in His obedience, perfect in His humility. . .perfect in every way.

Reading Plan: Leviticus 21–23

HOW IMPORTANT IS FAIRNESS TO GOD?

*And if thou sell ought unto thy neighbour, or buyest ought
of thy neighbour's hand, ye shall not oppress one another.*
LEVITICUS 25:14

The following story sounds like an urban legend, but it's true. A collector and restorer of classic cars found an ultra-rare vehicle listed for sale online. When he arrived at the sellers' home, he and an associate determined that in its present condition, the car had a value in excess of fifty thousand dollars. He decided he wanted to buy it, so he began negotiating the price.

The elderly couple selling the car didn't know the car's worth, so they told him they'd sell it to him for less than half its value. But then the collector's sense of fairness kicked in.

"I can't buy it from you for that price," the collector said. "It's worth far more than that. Would you take fifty thousand?"

Some might say this man didn't understand the concept of negotiation. But whether or not he knew today's verse, he exemplified God's command to "not oppress one other."

There's nothing wrong with looking for a good deal, but always make sure to treat people fairly when making a purchase or a sale. By doing so, you glorify God and show others what following Him truly looks like.

Reading Plan: Leviticus 24–25

DO MY ACTIONS HAVE CONSEQUENCES?

If ye walk in my statutes, and keep my commandments, and do them; then I will give you rain in due season, and the land shall yield her increase, and the trees of the field shall yield their fruit.

LEVITICUS 26:3–4

Every decision we make has consequences, whether negative or positive. We choose how we're going to respond to other people, to our circumstances, and to our God. . .and all those choices affect our lives and the lives of others.

The apostle Paul used farming—something most ancient people understood well—as a metaphor when he wrote, "A man reaps what he sows. Whoever sows to please their flesh, from the flesh will reap destruction; whoever sows to please the Spirit, from the Spirit will reap eternal life" (Galatians 6:7–8 NIV).

In other words, our attitudes, thoughts, and actions all have consequences.

At the end of Leviticus, God listed the many wonderful blessings that awaited the Israelites if they simply obeyed Him. Those were the good consequences. But He also listed punishments they would suffer if they disobeyed. Those are the bad consequences.

Today, God gives you the same choice He gave the ancient Israelites. If you choose to sow seeds of disobedience, you'll harvest destruction. But when you sow seeds of faith and obedience, you'll harvest God's very best.

Reading Plan: Leviticus 26–27

WHAT IS NUMBERS ALL ABOUT?

Numbers begins with a census—hence the book's name. Fourteen months after the Israelites escape Egypt, they numbered 603,550 men, not including the Levites. This mass of people, the newly formed nation of Israel, began a march of approximately two hundred miles to the "promised land" of Canaan—a journey that would take *decades* to complete.

The delay was God's punishment of the people, who complained about their food and water, rebelled against Moses, and hesitated to enter Canaan because of powerful people already living there. Even though God described Himself as "longsuffering, and of great mercy, forgiving iniquity and transgression" (Numbers 14:18), His patience ran out with the cantankerous Israelites. He decreed that this entire generation would die in the wilderness, leaving the promised land to a new generation of more obedient people.

Even Moses missed out on the promised land, his punishment for disobeying God by striking, rather than speaking to, a rock from which water would miraculously appear (Numbers 20:1–13).

God hates sin, and He punishes it. We as Christians can be thankful that Jesus took that punishment for us.

Reading Plan: Numbers 1–2

HOW DID THE LEVITES FORESHADOW THE CHURCH?

According to the commandment of the Lord they were
numbered by the hand of Moses, every one according to
his service, and according to his burden: thus were they
numbered of him, as the Lord commanded Moses.

NUMBERS 4:49

The Kohathites, Gershonites, and Merarites were Levite families who filled Israel's priestly roles. In Numbers 4, God assigned each of these families specific responsibilities for when it was time to move the tabernacle from one place to another.

The Kohathites cared for the items associated with the sanctuary (4:4–14), the Gershonites for the sanctuary decorations (4:24–26), and the Merarites for the structural items that made up the tent of meeting (4:29–33).

In a way, these families greatly resembled what the New Testament calls "the body of Christ," another name for the universal church. First Corinthians 12 says that God gives each believer certain gifts and that we all work together for the common good.

Like the Levite tribes, each of us has our own God-given assignments. . .and the supernatural ability to carry them out. How might God want you to serve Him in your local congregation?

Reading Plan: Numbers 3–4

WHAT DOES "SET APART" MEAN?

And the Lᴏʀᴅ spake unto Moses, saying, Speak unto the children of Israel, and say unto them, When either man or woman shall separate themselves to vow a vow of a Nazarite, to separate themselves unto the Lᴏʀᴅ. . .

NUMBERS 6:1–2

In the Bible, Nazirites were people who took a vow to set themselves apart to God so that He could use them for a special purpose—in fact, the word *Nazirite* literally means "set apart." Most Nazirite vows were for a limited time.

When a man took the Nazirite vow, he promised to avoid cutting his hair, consuming grape products (including wine), or touching dead bodies. For Nazirites, the length of their hair publicly demonstrated their dedication to God.

Jesus has set you as a believer aside for a special purpose, and He wants others to see that purpose in you. The apostle Paul summarized that purpose when he wrote, "For you know that we dealt with each of you as a father deals with his own children, encouraging, comforting and urging you to live lives worthy of God, who calls you into his kingdom and glory" (1 Thessalonians 2:11–12 ɴɪᴠ).

We Christian men are called to live differently than those who live by the world's values. For that reason, we should examine ourselves regularly, asking whether our lives demonstrate holiness and whether our conduct proves our dedication to God.

Reading Plan: Numbers 5–6

WHAT WAS GOD'S PURPOSE FOR THE TABERNACLE?

*And it came to pass on the day that Moses had fully set up
the tabernacle, and had anointed it, and sanctified it, and
all the instruments thereof, both the altar and all the vessels
thereof, and had anointed them, and sanctified them. . .*

NUMBERS 7:1

Numbers 7 describes the tabernacle's dedication ceremony. Each of Israel's twelve tribes offered to the Lord, and the festivities went on for twelve days, one tribe per day.

With the tabernacle completed and dedicated, Moses could meet and speak with God there: "When Moses entered the tent of meeting to speak with the LORD, he heard the voice speaking to him from between the two cherubim above the atonement cover on the ark of the covenant law. In this way the LORD spoke to him" (Numbers 7:89 NIV).

God commissioned the tabernacle's construction for one reason: He wanted to spend time with His chosen people. Similarly, God sent Jesus into the world so that He could restore fellowship with us Christians. Today, He welcomes us to come into His presence just so we can spend time with Him and He with us. But now we don't need any manmade structure—we can enjoy this fellowship at any time or place.

Reading Plan: Numbers 7

WHY SHOULD I SHARE MY FAITH WITH OTHERS?

And Moses said unto Hobab, the son of Raguel the Midianite, Moses' father in law, We are journeying unto the place of which the LORD said, I will give it you: come thou with us, and we will do thee good: for the LORD hath spoken good concerning Israel. . . . And it shall be, if thou go with us, yea, it shall be, that what goodness the LORD shall do unto us, the same will we do unto thee.

NUMBERS 10:29, 32

What do you think makes many Christian men reluctant to share the good news of salvation through Jesus Christ? Fear of rejection? Not wanting to seem pushy? Assuming people don't want to hear any "God talk"?

When God saved you, He set you on a new, better life path and irrevocably reserved a place for you in His eternal kingdom. That's why the apostle Peter wrote, "Always be prepared to give an answer to everyone who asks you to give the reason for the hope that you have" (1 Peter 3:15 NIV).

In today's passage, Moses invited his father-in-law, Hobab, to travel with the Israelites as they departed Sinai for the promised land. Hobab knew the wilderness well, making him a valuable asset to Moses. But Moses had something much better to offer Hobab: the good things God was giving the Israelites (Numbers 10:29).

God's promises for Israel were too good for Moses *not* to share. The same is true of God's continual work in us through His Son, Jesus Christ.

Reading Plan: Numbers 8–10

HOW DID GOD RESPOND TO MOSES' DISCOURAGEMENT?

And I will come down and talk with thee there: and I will take of the spirit which is upon thee, and will put it upon them; and they shall bear the burden of the people with thee, that thou bear it not thyself alone.

NUMBERS 11:17

As the Israelites departed from Sinai in Numbers 10, Moses their leader voiced great optimism. "Rise up, LORD!" he prayed. "May your enemies be scattered; may your foes flee before you" (verse 35 NIV). But in Numbers 11, the ingratitude of the people he had led out of Egypt brought Moses so low that he cried to God, "If this is how you are going to treat me, please go ahead and kill me—if I have found favor in your eyes—and do not let me face my own ruin" (Numbers 11:15 NIV).

These are the words of a man whose heart and mind have moved past discouragement and settled in outright depression.

God didn't respond to Moses with anger. Instead, He directed him to appoint seventy of Israel's elders to stand with him during this very difficult time. Also, the Lord promised Moses, "I will take of the spirit which is upon thee, and will put it upon them; and they shall bear the burden of the people with thee, that thou bear it not thyself alone."

God know everything about us, including our weaknesses and discouragement. And like He did with Moses, He'll send us the perfect help we need to complete the tasks He has assigned.

Reading Plan: Numbers 11–12

WHY DIDN'T THE ISRAELITES IMMEDIATELY ENTER THE PROMISED LAND?

*And wherefore hath the Lord brought us unto this land,
to fall by the sword, that our wives and our children should
be a prey? were it not better for us to return into Egypt?*

NUMBERS 14:3

As the Israelites gathered at the border of Canaan, the promised land, Moses sent spies—one from each of the twelve tribes—to explore the region (Numbers 13). The spies spent forty days there, surveying the land, its food, its cities' fortifications, and its residents.

Upon their return, all twelve spies agreed that the land was a beautiful place to grow their crops, make their homes, and raise their families. But ten focused on the challenges of taking the land—specifically the giants who lived there—and began spreading fear among the people.

All this led to a rebellion. The people complained to Moses—and to God—that trying to take the land would be a fool's errand. So God, angry at His people's lack of faith, barred these unbelieving people from taking the promised land for another forty years.

If the Israelites' failure can teach us anything, it's this: God keeps His promises, and the one thing that keeps us from receiving His blessing is unbelief.

Reading Plan: Numbers 13–14

WHY DID KORAH REBEL?

*And it came to pass, as he had made an end of speaking all these
words, that the ground clave asunder that was under them: and the
earth opened her mouth, and swallowed them up, and their houses,
and all the men that appertained unto Korah, and all their goods.*

NUMBERS 16:31–32

Have you ever felt a twinge of jealousy when God used another person?
Maybe you felt like you could've done the job better. Or maybe you envied
the way others admired or praised that person for something you knew
you could do just as easily.

That's how Korah felt toward Moses. As a Levite, Korah served in the
tabernacle, doing a crucial job with great responsibility. But because
he wasn't a priest, he didn't have the same connection to God as
the priests enjoyed. So instead of faithfully seeing to his God-given
responsibilities, Korah complained against Moses and Aaron—and
gathered men to his cause.

Numbers 16:3 (NIV) says, "They came as a group to oppose Moses and
Aaron and said to them, 'You have gone too far! The whole community
is holy, every one of them, and the LORD is with them. Why then do you
set yourselves above the LORD's assembly?'"

Korah allowed his jealousy to consume him. Because of that, he lost
out on serving God—and was consumed by the earth at God's command.

If God has given you a task, do your best. Don't look at how He's using
anyone else—that could lead you down a destructive path of jealousy.

Reading Plan: Numbers 15–16

WHAT DOES THE MIRACLE OF THE BUDDING STAFF MEAN?

And it came to pass, that on the morrow Moses went into the tabernacle of witness; and, behold, the rod of Aaron for the house of Levi was budded, and brought forth buds, and bloomed blossoms, and yielded almonds.

NUMBERS 17:8

After Korah's rebellion, God instructed Moses to have each tribe of Israel present a staff with the tribe's name on it. "The staff belonging to the man I choose will sprout," God said (Numbers 17:5 NIV).

Moses then placed each staff—including his brother Aaron's—in the tabernacle before the Lord that night. The next day, the Israelites saw a miraculous sign. Aaron's staff—a dead stick like all the others—had sprouted buds, flowers, and ripe almonds. For the tribes of Israel, the sign was clear: God would work through His priests, at least for the foreseeable future.

This even not only proved that God had chosen Aaron's family, the Levites, to serve as priests, it also foreshadowed of the future arrival of Jesus Christ, God's great High Priest who has "made us alive. . .even when we were dead in transgressions" (Ephesians 2:5 NIV).

God's causing a dead stick to come to life, sprout flowers, and bear ripe almonds was an amazing miracle. But His resuscitation of spiritually dead men is a far greater one.

Never forget to praise and thank Him for giving you new life!

Reading Plan: Numbers 17–19

WHAT WAS THE SIGNIFICANCE OF THE BRONZE SERPENT?

The LORD said unto Moses, Make thee a fiery serpent, and set it upon a pole: and it shall come to pass, that every one that is bitten, when he looketh upon it, shall live. And Moses made a serpent of brass, and put it upon a pole, and it came to pass, that if a serpent had bitten any man, when he beheld the serpent of brass, he lived.

NUMBERS 21:8–9

The Israelites, having taken their eyes off God, began complaining against Him and Moses. "Why have you brought us up out of Egypt to die in the wilderness?" they protested. "There is no bread! There is no water! And we detest this miserable food!" (Numbers 21:5 NIV).

In response to their complaints, God sent venomous snakes into their camp. As people started dying, the Israelites came to Moses expressing sorrow over their sin. So he prayed for them. In response, God told Moses to make a bronze snake and place it atop a long pole. Moses obeyed, and anyone who was bitten could look at the statue and be healed (Numbers 21:4–9).

Many centuries later, Jesus compared Himself to the bronze serpent: "Just as Moses lifted up the snake in the wilderness," He said, "so the Son of Man must be lifted up, that everyone who believes may have eternal life in him" (John 3:14–15 NIV).

Jesus was indeed "lifted up"—on a cross, dying a terrible, agonizing death and shedding His blood. Now, by our simple, humble faith in Him, we can be forgiven of sin and live. . .forever.

Reading Plan: Numbers 20–21

WHY DID BALAAM'S DONKEY SPEAK?

*And the L<small>ORD</small> opened the mouth of the ass, and she
said unto Balaam, What have I done unto thee,
that thou hast smitten me these three times?*

NUMBERS 22:28

This is the strange—and humorous—story of how God got Balaam's attention.

Balaam was a devious prophet who tried to betray Israelites (Numbers 22–24). When Balak, the king of Moab, wanted to hire Balaam to curse the Israelites, God warned Balaam. But Balaam pushed ahead, the next morning saddling his donkey and heading out to meet with Balak.

However, God stopped Balaam by sending an angel to stand in front of his donkey, stopping it in its tracks. As Balaam beat the poor animal, God gave the donkey the ability to talk (Numbers 22:28). Immediately, God opened Balaam's eyes to see the angel, and he reacted just as the donkey did—by bowing down and falling on his face.

The angel rebuked Balaam's cruel treatment toward the animal, telling him he would have killed Balaam if his donkey hadn't stopped. Balaam—feeling sorry for his disobedience but perhaps sorrier for getting caught—replied, "I have sinned. I did not realize you were standing in the road to oppose me. Now if you are displeased, I will go back" (Numbers 22:34 NIV). The angel told Balaam to speak to Balak only the words God would give him.

This episode would probably be funnier if it didn't seem so familiar. Talking donkey or not, people are often blinded by sin. Our job is to live like Jesus so that others can truly see.

Reading Plan: Numbers 22–24

WHATEVER HAPPENED TO KORAH'S DESCENDANTS?

And the earth opened her mouth, and swallowed them up
together with Korah, when that company died, what time the
fire devoured two hundred and fifty men: and they became
a sign. Notwithstanding the children of Korah died not.

NUMBERS 26:10–11

Numbers 16 gives the terrible account of God's judgment on Korah, Dathan, and Abiram—men who openly rebelled against God's appointed leadership. Because of their sin, God caused the earth to swallow them and their unfaithful families. Today's passage, however, says that many of Korah's people lived—simply because they did not follow Korah in his rebellion.

Though Korah paid for his sin with his life, God was gracious to his descendants, many of whom went on to serve the Lord as composers, musicians, singers, worship leaders, and prophets. In fact, these noble men wrote most of Psalms 42–49 and Psalms 84–88.

The children of Korah are an important example to those of us with fathers—and other family members—who did not serve the Lord. The consequences for one generation's disobedience don't have to seep into the next. In Jesus, we can start anew.

Reading Plan: Numbers 25–27

HOW IMPORTANT IS PROMISE-KEEPING TO GOD?

And Moses spake unto the heads of the tribes concerning the children of Israel, saying, This is the thing which the Lord hath commanded. If a man vow a vow unto the Lord, or swear an oath to bind his soul with a bond; he shall not break his word, he shall do according to all that proceedeth out of his mouth.

NUMBERS 30:1–2

Jesus stressed the importance of keeping our word—to God and to humans—when He said, "Do not swear by your head, for you cannot make even one hair white or black. All you need to say is simply 'Yes' or 'No'; anything beyond this comes from the evil one" (Matthew 5:36–37 NIV).

Today's passage, as well as many others in the Bible, strongly affirms this teaching.

As Christian men, we are called to reflect God in every area of our lives. Just as He always keeps His word, so should we: "God is not human, that he should lie, not a human being, that he should change his mind. Does he speak and then not act? Does he promise and not fulfill?" (Numbers 23:19 NIV).

Before you make a promise, carefully consider whether you're fully committed to keeping it. God forgives all sins—including promise-breaking—but there are consequences to our careless speech. Why hurt our family and friends, our testimony and Lord, by making promises we don't keep?

Reading Plan: Numbers 28–30

WHAT DOES "BE SURE YOUR SINS WILL FIND YOU OUT" MEAN?

*But if ye will not do so, behold, ye have sinned against
the LORD: and be sure your sin will find you out.*

NUMBERS 32:23

As the Israelites drew closer to the promised land, the tribes of Reuben and Gad saw an excellent opportunity for themselves just outside the border in the area south of the Sea of Galilee. This was a great area to raise their families, farm, and keep livestock. The two tribes wanted this land, so they approached Moses and made him an offer: if the men of Reuben and Gad led the Israelites in taking the promised land, they should then settle in the land they desired.

It was an audacious offer, but Moses accepted it. However, he also warned them that if they didn't hold up their end of the bargain, they would be sinning against God. . .and God would certainly see it and make them suffer the consequences.

We must remember two things about sin. First, you can never hide it from God. Moses himself wrote, "You have set our iniquities before you, our secret sins in the light of your presence" (Psalm 90:8 NIV). Second, sin—whether it's promise-breaking, sexual sin, or idolatry—always has consequences.

God takes all sins very seriously—and so should we.

Reading Plan: Numbers 31–32

WHAT DO WE HAVE IN COMMON WITH THE ISRAELITES?

*These are the journeys of the children of Israel, which went
forth out of the land of Egypt with their armies under the
hand of Moses and Aaron. And Moses wrote their goings out
according to their journeys by the commandment of the LORD:
and these are their journeys according to their goings out.*

NUMBERS 33:1–2

Imagine being forced to travel in a vast wilderness, stopping only to sleep in a tent each night before tearing down your gear the next day to continue the journey. Would you ever feel like you were *home*?

Numbers 33 summarizes the journey the Israelites took through the wilderness before they finally settled in Canaan, the promised land. There was a lot of camping and departing—four decades' worth! But none of these pit stops were "home" for the Israelites. That label belonged only to one place: Canaan.

The same is true for every Christian in history—including you. Though we live on earth, it's not our ultimate home. As the writer of Hebrews says: "For here we do not have an enduring city, but we are looking for the city that is to come" (13:14 NIV).

God has given you a life to live for Him, so you should be grateful for every day He provides. But always remember that your ultimate home is with Him, forever.

Reading Plan: Numbers 33–34

WHAT IS A CITY OF REFUGE?

*Speak unto the children of Israel, and say unto them, When
ye be come over Jordan into the land of Canaan; then ye shall
appoint you cities to be cities of refuge for you; that the slayer
may flee thither, which killeth any person at unawares.*

NUMBERS 35:10–11

When the Israelites entered the promised land, specific regions were
allotted to the various tribes—all except for the Levites, the ministers,
who received cities throughout all the tribes' areas. Then God instructed
Moses to set aside six of the forty-eight Levite cities as cities of refuge.
These were established so that a person who accidentally killed someone
could have a safe place to live until the case went to trial. The cities
of refuge were Kedesh, Shechem, Hebron, Bezer, Ramoth, and Golan
(Joshua 20:7–8).

These cities were a picture of God's graciousness and His deep
concern for those who had not intentionally committed a crime against
a fellow human being. But they were also representative of a believer's
refuge in God Himself.

Psalm 46:1 (NIV) says, "God is our refuge and strength, an ever-
present help in trouble," and Hebrews 6:18 (KJV) promises that we
"have a strong consolation, who have fled for refuge to lay hold upon
the hope set before us."

Jesus is our refuge, and we don't need to flee to any particular place
for His help. He's already with each of us, every minute of the day.

Reading Plan: Numbers 35–36

WHAT IS DEUTERONOMY ALL ABOUT?

With a name meaning "second law," Deuteronomy records Moses' final words as the Israelites prepared to enter the promised land.

Forty years had passed since God handed down His laws on Mount Sinai, and the entire generation that experienced that momentous event was dead. So as they readied their entry into Canaan, Moses reminded the new generation of their national history and the God they served: "Hear, O Israel: The Lord our God is one Lord" (Deuteronomy 6:4). "Thou shalt love the Lord thy God with all thine heart, and with all thy soul, and with all thy might" (6:5). "The Lord thy God is a jealous God among you" (6:15).

The invasion of Canaan would occur under Joshua, as Moses only saw the promised land from Mount Nebo. "So Moses the servant of the Lord died there. . . . And he [God] buried him in a valley in the land of Moab. . .but no man knoweth of his sepulchre unto this day" (34:5–6). Moses was 120 years old.

Deuteronomy makes clear that God's rules and expectations aren't meant to limit and frustrate us but instead to benefit us: "Hear therefore, O Israel, and observe to do it; that it may be well with thee, and that ye may increase mightily, as the Lord God of thy fathers hath promised thee, in the land that floweth with milk and honey" (6:3).

Reading Plan: Deuteronomy 1–2

HOW IMPORTANT IS REMEMBERING?

Only take heed to thyself, and keep thy soul diligently,
lest thou forget the things which thine eyes have seen,
and lest they depart from thy heart all the days of thy
life: but teach them thy sons, and thy sons' sons.

DEUTERONOMY 4:9

Have you ever spent time with your family looking at old scrapbooks, watching old vacation videos, or just talking about pleasant memories? These kinds of activities can make for a wonderful evening at home, and they can strengthen family bonds.

It's good to do the same thing with your Father in heaven. In several scripture passages (such as today's), God encouraged His people to remember the amazing things He'd done for them. He did that to encourage and challenge them to remember His goodness so that they would not be tempted to turn away from Him.

So take time to remember God's goodness to you. Think about the moment He saved you and adopted you into His eternal family—and how He's helped you grow into the man of God you are today. Remember the times He's given you wisdom and helped you out of a terrible jam. And consider those instances when He stunningly answered a prayer.

Doing these things can move you to grateful praise, strengthen your faith, and embolden you to share Him with others.

Reading Plan: Deuteronomy 3–4

WHAT IS THE MOST IMPORTANT COMMANDMENT?

*Hear, O Israel: The Lord our God is one Lord: And thou
shalt love the Lord thy God with all thine heart, and
with all thy soul, and with all thy might.*

DEUTERONOMY 6:4–5

During Jesus' earthly ministry, a Jewish religious authority asked Him a very important question: "Master, which is the greatest commandment in the law?" (Matthew 22:36). Of course, this man knew that all of God's commandments were important. But he hoped to catch Jesus off-guard and trap Him in His words.

Jesus responded by directly quoting today's scripture passage: "'Love the Lord your God with all your heart and with all your soul and with all your mind.' This is the first and greatest commandment" (Matthew 22:37–38 NIV).

This commandment, which still applies today, is the first and greatest for one simple reason: if you love God with everything inside you, obedience will naturally follow. If you love God, you won't engage in idolatry, misuse His name, or do anything else that displeases Him.

Jesus once said to His followers, "If you love me, keep my commands" (John 14:15 NIV). Love rests at the center of your relationship with God—Jesus' love for you motivated Him to willingly go to the cross, and your love for Him motivates you to perform everything He calls you to do, willingly and joyfully.

Reading Plan: Deuteronomy 5–7

HOW CAN I HAVE A STRONG RELATIONSHIP WITH GOD?

And now, Israel, what doth the LORD thy God require of thee, but to fear the LORD thy God, to walk in all his ways, and to love him, and to serve the LORD thy God with all thy heart and with all thy soul, to keep the commandments of the LORD, and his statutes, which I command thee this day for thy good?

DEUTERONOMY 10:12–13

Moses was so connected to God that the Lord spoke to him like a friend (see Exodus 33:11). He desperately wanted his people to know God on that level too. That's why Moses, in today's scripture, told them what it took to have a real, personal relationship with the Lord:

Fear God: Fearing God isn't an attitude of dread but a deep, reverential awe of the One who miraculously brought the Hebrews out of Egyptian bondage.

Walk in God's ways: Walking with God means living exactly the way He wants us to live each day.

Love God: Loving God doesn't imply just an emotional attachment (although that should play a part) but a sense of unshakable devotion to Him, His Word, and His ways.

Serve God: Loving God means serving Him in any way He desires.

Keep God's commandments: As you read yesterday, true love for God always leads to doing what He wants.

Reading Plan: Deuteronomy 8–11

WHAT DOES "REJOICING IN THE LORD" MEAN?

And ye shall rejoice before the LORD your God, ye, and your sons, and your daughters, and your menservants, and your maidservants, and the Levite that is within your gates; forasmuch as he hath no part nor inheritance with you.

DEUTERONOMY 12:12

One of the main themes of Deuteronomy 12—and the rest of the Bible—is rejoicing before the Lord.

The Israelites had every reason to rejoice. After God had miraculously led them through decades of wandering in the wilderness, He was now preparing them to enter the land He had promised. But Moses still felt a need to remind the people to thank God for His greatness and love—for all He had done for them and for all He would continue to do.

However, the Bible teaches us not to let our circumstances and feelings keep us from rejoicing before the Lord. Even when we suffer, we can still rejoice—because Jesus has gifted us a joyous future in an indescribably wonderful place called heaven.

So in good times and tough times alike, purpose in your heart and mind to "rejoice in the Lord *always*. I will say it again: Rejoice!" (Philippians 4:4 NIV, italics added).

Reading Plan: Deuteronomy 12–14

HOW SHOULD I TREAT THE POOR?

For the poor shall never cease out of the land: therefore I command thee, saying, Thou shalt open thine hand wide unto thy brother, to thy poor, and to thy needy, in thy land.

DEUTERONOMY 15:11

When you encounter beggars on a downtown street or people holding signs asking for help, how do you respond?

You might think, *Well, if they'd just find some initiative, they wouldn't be in this position*, or *They're probably poor due to bad life decisions*.

Today's scripture verse, however, strongly discourages that attitude.

First, you can't know the reason for someone's terrible situation. Second, the reason shouldn't matter. Men and women end up in poverty for a variety of reasons: mental illness, addiction, or even the untimely loss of employment. No matter the reason, they need help—and you may be the man God wants to provide it.

So what can you do? Maybe start by researching local homeless ministries and outreaches. Ask God what steps He wants you to take. He may guide you to give money, volunteer at a local shelter, or work on behalf of the poor. Whatever He asks, do it! You'll bless others and glorify the Lord at the same time.

Reading Plan: Deuteronomy 15–17

WHO IS THE PROPHET IN DEUTERONOMY 18?

And the LORD said unto me, They have well spoken that which they have spoken. I will raise them up a Prophet from among their brethren, like unto thee, and will put my words in his mouth; and he shall speak unto them all that I shall command him.

DEUTERONOMY 18:17–18

Under inspiration of the Holy Spirit, Moses said that God would one day raise up a prophet like himself from among his fellow Israelites. Reading these words through the lens of the New Testament, we can see very clearly that this Prophet was Jesus Christ.

Indeed, Jesus would be born from their "fellow Israelites" as the ultimate fulfillment of God's promise to bless all the nations of the world through Abraham's offspring. Jesus would also be a Prophet who would "speak unto them" all that God had commanded Him. Jesus confirmed this truth about Himself when He said, "The words I say to you I do not speak on my own authority. Rather, it is the Father, living in me, who is doing his work" (John 14:10 NIV).

In other words, Jesus would be the Spokesman for the one true God.

Moses was a great and heroic servant of God, but Hebrews 3:3 (NIV) says, "Jesus has been found worthy of greater honor than Moses." While Moses was God's servant, Jesus was God's own Son. And while Moses passed God's law on to the Israelites, Jesus fulfilled the law for all of us (Matthew 5:17). The prophet of Deuteronomy 18 is your Lord and Savior!

Reading Plan: Deuteronomy 18–20

WHEN SHOULD WE HELP OTHERS?

*Thou shalt not see thy brother's ox or his sheep go
astray, and hide thyself from them: thou shalt in
any case bring them again unto thy brother.*

DEUTERONOMY 22:1

One of the Bible's many great messages is that we are to love others in word and deed. Leviticus 19:18 (NIV) states, "Love your neighbor as yourself," and during His earthly ministry, Jesus quoted this verse and labeled it as one of the two greatest commandments—the other being to love God with everything we have (see Mark 12:29–31).

The Bible is filled with practical ways to love others through our actions. For example, in today's scripture, God told His people that if they see someone's livestock on the run, having broken free from the rest of the herd (any farmer or rancher knows how easily this can happen), they shouldn't ignore it. Instead, they should return the animal to its owner.

Even if you never have the opportunity to capture and return another person's animal, the main principle of today's verse still stands: God wants you to take action when you meet someone who needs help. So when He gives you a chance to do a good deed, don't look the other way!

Reading Plan: Deuteronomy 21–23

HOW DOES GOD FEEL ABOUT DIVORCE?

*When a man hath taken a wife, and married her, and it come to pass
that she find no favour in his eyes, because he hath found some
uncleanness in her: then let him write her a bill of divorcement,
and give it in her hand, and send her out of his house.*

DEUTERONOMY 24:1

Jesus was God in human flesh, so the things that mattered to His Father mattered to Him—including the covenant relationship of marriage.

One day, a group of Jewish religious leaders approached Jesus and tried to trap Him with a question related to today's verse. Jesus had just told them that early in creation, God established marriage as an unbreakable relationship between husband and wife. "They are no longer two, but one flesh," Jesus said. "Therefore what God has joined together, let no one separate" (Matthew 19:6 NIV).

"Why then," these religious men responded, "did Moses command that a man give his wife a certificate of divorce and send her away?" (verse 7 NIV).

Like many today, these men were looking for a loophole. But God's Word clearly teaches that He wants us to honor our wedding vows and do everything possible to avoid divorce.

Divorce and its consequences are huge problems today. That's why seeking God is so important. Only He can empower us to keep our marriages intact, strong, and flourishing in Him.

Reading Plan: Deuteronomy 24–26

HOW COULD THE ISRAELITES RECEIVE GOD'S BLESSINGS?

*And it shall come to pass, if thou shalt hearken diligently
unto the voice of the Lord thy God, to observe and to do all his
commandments which I command thee this day, that the Lord
thy God will set thee on high above all nations of the earth:
and all these blessings shall come on thee, and overtake thee,
if thou shalt hearken unto the voice of the Lord thy God.*

DEUTERONOMY 28:1–2

Of the Israelites who were poised to enter into the promised land, very few had been alive during the Exodus. Moses knew that this younger generation needed some words of encouragement—and warning. So he gave both, first declaring that God wanted to bless them with victory (Deuteronomy 28:1–14). Then Moses strongly warning the people that God would curse them if they did not obey Him or "carefully follow all his commands and decrees" (28:15 NIV). In short, the Israelites' own choices would determine whether they were blessed or cursed.

In the thousands of years since Moses delivered the address in today's reading, God hasn't changed, and neither has His willingness to reward obedience and commitment.

Are you committed to following and loving God with your whole heart, soul, and mind? If so, you're ready to receive God's very best. If not, ask Him to strengthen your desire and willingness to serve and follow Him. This is a prayer God is happy to answer.

Reading Plan: Deuteronomy 27–28

WHAT DOES IT MEAN TO "CHOOSE LIFE"?

*I call heaven and earth to record this day against you, that I have
set before you life and death, blessing and cursing: therefore choose
life, that both thou and thy seed may live: That thou mayest love
the Lord thy God, and that thou mayest obey his voice, and that
thou mayest cleave unto him: for he is thy life, and the length of
thy days: that thou mayest dwell in the land which the Lord sware
unto thy fathers, to Abraham, to Isaac, and to Jacob, to give them.*

DEUTERONOMY 30:19–20

After wandering forty years in the wilderness with his fellow Israelites,
Moses prepared them to enter the promised land by offering some simple
choices: life or death, blessing or cursing.

Moses promised that the people could obtain life and blessing by
doing three things: loving God, obeying His commandments, and clinging
to Him each day. But if they didn't do these things, they would suffer
death and cursing.

The instructions were simple, but year after year, generation after generation, God's chosen people disobeyed, sinned, and rebelled against Him.

Though the Israelites were mostly faithless toward God, He remained
faithful to them. And because of His great love for us, God used these
ungrateful, rebellious people to bring into the world our source of life:
Jesus Christ. Today, let's be sure we choose life—our eternal salvation
and our daily sanctification in and through Him.

Reading Plan: Deuteronomy 29–31

DAY 72

WHY COULDN'T MOSES ENTER
THE PROMISED LAND?

*And the LORD said unto him, This is the land which I sware
unto Abraham, unto Isaac, and unto Jacob, saying, I will
give it unto thy seed: I have caused thee to see it with
thine eyes, but thou shalt not go over thither.*

DEUTERONOMY 34:4

Moses is the most important, revered character in the Old Testament. That is because God used this great man of faith to lead the Hebrews out of Egyptian bondage and into their promised land.

Tragically, however, Moses wasn't allowed to complete his mission. That's because he had, in a moment of frustration, failed to obey a simple command God had given him.

Here's what happened: the Israelites complained they were thirsty, so God told Moses to *speak* to a large rock, out of which a stream of drinkable water would miraculously spring. But instead of speaking to the rock, Moses instead *struck* the rock with his shepherd's staff—twice.

God still provided the water, but He told Moses, "Because you did not trust in me enough to honor me as holy in the sight of the Israelites, you will not bring this community into the land I give them" (Numbers 20:12 NIV). So instead of entering the promised land with his people, Moses died. . .within eyesight of the land God had promised His people (Deuteronomy 34:5).

Obedience to God's commands should be of the utmost importance for us as men of God. That's because God blesses those who follow His instructions and finish well.

Reading Plan: Deuteronomy 32–34

WHAT IS JOSHUA ALL ABOUT?

With Moses and an entire generation of disobedient Israelites dead, God told Joshua to lead the people into Canaan, their promised land. In Jericho, the first major obstacle, the prostitute Rahab helped Israelite spies and earned protection from the destruction of the city: God knocked its walls flat as Joshua's army marched outside, blowing trumpets and shouting.

Joshua led a successful military campaign to clear idol-worshipping people—Hittites, Amorites, Canaanites, Perizzites, Hivites, and Jebusites—from the land. At one point, God answered Joshua's prayer to make the sun stand still, allowing more time to complete a battle (Joshua 10:1–15). Major cities subdued, Joshua divided the land among the twelve tribes of Israel, reminding the people to stay true to the God who led them home: "Now therefore put away. . .the strange gods which are among you, and incline your heart unto the Lord God of Israel" (24:23).

Joshua is one of few major Bible characters who seemed to do everything right—he was a strong leader, completely committed to God, who never fell into recorded sin or disobedience. Only one mistake mars his record: his experience with the Gibeonites, one of the local groups he should have destroyed. Fearing for their lives, they appeared before Joshua dressed in old clothes, carrying dry, moldy bread, claiming they had come from a faraway land. Joshua and the Israelite leaders "asked not counsel at the mouth of the Lord" (Joshua 9:14) and agreed to a peace treaty. When Joshua learned the truth, he honored his agreement with the Gibeonites—but made them slaves.

Reading Plan: Joshua 1–2

WHAT MADE JOSHUA A GREAT LEADER?

*On that day the L*ORD *magnified Joshua in the sight of all Israel;*
and they feared him, as they feared Moses, all the days of his life.

JOSHUA 4:14

God gave Joshua an assignment that would have been impossible for any man to accomplish on his own. But God encouraged him, saying, "Have I not commanded you? Be strong and courageous. Do not be afraid; do not be discouraged, for the LORD your God will be with you wherever you go" (Joshua 1:9 NIV). Joshua responded in faith.

Later, as the Israelites prepared to cross the Jordan River, God made another promise to Joshua: "Today I will begin to exalt you in the eyes of all Israel, so they may know that I am with you as I was with Moses" (Joshua 3:7 NIV).

But many Israelites may have had their doubts about Joshua. Having grown accustomed to Moses' leadership, they probably wondered if they could trust Joshua. Could he really lead them into the promised land? They needed a sign from above. . .and God gave them one.

Assured by God's promise, Joshua meticulously followed His instructions for crossing the Jordan, and the water suddenly dried up. The people realized the significance of this miracle: God had given Joshua His seal of approval. As a result, God made Joshua a great leader in the eyes of all the Israelites.

If you want to do great things for God's kingdom, do as Joshua did: trust and obey the Lord. When you do, He'll put His seal of approval on all you do for Him.

Reading Plan: Joshua 3–5

WHAT CAN WE LEARN FROM ACHAN?

*And Joshua said unto Achan, My son, give, I pray thee, glory
to the Lord God of Israel, and make confession unto him;
and tell me now what thou hast done; hide it not from me.*

JOSHUA 7:19

Not long after the Israelites had taken Jericho (Joshua 6), God directed them to take a city called Ai. Joshua's men should have defeated Ai easily, but they lost the battle and had to flee. Joshua, believing God was punishing them for some sin, later found out that a man named Achan had taken silver, gold, and a robe from Jericho, despite God's command for Israel's warriors to acquire nothing.

The Israelites stoned Achan and his children to death for his sin (Joshua 7:19–26). Then they left a pile of stones at the site where he died as a reminder of the cost of disobeying the Lord.

Achan's story reminds us of the disastrous effects of sin. Achan's actions brought death upon himself, but also to his family. His poor choice had had terrible consequences for Joshua and Israel's army as well. We need to be aware of such outcomes when temptation tries to draw us into sin.

Obedience to God's commands is always best. By doing the right thing, we avoid disaster and find blessing.

Reading Plan: Joshua 6–8

HOW DID JOSHUA DEMONSTRATE INTEGRITY?

*And Joshua made peace with them, and made
a league with them, to let them live: and the
princes of the congregation sware unto them.*

JOSHUA 9:15

Joshua trusted God with all his heart and was a great hero to his people. But like all of us, he made some mistakes, the biggest of which was making a treaty with the Gibeonites (Joshua 9).

After the Israelites defeated Jericho and Ai, many of the nearby Canaanite cities united to form a huge army to fight Israel. The Gibeonites, however, deceived Joshua by pretending to be from a distant country. Rather than destroying them as God had commanded, Joshua made a peace agreement with the Gibeonites—without asking God first.

While agreements and negotiations aren't necessarily bad, this one could have potentially jeopardized the Israelites' ultimate mission. But despite Joshua's error, he still demonstrated integrity by dutifully honoring the treaty and defending the Gibeonites against their enemies (Joshua 10:1–15).

Centuries after Joshua's courageous leadership over the Israelites, another great leader named David wrote, "The one whose walk is blameless. . .keeps an oath even when it hurts, and does not change their mind" (Psalm 15:2, 4 NIV).

Reading Plan: Joshua 9–10

DAY 77

HOW DOES SERVING GOD CHANGE AS WE GROW OLD?

Now Joshua was old and stricken in years; and the LORD said unto him, Thou art old and stricken in years, and there remaineth yet very much land to be possessed.

JOSHUA 13:1

In case Joshua didn't already know that he was getting up there, God confirmed the fact by saying, "Thou art old and stricken in years." *As if I didn't already know that!* Joshua may have thought.

Those of us who have lived for more than three or four decades can relate. No matter how well we eat, how much we exercise, how much sleep we get, or how committed we are to avoiding unhealthy habits, we eventually feel the often-unpleasant effects of age.

But for the man of God, old age is never an excuse for "retiring" from serving God. While pastors, missionaries, and others in fulltime ministry may retire from their jobs, they know God still has work for them to do.

Even though Joshua was growing old, having lived his entire life as a man of faith and a respected leader of God's people, he still had plenty to do for the Lord and for the nation of Israel.

That was true for Joshua, and it's true for us today.

Reading Plan: Joshua 11–13

WHAT QUALIFIED CALEB TO LEAD?

*Then the children of Judah came unto Joshua in Gilgal: and Caleb
the son of Jephunneh the Kenezite said unto him, Thou knowest
the thing that the LORD said unto Moses the man of God concerning
me and thee in Kadeshbarnea. Forty years old was I when Moses
the servant of the LORD sent me from Kadeshbarnea to espy out the
land; and I brought him word again as it was in mine heart.*

JOSHUA 14:6–7

If you needed someone to lead an army into hostile territory, you probably wouldn't send an eighty-five-year-old man. But that's exactly what Joshua did when he chose Caleb.

You may remember Caleb as one of the twelve spies who scouted the promised land while the Israelites amassed at Canaan's border. Of those twelve, only Joshua and Caleb came back with a positive report, telling the Israelites they could easily take the land with God on their side. Sadly, the Israelites listened to the other ten, causing the entire nation to wander in the wilderness for forty years (see Numbers 13).

Forty-five years later, Caleb still possessed the same extraordinary faith as before. The Bible doesn't say whether Caleb was a great warrior, but it does tell us that he "followed the LORD, the God of Israel, wholeheartedly" (Joshua 14:14 NIV).

Caleb's story proves that God isn't nearly as concerned about age or qualifications as He is about a faith that declares, "With God I can do it!"

Reading Plan: Joshua 14–16

WHY DID SOME TRIBES HESITATE TO CLAIM THEIR LAND?

*And Joshua said unto the children of Israel, How long
are ye slack to go to possess the land, which the
Lord God of your fathers hath given you?*

JOSHUA 18:3

For reasons not spelled out in scripture, seven of Israel's twelve tribes hesitated to claim the land allotted to them. It was time for them to act, to claim what God had said was already theirs, but they still waited.

Joshua, realizing that the promise God had made to Abraham about a new homeland hundreds of years earlier was coming true before his eyes, scolded these seven tribes. "How long," he challenged them, "are ye slack to go to possess the land, which the Lord God of your fathers hath given you?"

In other words, *God has given you something great! What are you waiting for?*

Great question. And it's one that many of us can ask ourselves.

The Bible contains hundreds of God's promises to His people. And since God always keeps His promises, all we have to do is take a step of faith and claim what He's already said is ours.

What could ever keep you from claiming God's promises? Remember, God "is able to do immeasurably more than all we ask or imagine, according to his power that is at work within us" (Ephesians 3:20 NIV).

What are *you* waiting for?

Reading Plan: Joshua 17–19

WHAT DOES ISRAEL'S ESTABLISHMENT TEACH US ABOUT GOD?

And the Lord gave unto Israel all the land which he sware to give
unto their fathers; and they possessed it, and dwelt therein.
. . . There failed not ought of any good thing which the Lord
had spoken unto the house of Israel; all came to pass.

JOSHUA 21:43, 45

If you want a scripture passage that tells you all you need to know about God's reliability in keeping His promises, your search stops with Joshua 23:43–45. This short passage summarizes everything God did for His people—starting with His promise to Abraham to grow his offspring into a great nation that would bless the entire world, and ending with the miraculous settlement of His people in the land of promise.

Though the Israelites' disobedience and lack of faith had taken them on a path God hadn't intended, everything the Lord had promised eventually came to pass—*everything*!

When God makes a promise, He keeps it. . .not partially, not mostly, but 100 percent. And even though His timing or methods may not be what we expect, we can count on Him to do everything He's promised.

Here's what the New Testament says about the ultimate Promise Keeper, the One who promised and then established the nation of Israel: "The one who calls you is faithful, and he will do it" (1 Thessalonians 5:24 NIV).

Reading Plan: Joshua 20–22

WHAT IS JOSHUA'S LEGACY?

And Israel served the Lord all the days of Joshua, and all the
days of the elders that overlived Joshua, and which had known
all the works of the Lord, that he had done for Israel.

JOSHUA 24:31

Not long before Joshua died, he gathered the people together and reminded them of what God had done for them. Then he encouraged them to remain faithful to their God: "If serving the Lord seems undesirable to you, then choose for yourselves this day whom you will serve, whether the gods your ancestors served beyond the Euphrates, or the gods of the Amorites, in whose land you are living. But as for me and my household, we will serve the Lord" (Joshua 24:15 NIV).

Joshua—one of the Bible's greatest heroes—died at the age of 110 and was buried in a place called Timnath-serah. Over the three portions of his life—forty years in Egypt, forty years in the wilderness, and thirty years in Canaan—Joshua remained unshakably faithful to God.

Joshua's assignment would have been impossible for him to accomplish on his own, but because he responded to God with faith, "Israel served the Lord all the days of Joshua, and all the days of the elders that overlived Joshua, and which had known all the works of the Lord, that he had done for Israel."

Joshua's amazing faith in his heavenly Father made him a true hero. Let's all do our best to emulate him.

Reading Plan: Joshua 23–24

WHAT IS JUDGES ALL ABOUT?

After Joshua's death, the Israelites lost momentum in driving pagan people out of the promised land. "The children of Benjamin did not drive out the Jebusites that inhabited Jerusalem" (Judges 1:21) is a statement characteristic of many tribes, which allowed idol worshippers to stay in their midst—with tragic results. "Ye have not obeyed my voice" God said to His people. "They shall be as thorns in your sides, and their gods shall be a snare unto you" (2:2–3).

That's exactly what happened, as the Israelites began a cycle of worshipping idols, suffering punishment by attackers, crying to God for help, and receiving God's aid in the form of a human judge (or "deliverer") who restored order.

Lesser-known judges include Othniel, Ehud, Tola, Jair, and Jephthah, who had only one child, a daughter, whom he foolishly vowed to sacrifice to God in exchange for a military victory (Judges 11:30–40). More familiar figures in the book are Deborah, the only female judge, who led a military victory against the Canaanites; Gideon, who tested God's will with a fleece and defeated the armies of Midian; and the amazingly strong Samson, who defeated the Philistines. Samson's great weakness—his love for unsavory women such as Delilah—led to his downfall and death in a Philistine temple.

The ancient Israelites got into trouble when they "did that which was right in [their] own eyes" (Judges 17:6; 21:25) rather than what God wanted them to do. Let's not make that mistake ourselves!

Reading Plan: Judges 1–3

WHAT CAN WE LEARN FROM BARAK?

Barak said unto her, If thou wilt go with me, then I will go: but if thou wilt not go with me, then I will not go. And she said, I will surely go with thee: notwithstanding the journey that thou takest shall not be for thine honour; for the Lord shall sell Sisera into the hand of a woman. And Deborah arose, and went with Barak to Kedesh.

JUDGES 4:8–9

Deborah, the fourth judge listed in the book of Judges, was a wise and respected woman who obeyed God and spoke the words He gave her. So when God told her to order a man named Barak, a military general, to gather an army and march to Mount Tabor to fight against the Canaanite army, Deborah did.

Even though God had promised Israel victory over King Jabin's military, Barak hesitated. He eventually complied, but under one condition: Deborah would have to go with him into battle. Deborah agreed, and the two led the Israelites in victory.

Many Bible readers mistakenly think Barak lacked courage and faith. However, Hebrews 11:32 lists Barak as one of the Bible's "heroes of the faith"—mentioning him in the same sentence as King David and the prophet Samuel.

Barak was no coward. He faithfully served God without concern for personal glory. By asking Deborah to accompany him into battle, he was actually sharing the glory with others. Is that something we need to consider doing in our own lives?

Reading Plan: Judges 4–5

WHY DID GOD SHRINK GIDEON'S ARMY?

And the Lord said unto Gideon, The people that are with thee are too many for me to give the Midianites into their hands, lest Israel vaunt themselves against me, saying, Mine own hand hath saved me.

JUDGES 7:2

Out of all the judges in the Bible, Gideon was the greatest. At first, he doubted that he was good enough, strong enough, or brave enough—but God still used Gideon to free the people of Israel from the rule of the powerful, ruthless Midianites.

Gideon believed God would help him lead the people out of Midianite bondage, so he began to prepare for battle. First, he wanted to make sure he had enough soldiers, so he selected thirty-two thousand fighting men. God, however, had a different number in mind, so He cut the number twice, leaving Gideon with just three hundred soldiers.

Humanly speaking, a band of three hundred Israelites versus a vast army of more than one hundred thousand Midianites wouldn't stand a chance. But with God on their side, the Israelites quickly and easily routed their enemy.

God pared down Gideon's army for one reason, a reason that applies to all of us today: He wanted Gideon and the Israelites to know that *He*, not their own power, had delivered them. God did for the Israelites what they never could have done for themselves.

He still works that way.

Reading Plan: Judges 6–8

WHAT CAN WE LEARN FROM ABIMELECH?

*Thus God rendered the wickedness of Abimelech, which he did
unto his father, in slaying his seventy brethren: and all the evil
of the men of Shechem did God render upon their heads: and
upon them came the curse of Jotham the son of Jerubbaal.*

JUDGES 9:56–57

Abimelech, the son of Gideon, was a gifted communicator who was passionate about leading the Israelites. But he had one fatal flaw: his ambitions ruled him because they were not submitted to the Lord. This led him down a path of seizing and keeping power through murder and deceit. He even murdered seventy potential rivals—his own brothers—upon a single stone (Judges 9:5).

Obviously, Abimelech would have never applied the apostle Paul's admonition, "Do nothing out of selfish ambition or vain conceit. Rather, in humility value others above yourselves, not looking to your own interests but each of you to the interests of the others" (Philippians 2:3–4 NIV).

Ambition isn't necessarily a bad thing—as long as it is godly (focused on glorifying God and expanding His kingdom) and not selfish (seeking its own desires).

Abimelech's story tragically illustrates what happens when a man does not submit his ambitions to God, failing to pray from his heart, "Not my will, but yours be done" (Luke 22:42 NIV).

Reading Plan: Judges 9

WHAT WAS JEPHTHAH'S FOOLISH VOW?

And Jephthah vowed a vow unto the Lord, and said, If thou shalt without fail deliver the children of Ammon into mine hands, then it shall be, that whatsoever cometh forth of the doors of my house to meet me, when I return in peace from the children of Ammon, shall surely be the Lord's, and I will offer it up for a burnt offering.

JUDGES 11:30–31

Jephthah, the eighth judge of Israel listed in the book of Judges, was "a mighty warrior" (Judges 11:1 NIV) who led the Israelites in battle against the Ammonites. At first, Jephthah tried to avoid war by sending a message to the Ammonite king. But after the king rejected his message, Jephthah knew that Israel would have to fight.

That's when Jephthah made an unnecessary—and quite foolish—vow to God, promising that if God gave him victory over the Ammonites, he would offer as a burnt offering whatever came out of the door of his house. After Jephthah defeated the Ammonites and returned home, his daughter stepped out of the house to greet him.

The Bible doesn't specify what happened to Jephthah's daughter. Some believe she wasn't literally sacrificed but lived the rest of her life in exile from the other Israelites. Either way, this story reminds us of the importance of thinking carefully before we speak. Our words have great power, for both good and ill. . .so let's make sure we mean what we say and say what we mean.

Reading Plan: Judges 10–12

HOW COULD GOD USE SAMSON?

And the Spirit of the Lord came upon him, and he went down to Ashkelon, and slew thirty men of them, and took their spoil, and gave change of garments unto them which expounded the riddle. And his anger was kindled, and he went up to his father's house.

JUDGES 14:19

Today's scripture reading (Judges 13–16) covers the story of Samson, the twelfth and final judge from the book of Judges. Samson was a Nazirite, meaning he was set apart for God's service and expected to follow special rules. For example, he was not allowed to cut his hair or drink fermented drinks such as wine.

When Sampson was faithful to God, he had amazing courage and strength, enabling him to do mighty deeds for the Lord and His people. But Samson was far from perfect. He rarely considered the consequences of his actions, and he often pursued his unrighteous desire for women—even enemy Philistine women.

Samson seems like the last person God would use to accomplish great things for Himself. This judge was selfish, prideful, and always trying to get his own way, but God still chose him to lead Israel. And God "was with the judge" (Judges 2:18 NIV), even when those judges messed up—which Samson certainly did.

In the end, who Samson was didn't matter as much as who God is.

Reading Plan: Judges 13–16

WHAT CAN WE LEARN FROM MICAH?

And the man Micah had an house of gods, and made an
ephod, and teraphim, and consecrated one of his sons, who
became his priest. In those days there was no king in Israel,
but every man did that which was right in his own eyes.

JUDGES 17:5–6

The final five chapters of Judges demonstrate how God's people—whom He had miraculously led out of Egyptian captivity and into the promised land—repeatedly violated His laws of worship.

In today's passage, a man named Micah (not to be confused with the prophet Micah) constructed a shrine to his own gods and appointed his son as priest. Even worse, a passing Levite—whose people had been appointed to serve God in the tabernacle—agreed to be Micah's priest as well.

The second half of today's scripture—"In those days there was no king in Israel, but every man did that which was right in his own eyes"—suggests that Micah wasn't the only person who attempted to create his own god. In the end, of course, Micah's efforts were futile.

Our culture strongly resembles that of the Israelites in Micah's day. Many people believe following their own hearts is the best choice, regardless of what God says.

Don't be like that. You have God's Word as your guide, so read it, study it, and obey it. You'll never regret that choice.

Reading Plan: Judges 17–19

WHAT SHOULD WE LEARN FROM JUDGES?

*In those days there was no king in Israel: every man
did that which was right in his own eyes.*

JUDGES 21:25

Today, you read the final two chapters of the book of Judges, which tells the tragic, often violent story of the Israelites' three-century cycle of rebellion, idol worship, oppression by invaders, temporary repentance, and deliverance through one of the several "judges" God appointed.

This period teaches a vital lesson about our relationship with our God—namely, that we must keep our eyes on Him each day. The Israelites failed miserably in that job, instead focusing on their own desires and perceptions of right and wrong. The results were disastrous.

Judges' main theme is found in today's verse: "Every man did that which was right in his own eyes"—a statement which largely describes our own culture, where it seems most people reject the idea of absolute truth and instead adopt a "whatever works for me" worldview.

For the modern man of God, such thinking is absolutely unacceptable. We should fix our hearts and minds "on Jesus, the pioneer and perfecter of faith" (Hebrews 12:2 NIV), building our lives on the truth of God's Word and following the Holy Spirit's leading each day. Never forget the warning of the Proverbs: "There is a way that appears to be right, but in the end it leads to death" (14:12 NIV).

Reading Plan: Judges 20–21

WHAT IS RUTH ALL ABOUT?

Ruth, a Gentile woman, married into a Jewish family who had escaped a famine in Judah by moving to Moab. When all the men of the family died, Ruth showed loyalty to her mother-in-law, Naomi, by staying with her and moving to Judah. Ruth's words to Naomi are well known: "Whither thou goest, I will go; and where thou lodgest, I will lodge: thy people shall be my people, and thy God my God" (Ruth 1:16).

As Ruth gleaned barley in a field, the wealthy farmer Boaz took an interest in her, ordering his workers to watch over her. Naomi recognized Boaz as her late husband's relative and encouraged Ruth to pursue him as a "kinsman redeemer," one who weds a relative's widow to continue a family line. She did, he married her, and something remarkable happened: Ruth, from the pagan land of Moab, became the great-grandmother of Israel's greatest king, David—and an ancestor of Jesus Christ.

Ruth and Naomi experienced many dark days. But they found, as we can, that God is trustworthy to provide. He will give what is needed, when it's needed—and He can work out our lives in ways that are better than we ever imagined.

Reading Plan: Ruth 1–4

WHAT IS 1 SAMUEL ALL ABOUT?

An infertile woman, Hannah, begged God for a son, promising to return him to the Lord's service. God answered her prayer, and Samuel was born. He was soon sent to the temple to serve under the aging priest, Eli.

Upon Eli's death, Samuel served as judge (or deliverer) of Israel, subduing the nation's fearsome enemy, the Philistines. As Samuel aged, Israel's tribal leaders rejected his sinful sons and asked for a king. Samuel warned that a king would tax the people and force them into service, but they insisted. . .and God told Samuel to anoint the notably tall and handsome Saul as Israel's first ruler.

King Saul started well but began making poor choices—and when he offered a sacrifice to God, a job reserved for priests, Samuel told Saul that he would be replaced. Saul's successor would be a young shepherd named David, who with God's help killed a giant Philistine warrior named Goliath. David's victory made him a hero in Israel, but the jealous king tried to kill him, and David ran for his life. Rejecting some seemingly perfect opportunities to kill Saul, David said, "I would not stretch forth mine hand against the Lord's anointed" (1 Samuel 26:23). At the end of 1 Samuel, Saul dies battling the Philistines, making way for David to become king.

Selfish choices—such as the Israelites' request for a king and Saul's decision to offer a sacrifice he had no business making—can have heavy, even tragic, consequences. Our good choices—such as David's refusal to harm the king—bless us and those around us.

Reading Plan: 1 Samuel 1–3

HOW COULD THE PHILISTINES STEAL THE ARK OF THE COVENANT?

*And when the people were come into the camp, the elders of Israel said, Wherefore hath the L*ORD *smitten us to day before the Philistines? Let us fetch the ark of the covenant of the L*ORD *out of Shiloh unto us, that, when it cometh among us, it may save us out of the hand of our enemies.*

1 SAMUEL 4:3

After losing four thousand men in a battle with the Philistines, the Israelites were shaken, wondering why God hadn't given them victory. But instead of directly asking God what they should do, the elders of Israel decided to take the ark of the covenant into their next battle with the Philistines.

The elders knew they needed God's presence, but they sought it incorrectly. They turned the ark into a kind of good luck charm.

The Philistines were terrified when they found out the Israelites were bringing the ark into battle, but they fought desperately, killing thirty thousand more Israelite soldiers and winning the battle (1 Samuel 4:2–11). In addition, they captured the ark and killed the sons of Eli the priest.

Israel's elders went terribly wrong by treating the ark of the covenant in a way God never intended or approved. That day, the ark became just a manmade box.

May we never lose our sense of awe at God. Yes, He's our Father, who has made us brothers of Jesus Christ. But He's not a good luck charm—He's the creator and sustainer of the entire universe!

Reading Plan: 1 Samuel 4–6

WHAT ARE CONDITIONAL PROMISES?

And Samuel spake unto all the house of Israel, saying, If ye do return unto the LORD with all your hearts, then put away the strange gods and Ashtaroth from among you, and prepare your hearts unto the LORD, and serve him only: and he will deliver you out of the hand of the Philistines.

1 SAMUEL 7:3

Any wise father knows that some promises to his children should be unconditional ("I will always love you!") and others conditional. ("If you clean your room, you can go to the movies with your friends.")

At the time the prophet Samuel spoke the words in today's scripture, the nation of Israel needed God's deliverance from an especially dangerous enemy. Speaking through Samuel, God promised to deliver Israel. . .if they abandoned their idols, returned to the Lord, and served Him with all their hearts.

Many of God's promises are conditional, meaning we must do our part before He does His. For example:

"Take delight in the LORD, and he will give you the desires of your heart" (Psalm 37:4 NIV).

"Trust in the LORD with all your heart and lean not on your own understanding; in all your ways submit to him, and he will make your paths straight" (Proverbs 3:5–6 NIV).

"If you remain in me and my words remain in you, ask whatever you wish, and it will be done for you" (John 15:7 NIV).

When you pursue God's promises of blessing, make sure you first understand what He expects of you.

Reading Plan: 1 Samuel 7–9

HOW IMPORTANT IS PRAYING FOR OTHERS?

Moreover as for me, God forbid that I should sin against the Lord in ceasing to pray for you.

1 SAMUEL 12:23

Today's scripture—spoken by Samuel, Israel's great and beloved prophet—is both a promise to his people and a call for all Christian men today. We must pray regularly about everything, especially for one another.

Samuel's audience had sinned terribly against God, even turning against Him by demanding a king to rule over them. Yet Samuel assured the Israelites that God had not rejected them, and he challenged them serve Him instead of other gods (verses 20–22). Then Samuel promised to pray for the people, for to do otherwise would be a sin against the Lord.

It's very important to God that we pray. Prayer is a wonderful privilege, but it's also a responsibility. The Lord wants us to come to Him with requests for ourselves, our families, our Christian brothers, our unsaved friends, and anyone or anything else He lays on our hearts.

Prayer is God's gift. When your heart feels burdened about anything, take it to God—He *wants* to hear from you.

Reading Plan: 1 Samuel 10–12

WHY DID GOD CALL DAVID "A MAN AFTER HIS OWN HEART"?

But now thy kingdom shall not continue: the LORD hath sought him a man after his own heart, and the LORD hath commanded him to be captain over his people, because thou hast not kept that which the LORD commanded thee.

1 SAMUEL 13:14

As you journey through 1 and 2 Samuel, you'll read of David's many mistakes and sins against God. David committed some of the worst sins in the Bible—and the consequences were terrible. . .for himself, his family, and the nation of Israel. Yet God, despite knowing of David's horrible failures beforehand, called him "a man after his own heart."

Why would God say such a thing?

Despite his many mistakes and blatant sins, David loved God, sought after Him, and tried to please Him. And when he failed, he always returned to the Lord, humbly confessing his sins and accepting the consequences.

Being a man after God's own heart doesn't mean being perfect— that's impossible on this side of heaven. It means loving God, wanting to please Him, and confessing to Him and repenting after each mistake.

Any of us can be a man after God's own heart.

Reading Plan: 1 Samuel 13–14

WHAT DOES GOD THINK OF OUR APPEARANCES?

But the LORD said unto Samuel, Look not on his countenance, or on the height of his stature; because I have refused him: for the LORD seeth not as man seeth; for man looketh on the outward appearance, but the LORD looketh on the heart.

1 SAMUEL 16:7

Our culture values physical appearance. If you don't believe that, just glance at most of the advertisements that air on television each hour.

Want to lose weight? Any number of new diets and exercise programs promise to make it happen. Trying to get rid of that wrinkled skin or gray hair? Find your "solution" in the countless creams and hair products. Countless companies look to separate you from your hard-earned cash by playing on your physical insecurities.

Most of us would say we're more concerned with what's inside a person than we are with physical appearance. For some, that statement is just a pleasantry. But when our God says it, He means it.

There's nothing wrong with taking care of yourself or trying to look better by staying fit. But never forget that your heavenly Father is far more concerned with the condition of your inner man than He is with the external. And you have far more control over your inner man!

Reading Plan: 1 Samuel 15–16

HOW CAN I SLAY THE GIANTS IN MY LIFE?

*Then said David to the Philistine, Thou comest to me
with a sword, and with a spear, and with a shield: but I
come to thee in the name of the Lord of hosts, the God
of the armies of Israel, whom thou hast defied.*

1 SAMUEL 17:45

We men tend to respect physical and emotional strength, intelligence, know-how, and wisdom. All of these are good qualities, but if we want to accomplish great things for God's kingdom, we must remember that we're powerless without Him.

The young shepherd boy David understood this truth as he faced a giant warrior named Goliath. There's some debate about Goliath's size, but we know his armor alone weighed 175 pounds. Goliath was a "man's man," and his awesome size and weapons made this match-up a no-contest.

Except. . .

Neither David nor Goliath had the smallest doubt their opponent would fall hard that day. But only David was right. From the beginning, he knew this confrontation wasn't going to end well for the giant. And David knew that for one reason: he was fighting in the name of his mighty, all-powerful God. It was no-contest indeed, but not in the way Goliath had hoped.

What giants do you face today? You can defeat them when you discard your own strength and realize that with God you can do anything.

Reading Plan: 1 Samuel 17–18

HOW NECESSARY ARE FRIENDS?

*Jonathan Saul's son delighted much in David: and Jonathan
told David, saying, Saul my father seeketh to kill thee:
now therefore, I pray thee, take heed to thyself until the
morning, and abide in a secret place, and hide thyself.*

1 SAMUEL 19:2

Perhaps no two men in all the Bible shared as close a relationship as Jonathan—the son of King Saul—and David. First Samuel 18:1 (NIV) reveals the depth of their friendship: "Jonathan became one in spirit with David, and he loved him as himself."

In one of David's darkest hours, after Saul had directed Jonathan and the rest of his servants to kill David on sight, the future king of Israel turned to his dear friend for help. At great risk to his own life, Jonathan betrayed his father's confidence and warned David to lay low until Jonathan had spoken with Saul. The king temporarily relented in his murderous plan, but Jonathan later had to intervene for David again (1 Samuel 20:30–33).

Having such a loving and loyal friend was a tremendous blessing for David—just as it is for any man. We all need a friend who "has your back" and is willing to intervene for us with other people or, most importantly, with the Lord.

Do you have—and can you *be*—that kind of friend?

Reading Plan: 1 Samuel 19–20

ARE CIRCUMSTANCES EVIDENCE OF GOD'S WILL?

*And it was told Saul that David was come to Keilah. And Saul
said, God hath delivered him into mine hand; for he is shut
in, by entering into a town that hath gates and bars.*

1 SAMUEL 23:7

King Saul wanted David—the man God had chosen as Israel's second king—dead, and he would stop at nothing, not even cold-blooded murder, to make that happen. In today's scripture, Saul rationalized that since an opportunity to kill David had presented itself, it must have been God's will for Saul to kill him.

Saul was wrong. God would never condone the taking of an innocent human life. David had not sinned against Saul—and certainly not in a way deserving of death. Saul's hatred rose from his own selfishness, jealousy, and fear that David was threatening his kingdom.

Our situations probably vary widely from Saul's. But it's still important to remember that mere circumstances don't always imply God's stamp of approval. Even when things seem to "fall into place" for us, we should always pray for God to reveal His will (see Proverbs 3:5–6). Here's an important truth: God's will for our lives never contradicts His Word.

Reading Plan: 1 Samuel 21–23

HOW DID ABIGAIL SAVE DAVID FROM A TERRIBLE SIN?

And David said to Abigail, Blessed be the LORD God of Israel, which sent thee this day to meet me: and blessed be thy advice, and blessed be thou, which hast kept me this day from coming to shed blood, and from avenging myself with mine own hand.

1 SAMUEL 25:32–33

Enraged, David had every intention of murdering a contentious, arrogant man named Nabal, who had offended David with his rudeness. But Abigail, Nabal's wife, stepped in to diffuse the situation, saving two men in the process—Nabal from certain death and David from himself.

Abigail calmed David, reminding him of his destiny as Israel's king and saying, "When the LORD has fulfilled for my lord every good thing he promised concerning him and has appointed him ruler over Israel, my lord will not have on his conscience the staggering burden of needless bloodshed or of having avenged himself. And when the LORD your God has brought my lord success, remember your servant" (1 Samuel 25:30–31 NIV).

David, acknowledging the truth of Abigail's words, thanked her for keeping him from committing a sin that would have haunted him for the rest of his life.

David's conflict with Nabal can teach us an important truth: being offended never justifies sinful attitudes and actions. As Jesus would say, "Love your enemies and pray for those who persecute you, that you may be children of your Father in heaven" (Matthew 5:44–45 NIV).

Reading Plan: 1 Samuel 24–25

WHY DIDN'T DAVID KILL SAUL?

*David said furthermore, As the LORD liveth, the LORD shall
smite him; or his day shall come to die; or he shall descend
into battle, and perish. The LORD forbid that I should
stretch forth mine hand against the LORD's anointed.*

1 SAMUEL 26:10–11

David knew King Saul desperately wanted him dead—but he knew better than to fight back. Instead, he ran and hid, trying to stay out of sight until it was time to take his rightful place on the throne.

David refused to kill Saul first—even when he had two chances to do it (see 1 Samuel 24 and 26). That was because Saul, as bad as he was, had still been made king of Israel by God. David respected and felt loyalty to him, even mourning after Saul died (2 Samuel 1).

By respecting King Saul and sparing him twice, David exemplified the apostle Paul's instruction to "be subject to the governing authorities, for there is no authority except that which God has established" (Romans 13:1 NIV).

In the United States, Christians have the freedom to oppose the government's positions and try to remove officials from office during elections. But according to scripture's teaching and example, we must always deal respectfully with our governmental leaders. Even the worst official is a human being made in God's image.

Reading Plan: 1 Samuel 26–28

HOW CAN I KNOW IF GOD APPROVES OF MY PLANS?

And David enquired at the Lord, saying, Shall I pursue after this troop? shall I overtake them? And he answered him, Pursue: for thou shalt surely overtake them, and without fail recover all.

1 SAMUEL 30:8

Most, if not all, of us have wondered if our plans to do something that we believe is necessary fall within God's will for us. We want assurance that God approves. But how do we find that?

In today's scripture, King David prayed, seeking God's go-ahead to pursue an enemy who had committed terrible atrocities against the city of Ziklag. When David asked God a very specific question to see if his military venture would be successful, God replied with a very pointed "Yes." So David launched the campaign, resulting in one of his finest hours.

None of us should embark on a life-altering venture without first seeking God's approval. He promises to hear our prayers and act on our behalf—and that includes giving us His approval when our plans line up with His will. So before you proceed, ask Him to guide and direct you, letting you know when to move, stop, or just wait on His timing. Then pause, allowing God to answer. Whatever you do, don't rush ahead of Him.

Reading Plan: 1 Samuel 29–31

WHAT IS 2 SAMUEL ALL ABOUT?

When King Saul died, David was made king by the southern tribe of Judah. Seven years later, after the death of Saul's son Ishbosheth, king of the northern tribes, David became ruler of all Israel.

Capturing Jerusalem from the Jebusites, David created a new capital for his unified nation, and God promised him, "Thy throne shall be established for ever" (2 Samuel 7:16). Military victories made Israel strong, but when David stayed home from battle one spring, he committed adultery with a beautiful neighbor, Bathsheba. Then he had her husband—one of his soldiers—murdered. The prophet Nathan confronted David with a story of a rich man who stole a poor man's sheep. David was furious until Nathan announced, "Thou art the man" (12:7). Chastened, David repented and God forgave his sins—but their consequences would affect the king powerfully. The baby conceived in the tryst died, and David's family began to splinter apart. One of David's sons, Amnon, raped his half-sister, and a second son, Absalom—full brother to the violated girl—killed Amnon in revenge. Absalom then conspired to steal the kingdom from David, causing his father to flee for his life. When Absalom died in battle with David's men, David grieved so deeply that he offended his own soldiers. Ultimately, David returned to Jerusalem to reassert his kingship, and raise another son born to Bathsheba—Solomon.

King David's story highlights the vital importance of the choices we make. Who would have guessed that such a great man could fall into such terrible sin?

Reading Plan: 2 Samuel 1–2

WHAT'S WRONG WITH REVENGE?

And when Abner was returned to Hebron, Joab took him aside in the gate to speak with him quietly, and smote him there under the fifth rib, that he died, for the blood of Asahel his brother. . . . So Joab, and Abishai his brother slew Abner, because he had slain their brother Asahel at Gibeon in the battle.

2 SAMUEL 3:27, 30

Doubtlessly, almost every man on earth has at one point felt the urge to take vengeance against another person. But God's Word warns, "Do not take revenge, my dear friends, but leave room for God's wrath, for it is written: 'It is mine to avenge; I will repay,' says the Lord" (Romans 12:19 NIV).

The story of Joab, who was King David's nephew and an outstanding military commander, illustrates the folly of seeking personal revenge. Joab plotted to kill Abner—David's former enemy—not to eliminate a threat to the kingdom but to avenge the death of Joab's brother in battle (2 Samuel 3:30). After David learned that Joab had murdered Abner, he pronounced a curse on Joab and his family (3:28–29).

Joab's thirst for revenge cost him everything (see 1 Kings 2:28–35), and the very same thing can happen to you. So when you're hit with the urge to avenge, pray for that person instead. . .and let God handle the matter.

Reading Plan: 2 Samuel 3–4

HOW CAN I KNOW GOD IS WITH ME?

*So David dwelt in the fort, and called it the city of David. And
David built round about from Millo and inward. And David went
on, and grew great, and the LORD God of hosts was with him.*

2 SAMUEL 5:9–10

David's dramatic story tells how a man rose from the humblest of
beginnings to great power and prestige. But his power didn't grow due
to his own wisdom and strength or because he was perfect. Far from it.
David's achievements occurred because God, who was always with him,
had called him to greatness.

God may not have planned to make you powerful, famous, or rich—in
fact, He probably hasn't. But He loves you, and He has plans for you to
live a life of greatness for Him, whatever that may entail.

How can you know that God is with you? What can you do to make
sure He stays with you every day? First, you can read His Word daily,
lingering over the passages about His love, goodness, and constant
presence. Then you can go to Him in prayer, thanking Him for always
being with you and asking Him to remind you of His wonderful presence
in every situation. And then, very importantly, you can step out in faith,
doing whatever He calls you to do.

Reading Plan: 2 Samuel 5–7

WHY SHOULD I EXPRESS GRATITUDE?

*And David said unto [Mephibosheth], Fear not: for I will
surely shew thee kindness for Jonathan thy father's sake,
and will restore thee all the land of Saul thy father;
and thou shalt eat bread at my table continually.*

2 SAMUEL 9:7

In 2 Samuel 9, David expressed his gratitude to his dear friend Jonathan—
who had died in battle many years earlier after doing David a tremendous
favor—by bringing Jonathan's son Mephibosheth to Jerusalem and
showing him kindness. After giving him all of Saul's belongings, including
farmland that David ordered to be cultivated, the king told Mephibosheth,
"You will always eat at my table" (2 Samuel 9:7 NIV). This meant David
had welcomed the young man into his home as his own son (9:11).

Centuries later, the apostle Paul expressed his gratitude to the church
in Philippi by writing, "I thank my God every time I remember you. In all
my prayers for all of you, I always pray with joy because of your partner-
ship in the gospel from the first day until now" (Philippians 1:3–5 NIV).

We can follow David and Paul's example by expressing our own
gratitude to others. When we do, we'll grow our relationships. . .and
encourage other people to do good things in Jesus' name.

Reading Plan: 2 Samuel 8–10

WHY DID DAVID SIN WITH BATHSHEBA?

And it came to pass in an eveningtide, that David arose from off his bed, and walked upon the roof of the king's house: and from the roof he saw a woman washing herself; and the woman was very beautiful to look upon. And David sent and enquired after the woman. And one said, Is not this Bathsheba, the daughter of Eliam, the wife of Uriah the Hittite?

2 SAMUEL 11:2–3

King David made a terrible mess of his life, his family, and his kingdom when he chose to sin sexually with Bathsheba. He made things even worse by trying to cover things up, arranging to have Uriah, Bathsheba's husband and one of David's top military men, killed in battle.

Notice that David's sin didn't start with "the act." Rather, his troubles began when he was walking on his rooftop and saw Bathsheba bathing. Right away, he could see that she was very beautiful. But David didn't stop there. Instead, he kept watching this beautiful, unclothed woman until his mind began plotting how he could have her.

David did nothing wrong by just seeing Bathsheba. But he opened himself to sin when he chose to keep looking.

If you want to keep your body sexually pure, you need to keep your mind pure. And to keep your mind pure, you must be careful what you allow your eyes to focus on. David didn't do that, and it led to disaster.

Reading Plan: 2 Samuel 11–12

HOW SHOULD WE RESPOND TO SINFUL SITUATIONS?

But when king David heard of all these things, he was very wroth.
And Absalom spake unto his brother Amnon neither good nor bad:
for Absalom hated Amnon, because he had forced his sister Tamar.

2 SAMUEL 13:21–22

After David's sin with Bathsheba, the prophet Nathan warned that the king's actions would have serious consequences for his family. True to Nathan's words, the king's son Amnon forced himself on his half-sister Tamar, another child of David. When David learned of this, he became very angry. . .but did nothing.

Of course, David's anger was justified. But he was 100 percent wrong—as a king and as a father—in choosing not to protect his daughter or discipline Amnon. David's lack of action led to more chaos in his family. Two years later, Amnon's half brother Absalom, full brother to Tamar, exacted revenge by killing the rapist.

Whether we're fathers, leaders at church, supervisors at work, or simply a friend aware of a sinful situation, we must respond. Doing nothing, as David did, is neither wise nor godly. Commit to speaking up, in a measured, loving, and firm way, and pray that God will deal with the sinning person's heart. You may not succeed. . .but it's better than not trying at all.

Reading Plan: 2 Samuel 13–14

HOW DID DAVID RESPOND TO HIS WORST CRISIS?

And David said unto all his servants that were with him at Jerusalem,
Arise, and let us flee; for we shall not else escape from Absalom:
make speed to depart, lest he overtake us suddenly, and bring
evil upon us, and smite the city with the edge of the sword.

2 SAMUEL 15:14

King David made many grievously bad decisions during his reign, including his sin with Bathsheba. That one terrible sin led to a series of disasters within his family, culminating in his son Absalom's revolt against David's kingdom.

When David learned of Absalom's intentions—and that Absalom had raised a ruthless army—he chose to avoid a bloody civil war by fleeing Jerusalem to wait until things cooled down.

With an army of men now on his trail, David did the one thing that could save him and his kingdom: he found a quiet place where he could be alone with God. There, he wrote these wonderful words:

LORD, how many are my foes! How many rise up against me! Many
are saying of me, "God will not deliver him." But you, LORD, are a
shield around me, my glory, the One who lifts my head high. I call
out to the LORD, and he answers me from his holy mountain.

PSALM 3:1–4 NIV

David's actions show that instead of immediately fighting back, it's sometimes best to retreat to a place where we can get alone with God—and then just listen.

Reading Plan: 2 Samuel 15–16

HOW DID ABSALOM'S REBELLION END?

*And the king said unto Cushi, Is the young man Absalom safe? And
Cushi answered, The enemies of my lord the king, and all that rise
against thee to do thee hurt, be as that young man is. And the king
was much moved, and went up to the chamber over the gate, and
wept: and as he went, thus he said, O my son Absalom, my son, my son
Absalom! would God I had died for thee, O Absalom, my son, my son!*

2 SAMUEL 18:32–33

Second Samuel 18 describes the tragic end of the life of Absalom, King
David's son who rebelled against his father's rule and attempted to
usurp the throne.

Absalom grew up as a child of privilege in his father's palace, where
he had everything he needed and wanted—except, apparently, some
strong spiritual training. David was Israel's greatest king, but he wasn't
a great father. Consequently, Absalom neither had a heart for God nor
respected his father's authority.

Absalom's story began with his revenge-killing of his half-brother
Amnon, who had raped Absalom's full sister. From there, Absalom's life
took many turns, culminating in his death on the battlefield.

Naturally, David was devastated when he learned of Absalom's death.
The Bible says that the king was shaken, shedding tears of grief over
the death of his son. . .and possibly his failure as a father.

Let's all approach our callings with the passion and energy of David
the king. But let's avoid the mistakes of David the father.

Reading Plan: 2 Samuel 17–18

HOW DID DAVID HANDLE THE DEATH OF ABSALOM?

And the victory that day was turned into mourning unto all the people: for the people heard say that day how the king was grieved for his son. And the people gat them by stealth that day into the city, as people being ashamed steal away when they flee in battle. But the king covered his face, and the king cried with a loud voice, O my son Absalom, O Absalom, my son, my son!

2 SAMUEL 19:2–4

Have you ever seen someone absolutely crushed by a big loss—the loss of a loved one, a relationship, or a job? Grieving is a healthy response to loss, and it's good to mourn with a grieving friend (see Romans 12:15)—but we must ensure our grief doesn't discourage those around us.

In 2 Samuel 19, King David was overcome with grief over the loss of his son Absalom, who had died trying to take Israel's throne from his father. What should have been a victorious celebration for David became a time of mourning. Eventually, the king's friend and military leader Joab chided him, urging David to look past his loss and focus on the good of his kingdom.

Grieving is natural and appropriate. But in the midst of our sorrows, we can't forget the words of the apostle Paul: "Rejoice always, pray continually, give thanks in all circumstances; for this is God's will for you in Christ Jesus" (1 Thessalonians 5:16–18 NIV). By making this conscious choice, we may shorten our time of grief and return to effective service for our Lord.

Reading Plan: 2 Samuel 19–20

HOW IS GOD OUR ROCK?

And [David] said, The Lord is my rock, and my fortress, and my deliverer; the God of my rock; in him will I trust: he is my shield, and the horn of my salvation, my high tower, and my refuge, my saviour; thou savest me from violence. I will call on the Lord, who is worthy to be praised: so shall I be saved from mine enemies.

2 SAMUEL 22:2–4

Our earth's surface is covered with rocks—some of them gigantic. According to geologists, the biggest rock in the world is Mount Augustus. Located in Western Australia, it stands 3,625 feet high and spans more than 35 square miles. Up close, you might imagine that Mount Augustus is immovable (at least by human power) or consider how an entire army could hide behind it for protection. Or you might just see it as a place to rest in the shade.

All these possibilities were likely going through David's mind when he wrote, "The Lord is my rock, my fortress and my deliverer" (2 Samuel 22:2, Psalm 18:2 NIV). The Psalms refer to God as a rock about twenty times, meaning you can always—without fail—depend on Him for protection from the world.

Things around us change all the time. But God never does. . .and never will. That's why He's our *only* Rock of protection (Psalm 18:31).

Reading Plan: 2 Samuel 21–22

HOW CAN I KEEP MY CONSCIENCE CLEAN?

And David's heart smote him after that he had numbered the people. And David said unto the Lord, I have sinned greatly in that I have done: and now, I beseech thee, O Lord, take away the iniquity of thy servant; for I have done very foolishly.

2 SAMUEL 24:10

No doubt you've heard the old saying "Let your conscience be your guide." That's not always good advice, considering that the human heart is "deceitful above all things, and desperately wicked" (Jeremiah 17:9). But for a Christian man whose heart and mind are controlled by the Holy Spirit, it's a great idea your conscience, when touched by God's Spirit, can keep you out of trouble and alert you to unconfessed sin.

Today's scripture tells how King David's conscience afflicted him after he had ordered one of his servants to take a count of all the Israelites. Though it's not entirely clear why this was sinful, . David later concluded that he had sinned against God. He confessed, but the Israelites suffered greatly because of their leader's choice.

Living victoriously for the Lord requires us to keep our conscience clean and sensitive to what He says to us through His Word and Holy Spirit. So listen to God, going to Him immediately when your conscience says it's time to make things right with Your heavenly Father. There's no shame in that. In fact, it's the only way to grow in your Christian life.

Reading Plan: 2 Samuel 23–24

WHAT IS 1 KINGS ALL ABOUT?

King David, in declining health, named Solomon, his son with Bathsheba, successor. After David's death, God spoke to Solomon in a dream, offering him anything he'd like—and Solomon chose wisdom. God gave Solomon great wisdom, along with much power and wealth. The new king soon built God a permanent temple in Jerusalem, and the Lord visited Solomon again to promise blessings for obedience and trouble for disobedience.

Sadly, Solomon's wisdom failed him, as he married seven hundred women, many of them foreigners who turned his heart to idols. When Solomon died, his son Rehoboam foolishly antagonized the people of Israel, and ten northern tribes formed their own nation under Jeroboam, a former official of Solomon's. Two southern tribes continued under Solomon's line in a nation called Judah.

Jeroboam began badly, initiating idol worship in the north; many wicked rulers followed. Judah would also have many poor leaders, though occasional kings, such as Asa and Jehoshaphat, followed the Lord. First Kings introduces the prophet Elijah, who confronted the evil King Ahab and Queen Jezebel of Israel regarding their worship of the false god Baal. In God's power, Elijah defeated 450 false prophets in a dramatic contest on Mount Carmel.

The book of 1 Kings provides a strong warning: Even the most blessed people can drift from God and make big mistakes. Let's make sure that never describes us!

Reading Plan: 1 Kings 1–2

HOW CAN I OBTAIN WISDOM?

*And God said unto him, Because thou hast asked this thing,
and hast not asked for thyself long life; neither hast asked riches
for thyself, nor hast asked the life of thine enemies; but hast
asked for thyself understanding to discern judgment; Behold, I
have done according to thy words: lo, I have given thee a wise
and an understanding heart; so that there was none like thee
before thee, neither after thee shall any arise like unto thee.*

1 KINGS 3:11–12

James 1:5 (NIV) tells us, "If any of you lacks wisdom, you should ask God, who gives generously to all without finding fault, and it will be given to you." What a great promise! Between work, family, ministry, and other important parts of your life, you have a lot on your plate—and you need wisdom every day. Every man does.

As Solomon prepared to assume the throne as Israel's third monarch, he knew he had much to learn. In fact, he didn't know if he was up for the job. So he did the only thing he could: ask God for wisdom. And God was more than happy to give Solomon just what he'd requested.

Here's the good news: God wants to give *you* wisdom as well. He won't look down on you when you ask for it—He'll always give it to you so that you can flourish in every area of your life. Count on it!

Reading Plan: 1 Kings 3–4

WHAT DOES THE COMPLETION OF SOLOMON'S TEMPLE AND PALACE SAY ABOUT PRIORITIES?

But Solomon was building his own house thirteen years, and he finished all his house.

1 KINGS 7:1

Today's scripture begins a chapter, so the word *but* might seem a little out of place. If, however, you look back at the previous verse—1 Kings 6:38—you'll see that the two verses make a comparison between the time Solomon spent building God's temple and the time he spent constructing his own palace.

Both buildings were magnificent and important. Some scholars believe the time difference resulted from Solomon's making the temple his priority, while others suggest it was because God had given Solomon perfect instructions for the temple. Either way, these two verses say something about *priorities*. Because God Himself was to be Israel's priority, He made building His temple Solomon's top job. From this point onward, the temple would lie at the center of the people's religious lives.

God gives every man a list of important responsibilities, but it's sometimes hard to prioritize those tasks. But when we make God our top priority, we'll become steadfast in meeting those responsibilities. Always ensure that spending time with Him—in prayer and in Bible reading—takes precedence over everything else.

Reading Plan: 1 Kings 5–7

HAS GOD PROMISED TO BE WITH ME ALWAYS?

The LORD our God be with us, as he was with
our fathers: let him not leave us, nor forsake us:
that he may incline our hearts unto him, to walk in all his
ways, and to keep his commandments, and his statutes,
and his judgments, which he commanded our fathers.

1 KINGS 8:57–58

Today's scripture is part of King Solomon's blessing over the Israelites at the dedication of the newly finished temple. In this prayer, Solomon spoke of how the people's ancestors enjoyed God's constant presence.

It's no coincidence that Solomon immediately followed his words about God's presence with a challenge for the people to obey God from their hearts and keep His commandments. In essence, he was saying, "Since God has promised to be with us always, we should respond in gratitude by turning our hearts to Him and obeying His laws."

Today, we have the privilege of enjoying God's constant, wonderful presence because of Jesus' sacrifice on our behalf. God's promise to the Israelites—"Never will I leave you; never will I forsake you" (Hebrews 13:5 NIV)—still stands for us today.

This promise should motivate you to a life of constant commitment and obedience to God—not because you're afraid He'll leave you but because you're grateful that He won't.

Reading Plan: 1 Kings 8–9

WHERE DID SOLOMON GO WRONG?

And the Lᴏʀᴅ was angry with Solomon, because his heart was turned from the Lᴏʀᴅ God of Israel, which had appeared unto him twice, and had commanded him concerning this thing, that he should not go after other gods: but he kept not that which the Lᴏʀᴅ commanded.

1 KINGS 11:9–10

God had promised Solomon that his kingdom would last forever—as long as Solomon followed the Lord the same way his father, David, had. But God also warned the king that if he turned away, terrible things would happen (1 Kings 9:4–7).

Sadly, Solomon didn't keep his end of the bargain. Later in his reign, the king broke several of God's laws. He married seven hundred wives and kept three hundred concubines (1 Kings 11:3), many of whom worshipped false deities instead of the one true God. Before long, they persuaded Solomon to build shrines for their idols.

One day, God told Solomon that the once-great kingdom of Israel would pay a heavy price because of his sin: "Since this is your attitude and you have not kept my covenant and my decrees, which I commanded you, I will most certainly tear the kingdom away from you and give it to one of your subordinates" (1 Kings 11:11 ɴɪᴠ).

God has made His people many "conditional" promises that are contingent on our obedience. Solomon went down the wrong path, and it cost him dearly.

Let's be sure we don't follow that tragic example. Instead, let's make every effort to live obediently to God, pleasing Him and receiving His very best in return.

Reading Plan: 1 Kings 10–11

WHAT HAPPENS WHEN I COMPROMISE?

And the man of God said unto the king, If thou wilt give me half thine house, I will not go in with thee, neither will I eat bread nor drink water in this place: for so was it charged me by the word of the Lord, saying, Eat no bread, nor drink water, nor turn again by the same way that thou camest.

1 KINGS 13:8–9

In today's world, compromise is seen as a good thing—and in many ways it is. Sometimes, "meeting someone halfway" is the best way to accomplish things fairly. But when it comes to obeying God's commands in the Bible, compromise can cost a man dearly.

First Kings 13 tells the sad story of an unnamed elderly prophet from Judah who compromised God's command for him not to eat or drink anything while he was in Bethel. The prophet had traveled from Judah to Bethel, where he'd spoken powerful words and performed an amazing miracle. When he obeyed, he triumphed. But when he compromised what he knew God had called him to do, he perished.

Many a Christian man's marriage, ministry, or business has been ruined because he compromised what he knew was right. Commit to doing exactly what God says, every time. There may be consequences from the world, but the heavenly rewards are entirely worth it.

Reading Plan: 1 Kings 12–13

WHY IS GOOD LEADERSHIP SO IMPORTANT?

Now in the eighteenth year of king Jeroboam the son of Nebat reigned Abijam over Judah. Three years reigned he in Jerusalem. And his mother's name was Maachah, the daughter of Abishalom. And he walked in all the sins of his father, which he had done before him: and his heart was not perfect with the Lord his God, as the heart of David his father.

1 KINGS 15:1–3

Chapters 14 and 15 of 1 Kings cover the reigns of several kings in both Israel and Judah. This passage demonstrates a truth found throughout the Old Testament: When a king loved and served the Lord, the kingdom generally prospered. But when evil, ungodly kings ruled, everything tended to go south.

In Old Testament times, good leadership drew out the best in people— loyalty, love for God, peace, and prosperity. Bad leadership, however, led mostly to rebellion, apostasy, turmoil, war, and other disasters.

This principle is as old as humanity itself—and it's still true today. Bad political, spiritual, business, and family leaders all lead, sooner or later, to chaos.

Are you a good leader in your family, workplace, and church? Whenever you lead as God intends, His blessings start to rain.

Reading Plan: 1 Kings 14–15

WHY DID ELIJAH PERFORM SO MANY MIRACLES?

And Elijah the Tishbite, who was of the inhabitants of Gilead, said unto Ahab, As the LORD God of Israel liveth, before whom I stand, there shall not be dew nor rain these years, but according to my word.

1 KINGS 17:1

The prophet Elijah, whose story is given in 1 Kings 17:1 through 2 Kings 2:11, certainly performed a lot of miracles—including the pronouncement of a drought on the wayward nation of Israel and the raising of a widow's son from the dead.

However, probably his greatest miracle happened when he challenged hundreds of prophets of the false god Baal at Mount Carmel—and won (see 1 Kings 18:17–40). This proved that Elijah's God was all-powerful and theirs was a powerless myth.

Not every Old Testament prophet performed miracles, but God gave Elijah this power so people could see that he really was God's representative. They needed to listen to him when he spoke.

Few of us will perform miracles, but God will still help us to glorify Him and expand His eternal kingdom. He'll do this by instilling in us the same qualities that made Elijah so great—immoveable faith, unshakable passion for His truth, and supreme confidence in His ability to work through His own.

Reading Plan: 1 Kings 16–17

WHAT CAN I DO WHEN I FEEL ALONE?

*I have been very jealous for the L*ORD *God of hosts: because the children of Israel have forsaken thy covenant, thrown down thine altars, and slain thy prophets with the sword; and I, even I only, am left; and they seek my life, to take it away.*

1 KINGS 19:14

Faithfully serving the Lord can feel lonely sometimes. Even Israel's greatest prophet knew that.

Elijah had just performed an incredible miracle, showing the Israelites the power of the one true God (see 1 Kings 18:17–40). Yet soon afterward, he was alone, having fled due to death threats. Elijah was so depressed that he complained to God how unfair it was that he, a faithful servant, should be alone in his suffering. He really believed that he was the only true prophet of God left in Israel.

But Elijah wasn't alone, as God would later prove to him. In his discouragement, though, he *felt* alone—just as all of us do sometimes.

When you feel alone, don't try to hide your emotions from your heavenly Father. Instead, tell Him how you feel and ask Him to encourage you with His presence. It may take some time—Elijah himself had to work through his depression with God—but the Lord is always present and always interested in your well-being.

Plus, God has people all around who can help you. There were seven thousand other Israelites who had "not bowed unto Baal" (1 Kings 19:18).

Reading Plan: 1 Kings 18–19

HOW DID KING AHAB CROSS THE LINE?

Ahab spake unto Naboth, saying, Give me thy vineyard, that I may have it for a garden of herbs, because it is near unto my house: and I will give thee for it a better vineyard than it; or, if it seem good to thee, I will give thee the worth of it in money. And Naboth said to Ahab, The Lord forbid it me, that I should give the inheritance of my fathers unto thee.

1 KINGS 21:2–3

In the last of the Ten Commandments, God tells His people, "You shall not covet your neighbor's house. You shall not covet your neighbor's wife, or his male or female servant, his ox or donkey, or anything that belongs to your neighbor" (Exodus 20:17 NIV).

Covetousness may not seem as serious as other sins listed in the Bible. But God in His wisdom knew that our obsessive desire for another person's possessions can easily lead to terrible things. The wicked Ahab, king of Israel, exemplified this truth.

Ahab sealed his own fate when he allowed the murder of a man named Naboth—simply because he wanted Naboth's vineyard. Ahab had offered to buy the vineyard, but Naboth wouldn't sell it. So while Ahab sulked in his palace, Jezebel, his wife, had Naboth killed. With Naboth dead, Ahab took the vineyard for himself. Elijah confronted Ahab, telling him he would die for his actions.

So how bad is covetousness? It doesn't always lead directly to death, but it will certainly take you places you don't want to go.

Reading Plan: 1 Kings 20–21

HOW CAN I BOLDLY SPEAK GOD'S TRUTH?

And the messenger that was gone to call Micaiah spake unto him,
saying, Behold now, the words of the prophets declare good unto
the king with one mouth: let thy word, I pray thee, be like the word
of one of them, and speak that which is good. And Micaiah said,
As the Lord liveth, what the Lord saith unto me, that will I speak.

1 KINGS 22:13–14

Speaking God's truth, even from a heart of love, can be frightening. But whenever we know God wants us to speak an uncomfortable truth, we should follow Micaiah's example.

In that man's day, four hundred "counselors"—actually false prophets who had no regard for the Lord or His message—told Ahab, the wicked king of Israel, only what he wanted to hear. Micaiah, on the other hand, was fully committed to speaking only the words God gave him.

What would you do if God was prompting you to say something, but you felt like the people around wanted you to speak only inoffensive words? Would you follow Ahab's prophets' example, or Micaiah's?

In today's culture, we as men of God may hesitate to speak His truth, fearing it may cost us more than we're willing to pay. But God's rewards are always greater than man's punishment. Today, let's commit ourselves to speaking the truth in love, knowing that God will provide the words if we're willing to obey Him (see Matthew 10:19–20).

Reading Plan: 1 Kings 22

WHAT IS 2 KINGS ALL ABOUT?

The story of 1 Kings continues, with more bad rulers, a handful of good ones, some familiar prophets, and the ultimate loss of the two Hebrew nations.

Early in 2 Kings, Elijah becomes the second man (after Enoch in Genesis 5:24) to go straight to heaven without dying. His successor, Elisha, performed many miracles and shared God's Word with the "average people" of Israel. The northern kingdom's rulers were entirely wicked, and Israel, under its last king, Hoshea, was "carried. . .away into Assyria" (17:6) in 722 BC. Judah, with occasional good kings such as Hezekiah and Josiah, lasted a few years longer—but in 586 BC the southern kingdom's capital of Jerusalem "was broken up" (25:4) by Babylonian armies under King Nebuchadnezzar. Besides taking everything valuable from the temple and the king of Judah's palace, the Babylonians also "carried away all Jerusalem, and all the princes, and all the mighty men of valour, even ten thousand captives, and all the craftsmen and smiths" (24:14). Ending on a slight up note, 2 Kings describes a new king of Babylon, Evil-merodach, showing kindness to Jehoiachin, the last real king of Judah, by giving him a place of honor in the Babylonian court.

Both Israel and Judah found that there were terrible consequences to sin. Their bad examples can be helpful to us, if we decide not to do the things that brought them trouble.

Reading Plan: 2 Kings 1–3

WHAT WAS ELISHA ALL ABOUT?

*Elisha said unto her, What shall I do for thee? tell me, what hast thou
in the house? And she said, Thine handmaid hath not any thing in
the house, save a pot of oil. Then he said, Go, borrow thee vessels
abroad of all thy neighbours, even empty vessels; borrow not a few.*

2 KINGS 4:2–3

Before Elijah was taken to heaven, God instructed him to appoint Elisha
as Israel's new leading prophet. Like Elijah, Elisha performed many miracles through God's power—a total of sixteen throughout 2 Kings 2–13.

Elisha performed about twice as many miracles as his mentor
Elijah, and more than any Old Testament character but Moses. Also,
while Elijah's miracles often demonstrated God's wrath and judgment,
Elisha's focused on His love and grace.

While these prophets' ministries highlighted two very real aspects
of God's character, their objectives were identical: to turn the Israelites
away from idolatry and back toward the one true God.

Elisha and Elijah both represented an important truth about our God:
He is all-loving and all-merciful, but He is also all-holy. God's nature
requires that He punish sin and discipline those He loves (see Romans
11:22). Be sure you don't overemphasize either side of God's nature. He
is a unified whole in His love and wrath.

> **Reading Plan: 2 Kings 4–5**

HOW CAN I SEE BEYOND THE NATURAL?

And when the servant of the man of God was risen early, and gone forth,
behold, an host compassed the city both with horses and chariots.
And his servant said unto him, Alas, my master! how shall we do?

2 KINGS 6:15

In 2 Corinthians 4:18 (NIV), the apostle Paul joyfully wrote that we Christians "fix our eyes not on what is seen, but on what is unseen, since what is seen is temporary, but what is unseen is eternal."

Focusing on the unseen is not always easy. That's why Elisha's servant was so frightened when he woke up one morning and saw a huge army of Arameans surrounding the two men and the entire city of Dothan. To this servant, it was curtains for him and Elisha.

Elisha, however, saw things very differently. "Don't be afraid," he answered. "Those who are with us are more than those who are with them" (2 Kings 6:16 NIV). Then Elisha prayed, "Open his eyes, LORD, so that he may see" (verse 17 NIV). Immediately, Elisha's servant looked up and saw legions of horses and chariots of fire all around Elisha.

God didn't open the servant's physical eyes—they were working just fine. God opened the young man's spiritual eyes to comfort and encourage him. Knowing that God was in control, the servant now had nothing to fear.

When you feel frightened or anxious, ask God to do for you what He did for Elisha's servant: to open your eyes that you might see Him working on your behalf!

Reading Plan: 2 Kings 6–8

WHAT CAN WE LEARN FROM KING JEHU'S FAILURE?

And [Jehu] said, Come with me, and see my zeal for the Lord. So they made him ride in his chariot. And when he came to Samaria, he slew all that remained unto Ahab in Samaria, till he had destroyed him, according to the saying of the Lord, which he spake to Elijah.

2 KINGS 10:16–17

As the new king of Israel, Jehu enthusiastically accepted the responsibility of following God's instructions to destroy Ahab's family and the rampant Baal worship in the kingdom.

Jehu zealously fulfilled God's commands to the very last detail, even destroying Baal's temple and everything in it. In 2 Kings 10:30 (NIV), God commended Jehu: "Because you have done well in accomplishing what is right in my eyes and have done to the house of Ahab all I had in mind to do, your descendants will sit on the throne of Israel to the fourth generation."

Jehu had forward momentum on his side, and he might have led Israel into national revival. Sadly, however, his compromise led to another kind of idolatry: "Jehu was not careful to keep the law of the Lord, the God of Israel, with all his heart. He did not turn away from the sins of Jeroboam, which he had caused Israel to commit" (verse 31 NIV).

Jehu represents a man who can accomplish great things for the Lord, only to have it come to nothing. If we get distracted along the way and don't finish well, what have we gained?

Reading Plan: 2 Kings 9–10

HOW DID KING JEHOASH DEMONSTRATE THE IMPORTANCE OF FOCUS?

But it was so, that in the three and twentieth year of king Jehoash the priests had not repaired the breaches of the house. Then king Jehoash called for Jehoiada the priest, and the other priests, and said unto them, Why repair ye not the breaches of the house? now therefore receive no more money of your acquaintance, but deliver it for the breaches of the house.

2 KINGS 12:6–7

After the sons of Judah's wicked queen Athaliah robbed and trashed the temple (see 2 Chronicles 24:7), King Jehoash worked with the priests of Judah on a plan to raise funds to repair it.

The fundraising was going well, but twenty-three years after Jehoash's order to restore the temple, the work still wasn't finished. So Jehoash summoned the priests, including Jehoiada, and asked them what was taking so long. Jehoash then fired all the fund-raising priests—except for Jehoiada—and the two men formulated another plan.

Jehoash had discovered the core problem plaguing the fund-raising efforts: distraction. The fund-raising priests, as much as they loved God's house, didn't focus on their task, leading to procrastination and ultimately failure.

Good intentions are fine. Good planning is even better. But to really succeed in anything—especially our life of faith—we need focus. As with any of our struggles, God will be happy to help if we ask.

Reading Plan: 2 Kings 11–13

WHAT DOES "PRIDE COMES BEFORE DESTRUCTION" MEAN?

But Amaziah would not hear. Therefore Jehoash king of Israel went up; and he and Amaziah king of Judah looked one another in the face at Bethshemesh, which belongeth to Judah. And Judah was put to the worse before Israel; and they fled every man to their tents.

2 KINGS 14:11–12

Wise Solomon once wrote, "Pride goes before destruction, a haughty spirit before a fall" (Proverbs 16:18 NIV). In other words, nothing good comes from pride.

For a perfect example of this timeless truth, look at the reign of Amaziah, Judah's ninth king. Second Kings 14:3 (NIV) says that Amaziah "did what was right in the eyes of the Lord, but not as his father David had done."

But not as his father David had done. That qualifier spelled disaster for Amaziah's reign.

After Amaziah's overwhelming victory over the Edomites, he brought back the enemy's idols—despite warnings by God's prophets (see 2 Chronicles 25). Amaziah, now feeling full of himself, arrogantly challenged Israel's king Jehoash to meet him on the battlefield. Jehoash warned Amaziah that he was overestimating Judah's military power, but Amaziah wouldn't listen.

Amaziah and Judah didn't just lose the battle—they were humiliated.

When you accomplish something great at work, in your ministry, or in your personal life, thank God for His kindness. But always stay humble. It is only God who gives you the ability to prosper anyway (see Deuteronomy 8:18).

Reading Plan: 2 Kings 14–15

WHAT DID ISRAEL'S SIN ACCOMPLISH?

Therefore the Lord was very angry with Israel, and removed them out of his sight: there was none left but the tribe of Judah only.

2 KINGS 17:18

Second Kings 17:7–17 lists the Northern Kingdom of Israel's sins against God. As this passage explains, the Israelites worshipped and feared false gods rather than the one true God, engaged in pagan religious practices (such as witchcraft, soothsaying, and other forbidden behaviors), and rejected God's "decrees and the covenant he had made with their ancestors and the statutes he had warned them to keep" (2 Kings 17:15 NIV).

Hoshea, Israel's last ruler, was just as evil as his predecessors, doing everything he could to lead the people away from God. The people followed, and in 722 BC, God's judgment finally fell upon them in the form of an Assyrian invasion. The Northern Kingdom then dissolved as the people paid the ultimate price for their sins.

Romans 6:23 (NIV) says, "The wages of sin is death"—and the Northern Kingdom was a physical example of this truth. Today, sin continues to bring eternal spiritual death to people around the world. The second half of this verse, however, tells the good news: "but the gift of God is eternal life in Christ Jesus our Lord."

If you have accepted that gift, take a moment to thank God for His mercy. If you haven't received God's kindness yet, why not now?

Reading Plan: 2 Kings 16–17

WHY WOULD GOD ALLOW EVIL PEOPLE TO BESIEGE ISRAEL?

And the king of Assyria did carry away Israel unto Assyria, and put them in Halah and in Habor by the river of Gozan, and in the cities of the Medes: because they obeyed not the voice of the LORD their God, but transgressed his covenant, and all that Moses the servant of the LORD commanded, and would not hear them, nor do them.

2 KINGS 18:11–12

Between about 900–700 BC, the powerful empire Assyria conquered a huge area that covered modern-day Iraq, Syria, Jordan, and Lebanon. The Assyrians did terrible things to their enemies.

Beginning around 733 BC, the Assyrian king Tilgath-pileser invaded the Northern Kingdom of Israel and took many of its people captive (2 Kings 15:29). In 721 BC another Assyrian king, Shalmaneser, attacked Samaria, Israel's capital. The city fell three years later (2 Kings 18:9–12), fulfilling Isaiah's prophecy that God would use the Assyrian Empire to punish Israel for its idolatry (Isaiah 10:5–19).

It's hard for us to understand why God would use an evil army to judge His own people—unless we focus on God's sovereignty, His absolute control over all things. God is God, and He can choose whatever means He wants to accomplish His will. He used the Assyrians to judge the Northern Kingdom of Israel, and He later used the Babylonians to judge the Southern Kingdom of Judah. Right now, He may be using difficult people and situations in your own life.

Reading Plan: 2 Kings 18–19

WHY WOULD GOD ADD YEARS TO HEZEKIAH'S LIFE?

Turn again, and tell Hezekiah the captain of my people, Thus saith the LORD, the God of David thy father, I have heard thy prayer, I have seen thy tears: behold, I will heal thee: on the third day thou shalt go up unto the house of the LORD.

2 KINGS 20:5

During a perilous time for the kingdom of Judah, Hezekiah received some dreadful news about his sickness. In 2 Kings 20:1 (NIV), the prophet Isaiah told him, "This is what the LORD says: Put your house in order, because you are going to die; you will not recover."

But instead of following the prophet's orders, Hezekiah tearfully begged God to allow him to live longer. Before Isaiah had even left the king's palace, God told him to go back and tell Hezekiah that God had heard his prayers—the king would live another fifteen years.

Hezekiah's response was exemplary: "Surely it was for my benefit that I suffered such anguish. In your love you kept me from the pit of destruction" (Isaiah 38:17 NIV). David expressed the same sentiment when he wrote, "It was good for me to be afflicted so that I might learn your decrees" (Psalm 119:71 NIV).

During difficult situations, it's always good to thank God for acting on your behalf. But it's even better to ask Him what He wants you to learn from the difficulty itself.

Reading Plan: 2 Kings 20–21

WHAT CAN WE LEARN FROM KING JOSIAH?

*Josiah was eight years old when he began to reign, and he reigned
thirty and one years in Jerusalem. . . . And he did that which was
right in the sight of the Lord, and walked in all the way of David
his father, and turned not aside to the right hand or to the left.*

2 KINGS 22:1–2

The story of Judah's king Josiah is an unusual one. First, he ascended
the throne at eight years of age, making him one of the youngest kings
in history. Second, his birth and reign were predicted in 1 Kings 13:2—
about three hundred years before he was born.

Even though Josiah's father (Amon) and grandfather (Manasseh)
had been evil kings, Josiah was godly. Second Kings 22:2 (NIV) says, "He
did what was right in the eyes of the Lord and followed completely the
ways of his father David, not turning aside to the right or to the left."
Josiah's love for God and His written Word enabled him to lead Judah
into spiritual revival.

Even though he didn't come from a family who nurtured his heart
for God, Josiah became one of the Old Testament's greatest kings. His
story proves that a great spiritual pedigree isn't necessary for us to
accomplish great things for God's kingdom.

If you have a rich spiritual heritage, thank God. If not, commit to
beginning one. Either way, God will be honored.

Reading Plan: 2 Kings 22:1–23:30

WHAT CAN WE LEARN FROM KING JEHOIACHIN?

Jehoiachin was eighteen years old when he began to reign, and he reigned in Jerusalem three months. And his mother's name was Nehushta, the daughter of Elnathan of Jerusalem. And he did that which was evil in the sight of the LORD, according to all that his father had done.

2 KINGS 24:8–9

Sadly, most of Israel's and Judah's kings did "evil in the sight of the Lord"—including Jehoiachin, the nineteenth king of Judah.

Jehoiachin's story is especially tragic because God gave him, as He did many other Old Testament kings, a chance to humble himself and repent; however, the king still "did evil in the eyes of the LORD his God and did not humble himself before Jeremiah the prophet, who spoke the word of the LORD" (2 Chronicles 36:12 NIV).

The Bible repeatedly tells us that God blesses, forgives, and restores those with humble hearts. The apostle James wrote very plainly, "Humble yourselves before the Lord, and he will lift you up" (James 4:10 NIV).

Jehoiachin didn't humble himself before God, so his reign ended in utter disaster. Had he simply listened to God's prophet Jeremiah, his kingdom may well have prospered.

God gives us the same choice today: to defer to His guidance in our lives or continue in our own pride. In the latter case, we'll leave a legacy of "what could have been."

Reading Plan: 2 Kings 23:31–25:30

WHAT IS 1 CHRONICLES ALL ABOUT?

The book of 1 Chronicles provides a history of Israel, going as far back as Adam. The unnamed author—tradition attributes the writing to Ezra the priest—covers much of the same information as the book of 2 Samuel but skips over some of the seedier aspects of David's life. . .things like his adultery with Bathsheba and the engineered killing of her husband, Uriah.

Despite his many flaws, David was clearly Israel's greatest king, and 1 Chronicles puts a special emphasis on his leadership of national worship. Another important focus is on God's promise that David would have an eternal kingly line through a descendant we know to be Jesus Christ.

The positive spin of 1 Chronicles was apparently designed to remind the Jews that despite the punishment they were suffering for sin, they were still God's special people. When God makes a promise, He keeps it.

Reading Plan: 1 Chronicles 1–4

WHAT DIFFERENCE DOES PRAYER MAKE?

*And they were helped against them, and the Hagarites
were delivered into their hand, and all that were with them:
for they cried to God in the battle, and he was intreated
of them; because they put their trust in him.*

1 CHRONICLES 5:20

First Chronicles 5 tells of a battle between three eastern Israelite tribes—Reuben, Gad, and the half-tribe of Manasseh—and the Hagarites, one of Israel's many enemies (see Psalm 83:6).

These three tribes included 44,760 men who were willing and able to fight. They knew how to handle their weapons, and they were well-trained for battle (1 Chronicles 5:18–19).

But the Bible doesn't credit their numbers, fighting skills, or training as the key to their victory. Today's verse says they were victorious because they "cried to God in battle," believing He would act on their behalf and give them victory.

The Bible—Old Testament and New Testaments alike—repeatedly teaches that God responds to His people's prayers. Prayer, when offered in faith and with the right motivation, has the power to change people's hearts, minds, and circumstances.

So believe in the power of prayer. As the apostle Peter said, "The eyes of the Lord are on the righteous and his ears are attentive to their prayer" (1 Peter 3:12 NIV).

Reading Plan: 1 Chronicles 5–7

HOW CAN I WALK HUMBLY IN MY FAITH?

So Saul died for his transgression which he committed against the LORD, even against the word of the LORD, which he kept not, and also for asking counsel of one that had a familiar spirit, to enquire of it; and enquired not of the LORD: therefore he slew him, and turned the kingdom unto David the son of Jesse.

1 CHRONICLES 10:13–14

God chose Saul to serve as Israel's first monarch, but his life soon took a tragic turn. Instead of consistently living a humble life of faith in his God, he often made selfish decisions that led to his downfall and death.

First, Saul made an unauthorized sacrifice to God instead of waiting for Samuel as he had been instructed (1 Samuel 13:1–15). Later, he spared the Amalekite king and his best livestock, even after God had instructed him otherwise (1 Samuel 15:1–9). And finally, he committed a grievous sin by consulting a medium instead of the Lord for guidance.

Because faithlessness and disobedience, Saul lost his kingdom through death in battle. He became an extreme example of the high cost of sin. We have all sinned and not immediately died, but sin always has consequences—and our disobedience can cost us dearly in our relationships, our professional life, and our walk with God.

That's why every Christian man can benefit from a little self-examination. Take time regularly to seek the Lord and ask Him where you may be falling short. Then humbly confess your sins, asking God to help you make any necessary course corrections.

Reading Plan: 1 Chronicles 8–10

HOW CAN I UNDERSTAND THE TIMES?

And of the children of Issachar, which were men that had
understanding of the times, to know what Israel ought
to do; the heads of them were two hundred; and all
their brethren were at their commandment.

1 CHRONICLES 12:32

Israel was facing a major transition during the period covered in 1 Chronicles 1–12. The reign of Saul, Israel's first king, had been a disaster, and now that he was dead, David was about to take the throne. To paraphrase an old song, *The times they were a-changin'*.

Though God had clearly chosen David as Israel's second king, political intrigue surrounded his ascension to the throne. That's why it was important that the men of Issachar "had understanding of the times, to know what Israel ought to do." Here, the word *understanding* refers to the insight they needed to act with judiciousness.

Every era in human history—including our twenty-first century—has had its own set of challenges. That's why modern men of God should ask Him for the wisdom to understand these unique problems.

As you spend time with God in prayer, ask Him to give you the same kind of understanding that He gave the men of Issachar centuries ago. You—and your world—need that.

Reading Plan: 1 Chronicles 11–14

HOW DID DAVID RESPOND TO GOD'S PROMISES?

Therefore now, LORD, let the thing that thou hast spoken
concerning thy servant and concerning his house be
established for ever, and do as thou hast said.

1 CHRONICLES 17:23

First Chronicles 17:11–14 summarizes the "Davidic Covenant"—God's unconditional promise to David that He would establish an everlasting kingdom through David's descendant. (The entire covenant is found in 2 Samuel 7.)

After the prophet Nathan relayed God's covenant to David, the king went before the Lord with a powerful prayer. By boldly asking God to fulfill His promise, David expressed his confidence in God's faithfulness.

God wants us to pray with the same kind of confidence. He wants us to search the scriptures for His promises and then confidently claim them in prayer: "This is the confidence we have in approaching God: that if we ask anything according to his will, he hears us. And if we know that he hears us—whatever we ask—we know that we have what we asked of him" (1 John 5:14–15 NIV).

God has promised us many wonderful things—forgiveness of sins (1 John 1:9), spiritual growth (Philippians 1:6), guidance (Psalm 32:8), among countless others.

What do you need today?

Reading Plan: 1 Chronicles 15–17

DOES GOD EVER TEMPT PEOPLE TO SIN?

*And Satan stood up against Israel, and provoked David to
number Israel. And David said to Joab and to the rulers of
the people, Go, number Israel from Beersheba even to Dan;
and bring the number of them to me, that I may know it.*

1 CHRONICLES 21:1–2

Second Samuel 24:1 (NIV) says, "The anger of the LORD burned against Israel, and he incited David against them, saying, 'Go and take a census of Israel and Judah.'" This counting clearly offended God. So why does this verse seem to say the Lord temped David to do it?

According to James 1:13 (NIV), "When tempted, no one should say, 'God is tempting me.' For God cannot be tempted by evil, nor does he tempt anyone." Since God can't be tempted, He'll never tempt anyone else. Therefore, we need to look a little deeper into the story.

Today's scripture covers the same incident as 2 Samuel 24 records, but from a new angle that helps us understand what really happened. God didn't tempt David to sin—He *allowed* David to be tempted, by Satan, because that served the Lord's purposes at the time.

God will never tempt you to sin! In fact, as the apostle Paul wrote, "God is faithful; he will not let you be tempted beyond what you can bear. But when you are tempted, he will also provide a way out so that you can endure it" (1 Corinthians 10:13 NIV).

Reading Plan: 1 Chronicles 18–21

HOW DID DAVID PREPARE SOLOMON TO BUILD THE TEMPLE?

Now, my son, the LORD be with thee; and prosper thou, and build the house of the LORD thy God, as he hath said of thee. Only the LORD give thee wisdom and understanding, and give thee charge concerning Israel, that thou mayest keep the law of the LORD thy God. Then shalt thou prosper, if thou takest heed to fulfil the statutes and judgments which the LORD charged Moses with concerning Israel: be strong, and of good courage; dread not, nor be dismayed.

1 CHRONICLES 22:11–13

As King David spoke these words to his son Solomon, the look of a proud father must have rested on his face. David knew God had appointed Solomon to lead Israel and build the temple in Jerusalem—a project David had wanted to take on himself.

Knowing Solomon's task would be difficult, David spoke amazing words of blessing and encouragement to him. He also challenged him to do four things:

- walk in God-given wisdom
- provide leadership for the Israelites
- keep God's law
- be strong and courageous

God's calling for you may not resemble what you'd hoped for, but that doesn't mean you can't play an important part in His kingdom. If you know someone else who has received the "exciting" call, follow David's example by speaking sincere words of encouragement.

Reading Plan: 1 Chronicles 22–24

HOW DID DAVID PREPARE FOR THE TEMPLE'S CONSTRUCTION?

Moreover David and the captains of the host separated to the service of the sons of Asaph, and of Heman, and of Jeduthun, who should prophesy with harps, with psalteries, and with cymbals.

1 CHRONICLES 25:1

King David passionately desired to see God's temple finished in his own lifetime. But 1 Chronicles 22 says that because he was a man of war, the Lord would not use David to build the temple in Jerusalem. That honor, God said, would go to David's son Solomon.

The disappointment David must have felt didn't hinder his passion for God and His temple. So he decided to make preparations for it.

David invested enormous amounts of his own resources to obtain the workers and materials necessary for such a magnificent place of worship. In addition, 1 Chronicles 25 says that David, "the sweet psalmist of Israel" (2 Samuel 23:1 KJV), appointed 288 skilled musicians to play beautiful music for the Lord. With both materiel and "cheerleaders," Solomon would be able to jump immediately into building the temple.

King David had many admirable qualities, but his humility and passion for worship are shown the most vividly in the last several chapters of 1 Chronicles. Whatever we may have accomplished ourselves, David did more. Let's be sure to follow his example of humility and service.

Reading Plan: 1 Chronicles 25–27

HOW CAN I FOLLOW GOD'S CALLING?

And thou, Solomon my son, know thou the God of thy father,
and serve him with a perfect heart and with a willing mind:
for the LORD searcheth all hearts, and understandeth all the
imaginations of the thoughts: if thou seek him, he will be found
of thee; but if thou forsake him, he will cast thee off for ever.

1 CHRONICLES 28:9

As King David's death drew near, he challenged and encouraged Solomon, his son and successor as king of Israel, to build God's temple and serve God with his whole heart and mind. Today's scripture—located in the midst of this speech—is a call for all men of God to focus themselves on serving, loving, and obeying God.

David understood that "the Lord searcheth all hearts, and understandeth all the imaginations of the thoughts" and that a sinful mind and heart would keep his son from serving God wholeheartedly.

You'll never completely escape sin on this side of heaven, but if your heart is fully devoted to God—as David's was—you'll be quick to confess when you fail. However, if you cling to "pet sins" in your heart and mind, they will certainly pull you away from God.

What does the Lord see right now as He searches your heart?

Reading Plan: 1 Chronicles 28–29

WHAT IS 2 CHRONICLES ALL ABOUT?

The book of 2 Chronicles covers Israelite history from about 970 BC (the accession of King Solomon) to the 500s BC (when exiled Jews returned to Jerusalem). The book continues the positive emphasis on Israel's history that 1 Chronicles began, since originally these two books were a single unit.

David's son Solomon is highlighted in 2 Chronicles. He was made king, built the temple in Jerusalem, and became one of the most prominent rulers ever. But when he died, the Jewish nation divided. In the remainder of 2 Chronicles, the various kings of the relatively godlier southern nation of Judah are profiled right down to the destruction of Jerusalem by the Babylonians. The book ends with King Cyrus, of the new world power Persia, allowing exiled Jews to return to Jerusalem to rebuild their devastated temple. Interestingly, the final two verses of 2 Chronicles are repeated almost verbatim at the beginning of the following book of Ezra.

The history of God's people is often dark and difficult. These Old Testament accounts show that God's punishment isn't intended to hurt sinful people, but to bring them back to Him.

Reading Plan: 2 Chronicles 1–4

WHO GETS THE CREDIT?

And the king turned his face, and blessed the whole congregation
of Israel: and all the congregation of Israel stood. And he said,
Blessed be the Lord God of Israel, who hath with his hands fulfilled
that which he spake with his mouth to my father David.

2 CHRONICLES 6:3–4

Second Chronicles 6 recounts Solomon's address to the Israelites at the dedication of the temple in Jerusalem. As the culmination of a promise God had made many years before, the day was solemn yet joyful.

After introducing the magnificent temple to the people, Solomon gave God all the credit for its construction: "Praise be to the Lord, the God of Israel, who with his hands has fulfilled what he promised with his mouth to my father David" (verse 4 NIV).

Solomon later wrote, "Unless the Lord builds the house, the builders labor in vain" (Psalm 127:1 NIV). Though many men had worked countless hours building the temple, they were merely human instruments in God's hands.

Think of the things God has enabled you to accomplish, as well as the things He's given you. Never forget to give credit where it's due—in your time alone with God, when you're talking with brothers and sisters in Christ, or when you're interacting with unbelievers who desperately need to hear of the Lord's goodness.

Reading Plan: 2 Chronicles 5–7

WHEN DID SOLOMON'S DOWNFALL BEGIN?

And Solomon brought up the daughter of Pharaoh out of the city of David unto the house that he had built for her: for he said, My wife shall not dwell in the house of David king of Israel, because the places are holy, whereunto the ark of the LORD hath come. Then Solomon offered burnt offerings unto the LORD on the altar of the Lord, which he had built before the porch.

2 CHRONICLES 8:11–12

Solomon got his reign as Israel's king off to an amazing start. But he gradually drifted away from the Lord, largely because he disobediently married seven hundred women—many of whom did not believe in the one true God.

The first of these marriages grew out of political convenience. After marrying the Egyptian Pharaoh's daughter, he moved her into her own palace. "My wife," he reasoned, "must not live in the palace of David king of Israel, because the places the ark of the LORD has entered are holy" (2 Chronicles 8:11 NIV).

In today's passage, we see an example of Solomon's "compartmentalizing." Immediately after disobeying God by marrying an Egyptian woman, Solomon went to the temple to worship God with a burnt offering. In a sense, two Solomons existed—the political Solomon and the religious one.

Eventually, Solomon's duplicity led to the downfall of the kingdom he had worked so hard to build. His story illustrates the importance of surrendering to God every aspect of our lives, including the "secular" parts.

Reading Plan: 2 Chronicles 8–9

WHERE DID REHOBOAM GO WRONG?

*And king Rehoboam took counsel with the old men that had stood
before Solomon his father while he yet lived, saying, What counsel
give ye me to return answer to this people? And they spake unto
him, saying, If thou be kind to this people, and please them, and
speak good words to them, they will be thy servants for ever.*

2 CHRONICLES 10:6–7

As Rehoboam, Solomon's son and successor to the throne, began his reign as king of Israel, he asked the wise men who had served his father how he could win the loyalty of his country's citizens. Their advice was simple: if he treated the people with kindness, they'd happily follow his leading.

Sadly, Rehoboam didn't listen to these older, wiser counselors. Instead, he consulted young men, who advised him to rule with an iron fist. They advised Rehoboam to tell the people, "My father laid on you a heavy yoke; I will make it even heavier. My father scourged you with whips; I will scourge you with scorpions" (2 Chronicles 10:11 NIV).

Rehoboam followed his young advisers' counsel, largely because it reflected his own approach. Bad decision! Because the new king ignored wise counsel, he eventually lost more than half of Israel's once-great kingdom.

We can find two important lessons in Rehoboam's error. First, be careful who you listen to—while advanced age isn't a guarantee of wisdom, older people have a lot more life experience than the young. And second, when it comes to how we treat people, kindness—in word and action—is always the best choice.

Reading Plan: 2 Chronicles 10–13

WHERE DID KING ASA GO WRONG?

And he went out to meet Asa, and said unto him, Hear ye me, Asa, and all Judah and Benjamin; The LORD is with you, while ye be with him; and if ye seek him, he will be found of you; but if ye forsake him, he will forsake you.

2 CHRONICLES 15:2

Asa was a descendant of King David and the third ruler of the Southern Kingdom of Judah. He was the son of Abijah, Judah's second king, who did much evil during his three-year reign.

Asa, however, "did what was good and right in the eyes of the LORD his God" (2 Chronicles 14:2 NIV). He ruled in Judah for forty-one years and instituted many religious reforms. He removed male shrine prostitutes, cut down Asherah poles, and commanded his people to follow God (see 2 Chronicles 14:4).

Though Asa had a heart for God, he made serious mistakes late in his reign—much like many other Old Testament kings—and began trusting in people rather than God for Judah's security. When a prophet named Hanani confronted him about his sin, Asa became enraged and had the prophet imprisoned (see 2 Chronicles 16:7–10). Even worse, he "brutally oppressed some of the people" (verse 10 NIV).

Asa went terribly wrong when he took his focus off the Lord. May we always resemble the Asa who trusted God and listened to His spokesman, not the Asa who responded in rage when confronted about his sin.

Reading Plan: 2 Chronicles 14–18

WHAT SHOULD I DO IN TIMES OF DESPERATION?

*O our God, wilt thou not judge them? for we have no
might against this great company that cometh against us;
neither know we what to do: but our eyes are upon thee.*

2 CHRONICLES 20:12

After receiving news about a legitimate threat to his kingdom, King Jehoshaphat was terrified. A vast army of Ammonites, Moabites, and others was marching toward Judah with the worst of intentions. Judah's forces were vastly outnumbered, and the kingdom's destruction seemed imminent.

Jehoshaphat, his army, and the rest of his subjects shook with fear as they considered their fate. The king, desperate and unsure of what to do, called on his people to pray in Jerusalem for God's protection and deliverance. Jehoshaphat admitted to God that Judah stood no chance against the approaching hoards, but his prayer also included a confession that would save his kingdom: "Our eyes are upon thee."

God answered Jehoshaphat's prayer, miraculously saving His people from certain death—without a single soldier in Judah going to battle.

It's been said that desperate times call for desperate measures. For the man of God, those desperate measures could mean getting on your knees and seeking God for answers and deliverance.

Reading Plan: 2 Chronicles 19–21

WHERE DID KING JOASH GO WRONG?

*Now after the death of Jehoiada came the princes of Judah,
and made obeisance to the king. Then the king hearkened
unto them. And they left the house of the LORD God of their
fathers, and served groves and idols: and wrath came
upon Judah and Jerusalem for this their trespass.*

2 CHRONICLES 24:17–18

The story of Joash, Judah's eighth king, tragically illustrates how a wrong focus can derail a life of great accomplishments for the Lord. Second Chronicles 24:2 (NIV) says, "Joash did what was right in the eyes of the Lord all the years of Jehoiada the priest."

Notice the last words: *all the years of Jehoiada the priest.*

As a young man, Joash was passionately committed to restoring God's temple. He remained true to that calling as long as his mentor, the high priest Jehoiada, was alive. But after Jehoiada died, the king abandoned the temple's restoration, began listening to evil advisers, and started worshipping idols. God sent prophets to warn Joash, but he refused to listen. And when the prophet Zechariah, Jehoida's son, confronted Joash about his sin, the king had him killed. Joash was later assassinated by one of his own officials, leaving a legacy of rebellion and disobedience.

Joash went terribly wrong in serving one of God's prophets instead of God Himself. Sadly, this can happen today, when Christians are known more as disciples of a particular pastor or leader than for following Jesus. Today, commit to keeping your focus where it belongs. . .and avoid the kind of fall Joash experienced.

Reading Plan: 2 Chronicles 22–24

WHAT KIND OF KING WAS UZZIAH?

*And he did that which was right in the sight of the Lord, according
to all that his father Amaziah did. And he sought God in the days
of Zechariah, who had understanding in the visions of God: and
as long as he sought the Lord, God made him to prosper.*

2 CHRONICLES 26:4–5

The reign of Uzziah, Judah's tenth king, followed the pattern of other Old Testament kingships—it had a solid start but ended in disgrace. Uzziah began as a strong leader who "sought God in the days of Zechariah." And as long as He focused on the Lord, God blessed him with prosperity and military success.

But as Uzziah's power and wealth increased, he forgot the reason for his success—his relationship with God. His priorities soon shifted from serving God and his nation to gaining more success and power.

Consequently, Uzziah left a legacy of shame. After a particular egregious sin, his life ended terribly; the Bible says, "King Uzziah had leprosy until the day he died. He lived in a separate house—leprous, and banned from the temple of the Lord" (2 Chronicles 26:21 NIV).

What a sad ending to such a promising life.

We can't know for sure, but maybe the apostle Paul thought of Uzziah when he wrote, "Do nothing out of selfish ambition or vain conceit. Rather, in humility value others above yourselves, not looking to your own interests but each of you to the interests of the others" (Philippians 2:3–4 NIV).

Reading Plan: 2 Chronicles 25–28

WHAT DOES IT MEAN TO BE CHOSEN?

*My sons, be not now negligent: for the Lord hath chosen
you to stand before him, to serve him, and that ye
should minister unto him, and burn incense.*

2 CHRONICLES 29:11

Hezekiah, Judah's thirteenth king, was one of the few Old Testament rulers who served God consistently throughout his reign. Second Kings 18:5 (NIV) says, "Hezekiah trusted in the Lord, the God of Israel. There was no one like him among all the kings of Judah, either before him or after him."

Because Hezekiah prioritized his kingdom's worship of God, he called the priests and Levites to "purify" the temple by removing anything unclean. Before he set them to work, he told them, "The Lord has chosen you to stand before him and serve him, to minister before him and to burn incense" (2 Chronicles 29:11 NIV).

By calling the priests and Levites "chosen," Hezekiah was telling them that God had given them very specific work to do. It was an important responsibility and a wonderful honor for them to work in His holy temple.

As a follower of Jesus, you are a "chosen" man—chosen to glorify God and bring others into His kingdom through your words and deeds. The apostle Paul confirmed this truth when he wrote, "For we are God's handiwork, created in Christ Jesus to do good works, which God prepared in advance for us to do" (Ephesians 2:10 NIV).

> **Reading Plan: 2 Chronicles 29–30**

WHAT WAS MANASSEH'S "HAPPY ENDING"?

Wherefore the LORD brought upon them the captains of the host of the king of Assyria, which took Manasseh among the thorns, and bound him with fetters, and carried him to Babylon. And when he was in affliction, he besought the LORD his God, and humbled himself greatly before the God of his fathers.

2 CHRONICLES 33:11–12

Judah's history spanned a few godly kings and several evil ones. Oddly enough, one of Judah's best kings, Hezekiah, was the father of one of the worst, Manasseh. After taking the throne, Manasseh undid all his father's religious reforms and led his people into pagan worship.

But as evil as Manasseh was for nearly his entire reign, the Lord didn't give up on him. After trying in vain to get Manasseh's attention, God chose to deal with him the hard way. Second Chronicles 33:11 (NIV) says, "So the LORD brought against them the army commanders of the king of Assyria, who took Manasseh prisoner, put a hook in his nose, bound him with bronze shackles and took him to Babylon."

Manasseh knew he was in big trouble, so he prayed to the one true God. God listened to his prayers and brought him back to Jerusalem. Then, "Manasseh knew that the LORD is God" (2 Chronicles 33:13 NIV).

Although his story had a happy ending, things would have gone much easier for Manasseh had he listened to God from the start. The same is true for us.

Reading Plan: 2 Chronicles 31–33

WHAT IS GOD'S ULTIMATE REMEDY?

*And the LORD God of their fathers sent to them by his messengers,
rising up betimes, and sending; because he had compassion on his
people, and on his dwelling place: but they mocked the messengers
of God, and despised his words, and misused his prophets, until the
wrath of the LORD arose against his people, till there was no remedy.*

2 CHRONICLES 36:15–16

The reign of Zedekiah, Judah's last king, ended horribly for him and his people. Zedekiah was an evil king who "did evil in the eyes of the LORD his God and did not humble himself before Jeremiah the prophet, who spoke the word of the LORD" (2 Chronicles 36:12 NIV). During his reign, he and his people refused to listen to God and His prophets, instead continuing in their idolatry, adultery, mistreatment of others, and other terrible sins (Jeremiah 7:5–31).

God finally pronounced judgment on Judah, saying there was "no remedy" for the nation and its people. In about 586 BC, the Babylonians attacked Jerusalem and the rest of Judah (Jeremiah 52). They tore down the city walls, destroyed the temple, and set fires throughout the capital. Many people died, and many more were carted off into Babylon captivity for seventy years.

God is a God of love, but He is also a God of holiness. As a result, He *must* judge sin. One day, He will pronounce His final judgment on this world, though He has provided each of us a "remedy"—a way to escape His wrath. That remedy is Jesus, who came to earth to live a sinless life, then die in our place so that we could live with Him forever. His offer of salvation is free and available to all. Are you in?

Reading Plan: 2 Chronicles 34–36

WHAT IS EZRA ALL ABOUT?

About a half century after Babylonians sacked Jerusalem and carried Jews into captivity, Persia stood as the new world power. The Persian king, Cyrus, allowed a group of exiles to return to Judah to rebuild the temple. Some forty-two thousand people returned and resettled the land under a governor named Zerubbabel.

About seventy years after that, a priest named Ezra was part of a smaller group that also returned to Judah. He taught the law to the people, who had fallen away from God to the point of intermarrying with nearby pagan nations, something that was strictly forbidden by Moses (Deuteronomy 7:1–3). Even though God has said He hates divorce (see Malachi 2:16), Ezra urged Jewish men to separate from their foreign wives to maintain their spiritual purity.

In the book of Ezra, God showed His willingness to offer a second chance—allowing a nation that had been punished for disobedience to have a fresh start. Even today, He's still in the second-chance business.

Reading Plan: Ezra 1–3

HOW DID ZERUBBABEL HANDLE OPPOSITION?

Zerubbabel, and Jeshua, and the rest of the chief of the fathers of Israel, said unto them, Ye have nothing to do with us to build an house unto our God; but we ourselves together will build unto the LORD God of Israel, as king Cyrus the king of Persia hath commanded us.

EZRA 4:3

After Cyrus proclaimed that the Jews could return to their homeland, three waves of former captives left Persia for Judah. The first wave was led by a man named Zerubbabel, who supervised the rebuilding of God's temple in Jerusalem. After getting settled, the people got to work.

Before long, some enemies of the Israelites tried to halt the construction. One group approached Zerubbabel, offering to help out: "Let us help you build because, like you, we seek your God and have been sacrificing to him since the time of Esarhaddon king of Assyria, who brought us here" (Ezra 4:2 NIV).

Sounds like a great offer, right? But Zerubbabel saw through the ruse and realized that these "helpers" had ulterior motives. Rather than accept their offer, he sent them on their way.

Like Zerubbabel, we as Christian men will face opposition as we attempt great things for God. Also like Zerubbabel, we should use God's wisdom to identify the opposition, handling it as our Lord directs.

Reading Plan: Ezra 4–6

WHAT QUALIFIES US FOR GOD'S WORK?

*Ezra had prepared his heart to seek the law of the LORD, and
to do it, and to teach in Israel statutes and judgments.*

EZRA 7:10

Ezra was an impressive man whom God used to lead a second wave
of Jews out of Babylon and back to Jerusalem. After Zerubbabel—who
oversaw the reconstruction of God's temple—led the first group back
(Ezra 3:8), Nehemiah rebuilt the city walls (Nehemiah 1–2). Ezra, when
he arrived, restored worship in Jerusalem.

Ezra was a priest, and the Persian king Artaxerxes had given him
great religious and political authority over Jerusalem. But that's not
what gave Ezra his power.

Ezra 7:6 (NIV) says that he "was a teacher well versed in the Law of
Moses, which the LORD, the God of Israel, had given." In other words, Ezra
had studied the law for many years and was more than able to teach
others, helping them apply it to their lives. Today's scripture tells us why:
his heart was determined to learn God's Word. Ezra loved God and obeyed
Him, speaking His Word to people who desperately needed to hear it.

If you want God to use you to accomplish great things, be like Ezra.
Set your heart to study God's Word, do what it says, and teach it to others.

Reading Plan: Ezra 7–8

WHY WOULD EZRA PULL OUT HIS OWN HAIR?

*Now when these things were done, the princes came to
me, saying, The people of Israel, and the priests, and the
Levites, have not separated themselves from the people of
the lands, doing according to their abominations, even of
the Canaanites, the Hittites, the Perizzites, the Jebusites, the
Ammonites, the Moabites, the Egyptians, and the Amorites.*

EZRA 9:1

Around 458 BC, about seventy years after Zerubbabel's group had arrived, Ezra and a second wave of Jews arrived in Jerusalem after leaving Persia.

Upon arrival, Ezra could barely believe what he was told: God's people had begun engaging in the wicked practices of the surrounding nations. Not only that, the men had been marrying foreign women—an action that God had expressly forbidden. Even worse, the people's leaders were permitting these marriages (Ezra 9:1–3).

Heartbroken and stunned, Ezra "tore [his] tunic and cloak, pulled hair from [his] head and beard and sat down appalled" (Ezra 9:3 NIV). After mourning his people's disobedience, Ezra got busy correcting the situation (Ezra 9–10).

Ezra refused to let his sadness stop him. No matter how upset he'd been, he picked himself up and did everything he could to solve the problem. Undoubtedly, he spent time in prayer, asking God for strength. May we follow Ezra's example in our homes, workplaces, and neighborhoods.

Reading Plan: Ezra 9–10

WHAT IS NEHEMIAH ALL ABOUT?

The book of Nehemiah contains "the words of Nehemiah" (1:1), though Jewish tradition says those words were put on paper by Ezra.

Nehemiah served as "the king's cupbearer" (1:11) in Shushan, Persia. As a Jew, he was disturbed to learn that even though exiles had been back in Judah for nearly a hundred years, they had not rebuilt the city's walls, devastated by the Babylonians in 586 BC. Nehemiah asked and received permission from King Artaxerxes to return to Jerusalem, where he led a team of builders—against much pagan opposition—in reconstructing the walls in only fifty-two days. The quick work on the project shocked the Jews' enemies, who "perceived that this work was wrought of our God" (6:16).

Nehemiah's success in rebuilding Jerusalem's walls provides many leadership principles for today—especially his consistent focus on prayer.

Reading Plan: Nehemiah 1–3

HOW WERE JERUSALEM'S WALLS REBUILT SO QUICKLY?

*So the wall was finished in the twenty and fifth day of the month
Elul, in fifty and two days. And it came to pass, that when all our
enemies heard thereof, and all the heathen that were about us
saw these things, they were much cast down in their own eyes:
for they perceived that this work was wrought of our God.*

NEHEMIAH 6:15–16

The people of Judah, knowing that their enemies were planning to sabotage the reconstruction of Jerusalem's walls, prayed for God's protection—and armed themselves. According to Nehemiah 4:16–18, only half of Nehemiah's men worked on the wall—the others stood guard with spears, shields, and bows. Even the workers were prepared for battle, as "those who carried materials did their work with one hand and held a weapon in the other" (verse 17 NIV).

Though Jerusalem's enemies didn't want the walls rebuilt, the people finished the work in a miraculous fifty-two days. Even the Jews' enemies saw this feat as proof of God's power: "When all our enemies heard about this, all the surrounding nations were afraid and lost their self-confidence, because they realized that this work had been done with the help of our God" (Nehemiah 6:16 NIV).

Nehemiah's miraculous story proves that when God does a great work through us, people —even our enemies—will notice. And, as the apostle Peter would write centuries later, those enemies might even become friends. "Live such good lives among the pagans," he said, "that, though they accuse you of doing wrong, they may see your good deeds and glorify God on the day he visits us" (1 Peter 2:12 NIV).

Reading Plan: Nehemiah 4–6

WHAT DOES "THE JOY OF THE LORD IS YOUR STRENGTH" MEAN?

Then he said unto them, Go your way, eat the fat, and drink the sweet, and send portions unto them for whom nothing is prepared: for this day is holy unto our LORD: neither be ye sorry; for the joy of the LORD is your strength.

NEHEMIAH 8:10

God had brought His people back to their homeland after the seventy-year Babylonian captivity. Once the walls around Jerusalem had been completed, the people gathered at the town square to hear Ezra the priest read from the law.

At first, the people cheered as Ezra read, but as the priest continued, their hearts sank—

they realized how far they had drifted from God. Men and women alike began weeping, overwhelmed with feelings of condemnation.

God's Word brought deep conviction of sin, just as God had intended it to (see Hebrews 4:12). Though the people were now despondent, Nehemiah spoke words of encouragement, reminding them to celebrate what God had done for them. "Do not grieve," he said, "for the joy of the LORD is your strength" (Nehemiah 8:10 NIV).

Nehemiah wanted the people to know that despite their deep imperfections, they were still God's chosen people. He took great joy in them, and His joy would be their source of power for everyday living. That is still true for Christians today.

Reading Plan: Nehemiah 7–9

DOES GOD WANT OUR VOWS?

They clave to their brethren, their nobles, and entered into a curse,
and into an oath, to walk in God's law, which was given by Moses
the servant of God, and to observe and do all the commandments
of the LORD our Lord, and his judgments and his statutes.

NEHEMIAH 10:29

The leaders of those Israelites who had returned from the Babylonian captivity knew the importance of keeping promises. So as the people all determined to enter a covenant of recommitment with the one true God—the God who had remained faithful to them—a sense of solemnity and reverence must have hung heavily in the air.

Centuries before, God had promised Abraham that he would be the patriarch of a nation through which God would bless the whole world. As God had promised, Abraham's descendants grew into the nation of Israel. However, God's chosen people gradually drifted further and further from Him—and eventually God judged them by removing them from their homeland.

Now that Nehemiah and God's people were home, they renewed their vows to God, promising to faithfully obey every word of His law.

Such commitments are good. But the bigger issue is whether we live up to our promises. When we tell God we're going to do something—whether following Jesus in salvation or performing some specific duty—we need to honor that commitment. Vows are only as good as their fulfillment.

Reading Plan: Nehemiah 10–11

WHAT MADE NEHEMIAH SO ANGRY?

And I contended with them, and cursed them, and smote certain
of them, and plucked off their hair, and made them swear by
God, saying, Ye shall not give your daughters unto their sons,
nor take their daughters unto your sons, or for yourselves.
Did not Solomon king of Israel sin by these things?
NEHEMIAH 13:25–26

Nehemiah, after temporarily returning to the Persian king Artaxerxes, came back to Jerusalem to see how the Lord's work was progressing among his people. Upon arrival, he was heartbroken and enraged to learn that some Jewish men had married women from places like Ashdod, Ammon, and Moab. Nehemiah was so angry that he called down curses on them, beating some of them and pulling out their hair (Nehemiah 13:25).

Why did Nehemiah respond so angrily? First, these men had openly disobeyed God by becoming romantically involved with women who did not love God. Second, Nehemiah remembered how Solomon's relationships with foreign women had led directly to the fall of the once great nation of Israel.

How would you respond if you found out that a fellow Christian had intentionally started down a path of sin? A physical confrontation isn't the best idea, but just standing by and saying nothing would be even worse. That's why Paul wrote, "If someone is caught in a sin, you who live by the Spirit should restore that person *gently*" (Galatians 6:1 NIV, italics added).

Reading Plan: Nehemiah 12–13

WHAT IS ESTHER ALL ABOUT?

In a nutshell, a beautiful Jewish girl becomes queen of Persia, and saves her fellow Jews from slaughter. In a slightly longer version, the Persian king Ahasuerus became angry with his queen, Vashti, for refusing to appear before his male advisers, who had been enjoying "wine in abundance" (1:7). Vashti was deposed, and Ahasuerus began looking for a replacement.

In a nationwide beauty contest, young Esther became queen of Persia without ever revealing her Jewish heritage. When a royal official plotted to kill every Jew in the country, Esther risked her own life to request the king's protection. The king, pleased with Esther, was shocked by his official's plan and had the man hanged—while decreeing that the Jews should defend themselves against the planned slaughter. Esther's people prevailed and began commemorating their victory with a holiday called Purim.

It is interesting to note that God's name is never mentioned in the book of Esther. Neither is prayer, though Esther asks her fellow Jews to fast for her before she approaches the king (4:16). God is certainly in the background of Esther's story, and its message resonates through the centuries: when we find ourselves in bad situations, it may be for the same reason Esther did—to accomplish something good.

Reading Plan: Esther 1–3

WHY WAS ESTHER WILLING TO DIE?

Then Esther bade them return Mordecai this answer, Go, gather
together all the Jews that are present in Shushan, and fast ye for
me, and neither eat nor drink three days, night or day: I also and
my maidens will fast likewise; and so will I go in unto the king,
which is not according to the law: and if I perish, I perish.

ESTHER 4:15–16

Esther loved her fellow Jews, especially her cousin and foster father Mordecai, so she was willing to do anything to prevent them from dying. But although Esther was the Persian king Xerxes's wife, she knew it was unlawful to approach him without being summoned (Esther 4:11). But Esther had no choice; she was going to approach Xerxes and plead her people's case. Doing so might mean death, but doing nothing would mean the certain death of countless Jews throughout Susa.

After asking Mordecai to gather all the Jews in Susa and fast three days for her, she prepared herself to approach the king.

By risking her life for her people, Esther became a living example of Jesus' words, "Greater love has no one than this: to lay down one's life for one's friends" (John 15:13 NIV). That's the extreme example. Are we willing to lay down some comfort, or money, or our reputation for a friend? Sacrifice is the calling of Christian men.

Reading Plan: Esther 4–6

HOW DID ESTHER FOIL HAMAN'S MURDEROUS PLOT?

Then Esther the queen answered and said, If I have found favour in thy sight, O king, and if it please the king, let my life be given me at my petition, and my people at my request: For we are sold, I and my people, to be destroyed, to be slain, and to perish.

ESTHER 7:3–4

Yesterday, you read about Esther's deep love for her people and how she hatched a plan to approach King Xerxes to plead with him to protect the Jews. Now, let's see what happened next.

Esther's heart was probably pounding as she approached the king, knowing he had the power to put her to death. So imagine her relief when Xerxes said to her, "Queen Esther, what is your petition? It will be given you. What is your request? Even up to half the kingdom, it will be granted" (Esther 7:2 NIV).

Not only did King Xerxes grant Esther's request, he had the evil Haman executed.

The courage Esther showed by approaching the king can only be explained as supernatural—and God promises to give each of us this courage when we cry out to Him. As David sang, "With your help I can advance against a troop; with my God I can scale a wall" (Psalm 18:29 NIV).

Reading Plan: Esther 7–10

WHAT IS JOB ALL ABOUT?

Head of a large family, Job was a wealthy farmer from a place called Uz. He was "perfect and upright" (1:1)—so much so, that God called Satan's attention to him. The devil, unimpressed, asked and received God's permission to attack Job's possessions—wiping out thousands of sheep, camels, oxen, donkeys, and worst of all, Job's ten children. Despite Satan's attack, Job kept his faith. But then Satan received God's permission to attack Job's health—still, in spite of terrible physical suffering, Job refused to "curse God, and die" as his desperate wife suggested (2:9).

Before long, though, Job began to question why God would allow him—a good man—to suffer so severely. Job's suffering was worsened by the arrival of four "friends" who accused him of causing his own trouble by secret sin. "Is not thy wickedness great?" asked Eliphaz the Temanite (22:5). In the end, though God Himself spoke, vindicating Job before his friends and also addressing the overarching issue of human suffering. God didn't explain Job's suffering but asked a series of questions that showed His vast knowledge—implying that Job should simply trust God's way. And Job did, telling God, "I know that thou canst do every thing" (42:2). By story's end, God had restored Job's health, possessions, and family, giving him ten more children.

Job's story proves that trouble isn't necessarily a sign of sin in a person's life. It may be something God allows to draw us closer to Him.

Reading Plan: Job 1–5

WHAT DOES JOB TEACH US ABOUT INTEGRITY?

*Even that it would please God to destroy me; that he would
let loose his hand, and cut me off! Then should I yet have
comfort; yea, I would harden myself in sorrow: let him not
spare; for I have not concealed the words of the Holy One.*

JOB 6:9–10

Job's three friends showed great compassion when they traveled to his place just to sit quietly with him and share in his suffering (Job 2:13). However, when Job finally broke the silence with an extended lament about his anguish (Job 3), Eliphaz the Temanite responded by calling him to repentance (Job 4–5).

But Job insisted that he was innocent, that sin had nothing to do with his suffering, and that he "had not denied the words of the Holy One"(Job 6:10 NIV).

In this world, we will have trouble. That's a promise from Jesus Himself (John 16:33). Job certainly experienced that, and though he faced many moments of anger and doubt, his deep-seated relationship with God ultimately pulled him through some of the worst trials we could imagine.

The Bible says that Job "was blameless and upright; he feared God and shunned evil" (Job 1:1 NIV). This should be our goal as well. When we live with that kind of integrity, we'll be able to enjoy the rest of Jesus' statement in John 16:33: "But take heart! I have overcome the world" (NIV).

Reading Plan: Job 6–10

HOW DOES GOD REVEAL HIMSELF IN CREATION?

But ask now the beasts, and they shall teach thee; and the fowls of the air, and they shall tell thee: Or speak to the earth, and it shall teach thee: and the fishes of the sea shall declare unto thee.

JOB 12:7–8

Many people love getting away and enjoying the outdoors. But for a man of God, these activities offer something more—a truly spiritual experience.

One of the best things about fishing, hunting, hiking, camping, or any other outdoor activity is the place itself. In these settings we can see and enjoy God's handiwork, free from manmade distractions.

The creation is not God Himself, just like a sculpture or painting isn't the artist who made it. But by enjoying the wonder of God's creation, you can learn great truths about His nature and character.

So the next time you embark on an outdoor excursion, don't forget to take your heavenly Father with you. Away from the world's noise, you can enjoy His company. . .and maybe even hear His voice.

Reading Plan: Job 11–14

WHAT CAN WE LEARN FROM JOB'S FRIENDS?

Then Job answered and said, I have heard many such things: miserable comforters are ye all. Shall vain words have an end? or what emboldeneth thee that thou answerest?

JOB 16:1–3

When Job's three friends—Eliphaz, Bildad, and Zophar—heard about all that had happened to Job, they traveled from their homes to visit him in Uz and try to comfort him, as any good friend would do. Upon arrival, they sat with him for seven days and seven nights without saying a word.

So far, so good.

Most of the book of Job (chapters 3–31) tells how Job's three friends tried to help him make sense of why such a good man should have to suffer so much. Sadly, however, instead of listening to him, praying with him, and offering real comfort, they spent much of their time accusing Job of foolishness and hidden wickedness.

"Miserable comforters" indeed!

Job told the three they were wrong and he was innocent. And they *were* wrong—about Job and about the God whom Job faithfully loved and served. Their biggest mistake was voicing their opinions without possessing all the facts.

Any of us can make this blunder. That's why it's crucial that we slow down, listening and thinking much before we speak just a little. Let's commit to gaining real understanding before we say uninformed, potentially hurtful words.

Reading Plan: Job 15–19

WHAT WILL BECOME OF THE WICKED?

They are exalted for a little while, but are gone and brought low; they are taken out of the way as all other, and cut off as the tops of the ears of corn. And if it be not so now, who will make me a liar, and make my speech nothing worth?

JOB 24:24–25

After listening to his three friends accuse him of many types of sin, Job spends much of chapter 24 pondering why evildoers often seem to prosper. Job thinks he knows what *should* happen to the wicked (verses 18–21), and he's not wrong. In today's scripture he concludes, evil men will be "brought low" and "taken out of the way."

"If it be not so now," Job declared, "who will make me a liar, and make my speech nothing worth?" In other words, even though followers of God may suffer while sinful people prosper, in the end God will judge the ungodly and bless the righteous.

Though Job had some great lessons to learn through his suffering, he was still a fundamentally godly man who would eventually receive the Lord's blessings. By not allowing false accusations to make him doubt his integrity, he became a stronger, better-grounded man of God.

Reading Plan: Job 20–24

HOW CAN I KEEP MY MIND SEXUALLY PURE?

I made a covenant with mine eyes; why then should I think upon a maid?

JOB 31:1

When we read God's seventh commandment—"You shall not commit adultery" (Exodus 20:14 NIV)—we might take comfort in knowing that we've never engaged in "the act" with someone other than our spouse. But Jesus offered some tough teaching on the subject—namely, it isn't just where we take our bodies, but even more importantly the impure places our thoughts can go (see Matthew 5:27–28).

So how can we keep those lustful desires from entering our minds? Job, a man who lived thousands of years before Jesus' birth, offers some practical advice: "I made a covenant with my eyes not to look lustfully at a young woman" (Job 31:1 NIV).

Job understood that what a man allows to enter his brain tends to stay there—as hard as he might try to make it go away. The key, he concluded, is to be extremely cautious about what we look at.

That's no easy task—especially today, when seemingly every other image that enters our field of view might be problematic. But this is a matter of commitment. . .to your spouse, your children, and your Father in heaven.

> **Reading Plan: Job 25–31**

WHAT CAN WE LEARN FROM ELIHU?

*Then was kindled the wrath of Elihu the son of Barachel the
Buzite, of the kindred of Ram: against Job was his wrath
kindled, because he justified himself rather than God. Also
against his three friends was his wrath kindled, because
they had found no answer, and yet had condemned Job.*

JOB 32:2–3

After speaking many half-truths and outright misunderstandings about
God and Job in chapters 3–31, Bildad, Eliphaz, and Zophar take a back
seat. A new character appears on the scene in chapter 32: a young man
named Elihu, who had apparently eavesdropped on the conversation.

Much has been written about Elihu's youth and his ability to humbly
hold his tongue while four men demonstrated their weak knowledge of
God. But today, let's focus on this key fact: Elihu was quite piqued at the
older men—Job because he had spent so much time defending himself
instead of God, and Job's three friends because they had condemned
a good man.

Yes, Elihu was angry *at* these four men, but he was probably also
angry *for* them because they had allowed Job's situation to take their
focus off God's goodness and justice.

Has one of your close friends or loved ones ever drifted away from
God? If so, you probably felt heartbroken or even angry. But that anger
doesn't have to be destructive. . .as long as it motivates you to lovingly
speak the truth and fervently pray for that wayward believer each day.

Reading Plan: Job 32–37

WHY DID GOD ASK JOB SO MANY QUESTIONS?

Then the Lord answered Job out of the whirlwind,
and said, Who is this that darkeneth counsel by words
without knowledge? Gird up now thy loins like a man;
for I will demand of thee, and answer thou me.

JOB 38:1–3

When the time was right, God appeared to Job through a whirlwind and spoke some much-needed truth. The Lord didn't directly answer any of Job's questions or complaints. Instead, He asked Job dozens of impossible-to-answer questions (Job 38–42), including: "Where were you when I laid the earth's foundation?" (Job 38:4 NIV).

These questions were asked so that Job could better understand God's greatness—as well as Job's smallness as a mere human. In the end, Job could never fully grasp God's magnificence, power, or reasons.

Job responded the only way he could: with deep humility, acknowledging his own humanity and lack of understanding (Job 40:3–5). Later, as God's questioning continued, Job repented deeply (Job 42:1–6).

A mature man of God is humble enough to know when he's wrong. That will happen often enough. When it does, let's admit our failure to our heavenly Father, who is faithful to forgive, cleanse, and reveal His own greatness.

Reading Plan: Job 38–42

WHAT IS PSALMS ALL ABOUT?

Over several centuries, God led various individuals to compose emotionally charged poems—of which 150 were later compiled into the book we know as Psalms. Many of the psalms are described as "of David," meaning they could be by, for, or about Israel's great king.

Highlights of the book include the "shepherd psalm" (23), which describes God as protector and provider; David's cry for forgiveness after his sin with Bathsheba (51); psalms of praise (100 is a powerful example); and the celebration of scripture found in Psalm 119, with almost all of the 176 verses making some reference to God's laws, statutes, commandments, precepts, word, and the like. Some psalms, called "imprecatory," call for God's judgment on enemies (see Psalms 69 and 109, for example). Many psalms express agony of spirit on the writer's part—but nearly every psalm returns to the theme of praise to God. That's the way the book of Psalms ends: "Let every thing that hath breath praise the LORD. Praise ye the LORD" (150:6).

The book of Psalms is the Bible's longest, in terms of both number of chapters (150) and total word count. It contains the longest chapter in the Bible (Psalm 119) and the shortest (Psalm 117, with only 2 verses). Psalm 117 is also the midpoint of the Protestant Bible, with 594 chapters before it and 594 after.

The psalms run the gamut of human emotion—which is why so many people turn to them in times of both joy and sadness.

Reading Plan: Psalms 1–10

WHAT IMPORTANT EVENT DID PSALM 16 PREDICT?

For thou wilt not leave my soul in hell; neither wilt
thou suffer thine Holy One to see corruption.

PSALM 16:10

Many centuries before God's only begotten Son came to live a perfect life on earth and willingly die for humanity's sins, God spoke through His prophets, foretelling many important events in Jesus' life and the impact they would have on His people.

When David wrote today's scripture, he was unknowingly writing about the resurrection of Jesus the Messiah—an event God would orchestrate many centuries later. But the apostle Peter knew. That's why he said, "God raised him from the dead, freeing him from the agony of death, because it was impossible for death to keep its hold on him" (Acts 2:24 NIV), explaining that this verse perfectly predicted Jesus' resurrection from the dead (see Acts 2:25–32).

That was no coincidence—it was God keeping a huge promise to His people.

By resurrecting Jesus after He had died on a cross to bear all of our sins, God proved that Jesus truly was His "Holy One" and that He had power over sin and death.

God's love and power are truly amazing. . .and He has directed them toward you. How does that change the way you live your life today?

Reading Plan: Psalms 11–18

DOES GOD KNOW
WHAT I'M THINKING?

Let the words of my mouth, and the meditation
*of my heart, be acceptable in thy sight, O L*ord,
my strength, and my redeemer.

PSALM 19:14

Have you at some point ever wanted to know exactly what another person was thinking?

Of course, it is humanly impossible to read people's minds—and honestly, being able to do so would probably create even more problems. But there is One who knows our every thought. As King David wrote of his God, "You know when I sit and when I rise; you perceive my thoughts from afar" (Psalm 139:2 NIV).

What a two-edged sword! On the one hand, we're grateful that God knows everything about us, even our thoughts, and loves us anyway. On the other hand, we'd all probably prefer Him not to know the frequently ugly, angry, lustful, doubtful things in our minds.

The fact that God knows your every thought should make you grateful for His immense, forgiving love but also motivate you to "guard your heart," knowing that "everything you do flows from it" (Proverbs 4:23 NIV).

Reading Plan: Psalms 19–27

WHAT IS CONFESSION AND WHY DOES IT MATTER?

When I kept silence, my bones waxed old through my roaring all the day long. For day and night thy hand was heavy upon me: my moisture is turned into the drought of summer.

PSALM 32:3–4

In Psalm 32, David celebrates God's willingness to forgive His people when they confess their sins to Him. This psalm opens with these wonderful words: "Blessed is the one whose transgressions are forgiven, whose sins are covered. Blessed is the one whose sin the Lord does not count against them and in whose spirit is no deceit" (verses 1–2 NIV).

However, in verses 3–4, David looks back on a time when he *didn't* confess his sins to God, remaining silent instead. During that time, David's guilt and misery so consumed him that he felt physically ill.

If you've ever had the burning urge to confess some wrongdoing to God (or maybe another person), you might know how David felt. But you might also remember how the guilt seemed to melt away when you humbly confessed and sought forgiveness.

Confession is a very important part of our relationship with God. It means admitting to God the things we've done or said that displease Him. God has promised to forgive our sins when we simply confess them to Him (see 1 John 1:9). King David exemplified this important truth when he wrote, "I said, 'I will confess my transgressions to the Lord.' And you forgave the guilt of my sin" (Psalm 32:5 NIV).

Reading Plan: Psalms 28–34

HOW SHOULD I RESPOND WHEN GOOD THINGS HAPPEN TO BAD PEOPLE?

Rest in the Lord, and wait patiently for him: fret not thyself
because of him who prospereth in his way, because of
the man who bringeth wicked devices to pass.

PSALM 37:7

Have you ever wondered why God allows evil people to prosper? Why does the person with questionable business ethics see his company grow? Why does the one who leaves his wife and children for another woman go on to live happily? Why do godless people seem to have it all?

In light of such questions, we might be tempted to cry out to God, "It's not fair!"

When King David wrote Psalm 37, he recognized life isn't always fair—that evil people often seem to receive good things *because* of their wrong deeds.

You've probably noticed that yourself. Even though it doesn't seem fair when dishonest, nasty people get their way, David had one message for good people who love God and try to please Him: don't worry about it!

"Do not fret when people succeed in their ways, when they carry out their wicked schemes," he wrote. "Refrain from anger and turn from wrath" (Psalm 37:7–8 NIV).

Many men in this fallen world seem to prosper from their sin. But that should never be true for the man of God. Seek and obey the Lord in every area of your life—that's a sure way to receive His very best in this life and in the life to come.

Reading Plan: Psalms 35–39

HOW CAN I OVERCOME NEGATIVE THINKING?

*Why art thou cast down, O my soul? and why art thou
disquieted in me? hope thou in God: for I shall yet
praise him for the help of his countenance.*

PSALM 42:5

Trials in this life have a way of messing with a man's head, don't they? At some point, nearly every one of us has examined our lives—or at least our current situations—and started thinking: *There's no way out of this. . . . Things aren't going to get better. . . . There's nothing I can do about it. . . . This just isn't fair!*

When life gets difficult, all sorts of voices vie for our attention—and among them is our own.

Of course, we believers should be careful to ignore the voices of the world and the lies of the devil, the enemy of our souls. But we should also make sure our own inner voices don't drown out the voice our loving heavenly Father.

So when you start muttering to yourself about how hopeless or unfair your situation is, stop—and turn your attention to God, who is big enough and more than willing to take control of it all.

As the apostle Peter put it, "Cast all your anxiety on him because he cares for you" (1 Peter 5:7 NIV).

Reading Plan: Psalms 40–47

WHAT SHOULD I DO WHEN I KNOW I'VE SINNED?

I acknowledge my transgressions: and my sin is ever before me. Against thee, thee only, have I sinned, and done this evil in thy sight: that thou mightest be justified when thou speakest, and be clear when thou judgest.

PSALM 51:3–4

Chapters 11 and 12 of 2 Samuel recount a series of shameful behaviors of King David—lust, adultery, and an attempted cover-up that included indirectly murdering one his top military men.

What a mess David made!

But despite these horrendous sins, God still loved David and had a plan for him, so He sent a prophet named Nathan to confront the wayward king. David, after acknowledging that he had sinned against God, penned Psalm 51. Verse 1 says, "Have mercy on me, O God, according to your unfailing love; according to your great compassion blot out my transgressions" (NIV).

David understood something that the apostle John wrote centuries later: "If we confess our sins, he is faithful and just to forgive us our sins, and to cleanse us from all unrighteousness" (1 John 1:9).

One of the Bible's most comforting themes is that God stands ready to forgive repentant sinners. So when you mess up—and you will—don't try to rationalize your sin, cover it up, or hide from God. Instead, run straight to Him in confession. He promises to make you right.

Reading Plan: Psalms 48–55

HOW DOES GOD RESPOND WHEN I'M IN DANGER?

*Be merciful unto me, O God, be merciful unto me: for my
soul trusteth in thee: yea, in the shadow of thy wings will
I make my refuge, until these calamities be overpast.*

PSALM 57:1

Can you imagine the fear and stress you'd feel if you knew someone were intending to physically harm you? David knew exactly how that felt. As King Saul hotly pursued David, intending to kill him because God had anointed him as the next king, David penned Psalm 57.

You probably won't ever find yourself in David's situation. But that doesn't mean you're immune to extreme stress or anxiety. During those times, do as David did: run to God for refuge. He promises to be your source of comfort, peace, encouragement, safety, and help.

Like David, you might sometimes feel like your life is one big disaster. But no matter how severe the situation, you can always run to God, who will protect you. How? "He shall cover thee with his feathers, and under his wings shalt thou trust. . . . Thou shalt not be afraid for the terror by night; nor for the arrow that flieth by day" (Psalm 91:4–5).

Reading Plan: Psalms 56–65

HOW CAN I KEEP MY HEAD ABOVE WATER?

*Save me, O God; for the waters are come in unto my soul.
I sink in deep mire, where there is no standing: I am come
into deep waters, where the floods overflow me.*

PSALM 69:1–2

David wrote Psalm 69 during a time of great sorrow and sadness, when he felt as though life's troubles were about to drag him under for good. But even through David's bitter complaints, this psalm still has hope.

Because David felt like he was sinking in "deep waters," he started his prayer with four vitally important words: "Save me, O God!"

Can you remember a time when your life was so stressful that you felt like you were sinking? Maybe someone was mistreating you or slandering your name. Maybe you lost your job and didn't know how you were going to provide for your family. Or maybe you were dealing with a son or daughter's rebellion and misbehavior.

Whenever it's humanly impossible to stay afloat, that's the time for God to do amazing things. He's always there for you, so when you feel like you're sinking, reach out for Him, remembering these four important words: "Save me, O God!" He won't let you down. . .or drown.

Reading Plan: Psalms 66–71

HOW CAN I DESIRE GOD MORE?

*Whom have I in heaven but thee? and there is none upon earth
that I desire beside thee. My flesh and my heart faileth: but
God is the strength of my heart, and my portion for ever.*

PSALM 73:25–26

The fourth and fifth century church leader Augustine of Hippo once prayed, "Lord, bring to me a sweetness surpassing all the seductive delights that I once pursued. Enable me to love You with all my strength that I may clasp Your hand with all my heart."

What a great request! Augustine confessed that he wanted— *needed*—to love and desire God the way Asaph, the writer of Psalm 73, did.

If we're honest with ourselves, we may confess that we don't always love and desire God the way we should. We may read Psalm 73 and think, *Why can't I love God and feel Asaph's incredible sense of devotion to and desire for Him?*

Here's the good news: we can. Just as a needy man once told Jesus, "I do believe; help me overcome my unbelief!" (Mark 9:24 NIV), we can come to God our Father and earnestly pray, "I love and desire You, Lord. Help me to love and desire You more."

That's the kind of prayer God loves to hear. . .and answer.

Reading Plan: Psalms 72–77

DOES GOD CARE FOR THE POOR AND NEEDY?

*How long will ye judge unjustly, and accept the persons
of the wicked? Selah. Defend the poor and fatherless:
do justice to the afflicted and needy. Deliver the poor
and needy: rid them out of the hand of the wicked.*

PSALM 82:2–4

Psalm 82 is different from most of the others because the psalmist, Asaph, wrote it in the form of a prophecy—specifically one against powerful, influential leaders who acted unjustly toward the vulnerable. Instead of defending the weak, fatherless, poor, and oppressed, these people showed favoritism to those in power.

If we're not careful, we can find ourselves doing the same. But God doesn't want us to be "respecters of persons" (Acts 10:34)—instead, He calls each of us to love and care for everyone, even those whom Jesus called "the least of these" (Matthew 25:40).

The prophet Micah echoed this sentiment when he wrote, "He has shown you, O mortal, what is good. And what does the LORD require of you? To act justly and to love mercy and to walk humbly with your God" (Micah 6:8 NIV).

God cares deeply about the poor, disadvantaged, and vulnerable—and He wants to love them through us. What can you do today to show God's love to someone who desperately needs it?

Reading Plan: Psalms 78–82

HOW DOES GOD RESPOND WHEN I CALL TO HIM?

*Give ear, O LORD, unto my prayer; and attend to the
voice of my supplications. In the day of my trouble
I will call upon thee: for thou wilt answer me.*

PSALM 86:6–7

Kids who grow up in loving homes are usually confident. These children just *know* Mom and Dad care about them and will joyfully meet their needs, even before they're able to ask. They also know their parents will defend and protect them against anything the world throws their way.

Love always gives and protects—it cannot do otherwise. That's true for a good parent. . .and even more so for our heavenly Father. So the apostle John wrote, "This is the confidence we have in approaching God: that if we ask anything according to his will, he hears us" (1 John 5:14 NIV), and it's why the author of Hebrews said, "Let us then approach God's throne of grace with confidence, so that we may receive mercy and find grace to help us in our time of need" (4:16 NIV).

Are you confident in God's love for you and His desire to provide for and protect you when you need it? If so, approach Him with both humility and boldness, knowing He has promised to fulfill your needs. If you're not so sure about God's care and compassion, reread today's scripture. Better yet, memorize it!

Reading Plan: Psalms 83–89

HOW SHOULD I RESPOND TO GOD'S BLESSINGS?

For thou, Lord, hast made me glad through thy work:
I will triumph in the works of thy hands.

PSALM 92:4

Have you ever worshipped God with all you have, overwhelmed by your love for Him and your gratitude for all the ways He blesses you each day? While you shouldn't base your relationship with God on emotion alone, it's still nice to enjoy those moments.

When you deeply ponder who God really is and the wonderful things He does for you (starting with your eternal salvation), gratitude and praise will start pouring out. He's more than worthy of your smiles, your words of praise, and the tears you'll cry as you think of these things.

Today, why not sit down with a pen and paper and start listing the wonderful things God has done for you—beginning with your adoption into His eternal family. Then tell Him how grateful you are for each.

Reading Plan: Psalms 90–99

HOW SHOULD I HANDLE REGRET?

*For as the heaven is high above the earth, so great is his mercy
toward them that fear him. As far as the east is from the
west, so far hath he removed our transgressions from us.*

PSALM 103:11–12

Do you ever feel a twinge of remorse over some sin that you've already humbly and sincerely confessed to God? A little regret isn't necessarily a bad thing, for it helps us to learn from our mistakes. But you should never allow that regret to become guilt—God has already forgiven you.

Today's scripture shows the completeness of God's forgiveness. Focus for a minute on the phrase "as far as the east is from the west" and then consider this: if you started at the North Pole and began traveling south, eventually you would start traveling north again. However, if you started traveling east from any spot on earth, you would keep going east forever. The only way you could travel west is by doing an about-face and heading the opposite direction.

The Bible says God is ready and willing to forgive our sins when we confess them to Him. When we do, He removes our sins and casts them far away—*infinitely* far away.

Reading Plan: Psalms 100–105

HOW CAN A HUNGRY SOUL BE SATISFIED?

Oh that men would praise the LORD for his goodness, and for his wonderful works to the children of men! For he satisfieth the longing soul, and filleth the hungry soul with goodness.

PSALM 107:8–9

When God created our bodies, He arranged them so that we would feel a hunger for nourishment and a thirst for hydration, both of which we need to survive. If we never felt hungry or thirsty, we would likely forget about food and water—and that would be disastrous for our health.

On a spiritual level, God instills in us something even more important: a hunger and thirst for Him. We need God every day.

Sadly, many men try to satisfy that longing for God with anything but Him. They try power, money, relationships, sex, and many other things, hoping to find a satisfaction that only God can give.

Jesus once told His followers, "Blessed are those who hunger and thirst for righteousness, for they will be filled" (Matthew 5:6 NIV). In other words, whenever we turn to God to satisfy our spiritual hunger and thirst, He will fill our souls and lives with the very best thing: Himself.

Reading Plan: Psalms 106–109

HOW TRUSTWORTHY IS GOD?

*It is better to trust in the Lord than to put
confidence in man. It is better to trust in the
Lord than to put confidence in princes.*

PSALM 118:8–9

On a scale of 1 to 100, how trustworthy do you think you are? Even if you consider yourself mostly dependable, you probably know you can't rate yourself at 100—or even 99 or 98. That's because you—and everyone else in this world—are a fallen human being and therefore prone to occasionally failing other people.

The writer of Psalm 118 (perhaps David) wrote of God's goodness, His never-ending mercy, and His other wonderful qualities. And he also wrote that we can place our absolute confidence in Him.

While we all sometimes fail our friends and loved ones—and others fail us—we should never question God's trustworthiness. We can depend on Him to keep 100 percent of His promises, 100 percent of the time. If He said it, He will do it!

Dependable friends and loved ones are blessings from God, and we should express our gratitude for them. But we must always remember that only God deserves our unwavering confidence.

Reading Plan: Psalms 110–118

HOW CAN I AVOID SIN?

*With my whole heart have I sought thee: O let me not
wander from thy commandments. Thy word have I hid
in mine heart, that I might not sin against thee.*

PSALM 119:10–11

On the cover of his Bible, the seventeenth-century Christian writer John Bunyan scrawled this note: "Either this book will keep you from sin, or sin will keep you from this book."

The writer of Psalm 119 would heartily agree. In today's scripture, he declares that keeping his heart and mind focused on God and His Word helps him avoid falling into sin.

If you want a good example of this kind of power, look no further than Jesus Himself.

In Matthew 4, the devil relentlessly tempted the Lord, but Jesus defeated each temptation by speaking the Word of God back to the enemy (see verses 4, 7, 10). In the end, Satan had no choice but to flee the scene of his attempted crime.

When you learn to walk in the tremendous power the Bible gives, you'll find the strength to say yes to the things that please God and no to the things that don't.

No weapon has more power against sin than scripture. Believe it! And then see how God can keep you from sin when you prioritize His Word in your life. Learn to wield this mighty sword by reading it, memorizing it, and meditating on it.

Reading Plan: Psalm 119

WHAT IS TRUE SUCCESS?

*Except the Lord build the house, they labour in
vain that build it: except the Lord keep the city,
the watchman waketh but in vain.*

PSALM 127:1

Today's scripture was written by a man (Solomon) who apparently understood the value of hard work. But more importantly, he realized that without God's guidance and blessing, his work would be still in vain.

The Bible is filled with examples of otherwise godly men who failed to place God's will at the center of their plans, trying instead to depend on their own wisdom or the wisdom of others. Things never ended well for them. In fact, they exemplified how *not* to find true success.

The Bible teaches that we can do nothing on our own. Only when God is at the center can we accomplish things of lasting value.

Something about our fallen nature causes us to trust in human efforts and wisdom. That's a big first step toward trouble. But recognizing this tendency is a big first step toward better things. When we put God not only *in* our plans but *at the center* of everything we do, we find true security and success.

Reading Plan: Psalms 120–134

HOW CAN I BECOME MORE INTIMATE WITH GOD?

Search me, O God, and know my heart: try me,
and know my thoughts: and see if there be any
wicked way in me, and lead me in the way everlasting.

PSALM 139:23–24

In Psalm 139, King David acknowledges that God created him and knows him infinitely better than he knows himself. However, at one point in this psalm, David invites the Lord to know him on an even deeper level.

In today's scripture, David takes a courageous step toward God, inviting Him to thoroughly search him and uncover what lies inside. He asks God to know his heart and thoughts and reveal any wickedness inside him.

These verses reveal David's humility. He was willing to allow the all-holy, all-loving Creator to show David what kind of man he was and to lead him "in the way everlasting" (verse 24).

Psalm 139 gives us a beautiful look into God's heart and the kind of relationship He wants to have with His people. Just as David desired a more intimate relationship with God, we should ask God for the humility and courage to seek Him and fellowship with Him more deeply each day.

Reading Plan: Psalms 135–142

HOW CAN I DEFEAT MY SPIRITUAL ENEMIES?

*Blessed be the Lord my strength which teacheth my hands
to war, and my fingers to fight: my goodness, and my
fortress; my high tower, and my deliverer; my shield, and he
in whom I trust; who subdueth my people under me.*

PSALM 144:1–2

Somehow, many modern followers of Jesus have been convinced that the Christian life is easy, quiet, and without conflict. But that's not what the Bible teaches. In fact, the apostle Paul enjoined his readers to "put on the full armor of God" as they engaged in spiritual warfare "against the rulers, against the authorities, against the powers of this dark world and against the spiritual forces of evil in the heavenly realms" (see Ephesians 6:10–20 NIV).

The writers of the Old Testament and New Testament alike compared a believer's earthly life to war. The Bible tells us that we are at war with our flesh, the world around us, and spiritual forces—the devil and his demons.

Christian man, it really is a war out there! But it's a war you don't have to fight alone.

In today's scripture, David thanks and praises God for empowering him to fight against his enemies. And our Lord does the same for us today.

When you let God train your hands for war and your fingers for battle, you'll reap the victory you'd never see on your own. But you'll need to be a humble student, willingly accepting His teaching and discipline.

Reading Plan: Psalms 143–150

WHAT IS PROVERBS ALL ABOUT?

Like the Psalms, Proverbs doesn't have a story line—these pithy, memorable sayings are a collection of practical tips for living, encouraging people to pursue wisdom.

Proverbs comes mainly from the pen of King Solomon, the wisest human being ever. (In 1 Kings 3:12, God said, "I have given thee a wise and an understanding heart; so that there was none like thee before thee, neither after thee shall any arise like unto thee.") But parts of Proverbs are attributed to "the wise" (22:17), Agur (30:1), and King Lemuel (31:1). The proverbs speak to issues such as work, money, sex, temptation, drinking, laziness, discipline, and child rearing. Underlying each proverb is the truth that "the fear of the LORD is the beginning of knowledge" (1:7).

"Wisdom," as Proverbs 4:7 indicates, "is the principal thing. . .with all thy getting get understanding." If you need help with that, just ask God, who is happy to help: "If any of you lack wisdom, let him ask of God, that giveth to all men liberally, and upbraideth not; and it shall be given him" (James 1:5).

Reading Plan: Proverbs 1–5

WHAT DOES "FEARING GOD" MEAN?

The fear of the Lord is the beginning of wisdom: and the
knowledge of the holy is understanding. For by me thy days shall
be multiplied, and the years of thy life shall be increased.

PROVERBS 9:10–11

Today, we hear much about the *love* of God, but not a lot about the *fear* of Him. Yet the Bible instructs us to fear God, and it includes many examples of men who did so. For example, the Bible says that Job "feared God and shunned evil" (Job 1:1 NIV).

When we think of the word *fear*, our minds usually go to the dread someone might feel toward a cruel tyrant or dictator. But that's not how God wants us to approach Him. God is the very definition of love. He's good, and He wants us to love Him so deeply and reverentially that we would never want to displease Him.

An unbeliever might fear God's eternal punishment, but the Christian man "fears" God by approaching Him with a blend of love and confidence, knowing He is worthy of the deepest reverence and awe. This moves him to surrender to God, who loves him and always has his best interests in mind.

When you understand that the fear of God and the love of God aren't contradictory—that they're two sides of the same coin—you can find the joy that comes by walking closely with Him.

Reading Plan: Proverbs 6–9

WHY SHOULD I GIVE?

There is that scattereth, and yet increaseth; and there is that withholdeth more than is meet, but it tendeth to poverty. The liberal soul shall be made fat: and he that watereth shall be watered also himself.

PROVERBS 11:24–25

Many Christian men today find it difficult to give of their own resources for God's work. One recent poll showed that Christians give at only 2.5 percent per capita, a rate worse than during the Great Depression.

Clearly, something is amiss in the body of Jesus Christ!

God strongly encourages His followers to give generously: "Each of you should give what you have decided in your heart to give, not reluctantly or under compulsion, for God loves a cheerful giver" (2 Corinthians 9:7 NIV).

Also, the Old Testament prophet Malachi wrote "'Bring the whole tithe into the storehouse, that there may be food in my house. Test me in this,' says the LORD Almighty, 'and see if I will not throw open the floodgates of heaven and pour out so much blessing that there will not be room enough to store it'" (Malachi 3:10 NIV).

In light of this verse, isn't it possible that our reluctance to give toward God's work has less to do with simple selfishness and more to do with our lack of trust in Him to provide for us?

The Bible says this is backwards thinking. According to God, giving puts you in a position to receive blessings from above.

Reading Plan: Proverbs 10–14

HOW CAN I SPEAK WISELY?

A fool's mouth is his destruction,
and his lips are the snare of his soul.

PROVERBS 18:7

Most of us at some point have known *that* guy—the one who boasts that he "tells it like it is" but in fact is just a big-mouth with no inner editor. You may have noticed that he sometimes gets himself in trouble or damages his reputation by saying foolish things.

The Bible has much to say about the words we should speak—as well as the ones we shouldn't. Here's a good summary of God's guideline: only speak words that glorify God and build others up, and avoid speaking in a way that dishonors God and tears others down.

The apostle Paul also gave some solid advice when he wrote, "Do not let any unwholesome talk come out of your mouths, but only what is helpful for building others up according to their needs, that it may benefit those who listen" (Ephesians 4:29 NIV).

That's what speaking wisely means.

So before you speak, ask yourself, *Are these words going to glorify God and build others up?* If the answer is no, hold your tongue. If it's yes, speak up. . .and bless others with your words.

Reading Plan: Proverbs 15–19

HOW CAN I GUARD MY REPUTATION?

A good name is rather to be chosen than great riches,
and loving favour rather than silver and gold.

PROVERBS 22:1

Benjamin Franklin once wisely observed, "It takes many good deeds to build a good reputation, and only one bad one to lose it." Franklin, often known as "The First American," obviously understood the value of a good name. So did Solomon, the author of today's scripture.

History—ancient and modern—is filled with highly esteemed men who ruined their reputations (as well as their careers, ministries, and families) with one highly publicized misdeed. And a destroyed reputation is exceedingly difficult, sometimes impossible, to restore.

Your errors may never make headlines, but you should still guard your reputation. The news crew may not be watching, but others are—your family, coworkers, business associates, partners in ministry. . .and even friends who know that you follow Jesus and may be interested in following.

Many things in life are well worth guarding, especially your personal reputation. So make sure your conduct consistently reflects who you are. . .and whom you belong to.

Reading Plan: Proverbs 20–23

HOW SHOULD I RESPOND WHEN AN ENEMY FAILS?

Rejoice not when thine enemy falleth, and let not thine heart be glad when he stumbleth: lest the Lord see it, and it displease him, and he turn away his wrath from him.

PROVERBS 24:17–18

Have you ever felt a small twinge of satisfaction when someone you know—maybe a business competitor or someone you think has treated you unfairly—fell on difficult times? If so, take note of today's scripture.

There's a term for feeling joy over another person's troubles: the German word *schadenfreude*. It doesn't have an exact English equivalent, but it reflects an emotion that's quite common in fallen humanity.

Jesus instructed His followers, not to wish ill on their enemies or rejoice at their downfall, but to pray for them (see Matthew 5:44). By obeying this command, you're proclaiming, "God is bigger than any conflict I have with another person, so I'm going to trust Him enough to respond to someone's suffering in a way that pleases Him."

Ask God to guard your heart from rejoicing over an adversary's failure. Instead, pray for that person, knowing that God will deal with him as He sees fit.

Reading Plan: Proverbs 24–28

SHOULD I CARE ABOUT THE DISADVANTAGED?

The righteous considereth the cause of the poor:
but the wicked regardeth not to know it.

PROVERBS 29:7

The Bible consistently calls God's people to pursue justice and care for the poor and disadvantaged. For example, Micah tells us to "act justly and to love mercy and to walk humbly with your God" (6:8 NIV), and Isaiah says, "Learn to do right; seek justice. Defend the oppressed. Take up the cause of the fatherless; plead the case of the widow" (1:17 NIV).

The Bible consistently teaches that salvation comes from God's grace and your faith in Jesus' work on the cross—it can't be earned (see Ephesians 2:8–9). But it also says that saving faith will produce a compassionate heart for those whom Jesus called "the least of these" (Matthew 25:40). That's why the apostle James wrote, "Faith, if it hath not works, is dead" (James 2:17).

Your concern for the less fortunate won't save you, and neither will any amount of humanitarian work. Rather, your love for others serves as evidence of your commitment to Jesus.

When you trust God for your salvation through Jesus Christ, God will motivate and empower you to serve others and help those in difficult life situations.

Reading Plan: Proverbs 29–31

WHAT IS ECCLESIASTES ALL ABOUT?

A king pursued the things of this world, only to find them unfulfilling. Learning, pleasure, work, laughter—"all is vanity," he wrote (1:2). The king also lamented the inequities of life: People live, work hard, and die, only to leave their belongings to someone else; the wicked prosper over the righteous; the poor are oppressed.

The author of Ecclesiastes is not stated, but many indicators point to Solomon. The writer is identified as "the son of David" (1:1) and "king over Israel in Jerusalem" (1:12) and says he had "more wisdom than all they that have been before me" (1:16). The book's generally negative tone makes some readers wonder if Solomon wrote it late in life, after his hundreds of wives led him to stray from God.

Still, by the end of Ecclesiastes, the author-king realized "the conclusion of the whole matter: Fear God, and keep his commandments: for this is the whole duty of man" (12:13). Even when life doesn't make sense to us, there's always a God who understands. And He's just waiting for us to draw near.

Reading Plan: Ecclesiastes 1–6

WHY SHOULD I READ A DEPRESSING BOOK LIKE ECCLESIASTES?

Let us hear the conclusion of the whole matter: Fear God, and keep his commandments: for this is the whole duty of man.

ECCLESIASTES 12:13

The first time you read Ecclesiastes, you might wonder why it's even in the Bible. Much of it seems to teach that this life is meaningless, that the best we can hope for is just to get through it.

But if you read the whole book, you'll see Solomon's main point: life on earth really is meaningless—*without God*.

A famous mid-seventeenth-century document called the Westminster Shorter Catechism, which was written in a question-answer format, opened with the following:

Q1: "What is the chief end of man?"

A1: "Man's chief end is to glorify God, and to enjoy him forever."

This exact response doesn't appear anywhere in the Bible, but its message can be drawn from today's scripture. After writing at length about the futility of life, Solomon states in the last two verses that everyone's purpose can be summarized like this: "Fear God, and keep his commandments."

As a man of God, you never have to wonder why God made or saved you. The Bible's overarching theme is that God created you to pursue Him, love Him, honor Him, live for Him, and be the man He made you to be.

Reading Plan: Ecclesiastes 7–12

WHAT IS SONG OF SOLOMON ALL ABOUT?

A dark-skinned beauty was marrying the king, and both were thrilled. "Behold, thou art fair, my love; behold, thou art fair; thou hast doves' eyes," he told her (1:15). "Behold, thou arl fair, my beloved, yea, pleasant: also our bed is green," she responded (1:16). Through eight chapters and 117 verses, the two lovers admire each other's physical attributes, expressing their love and devotion.

The Song of Solomon could certainly have been written by the third king of Israel, since Solomon ultimately had seven hundred wives (1 Kings 11:3). But some wonder if the song "of Solomon" is like the psalms "of David"—which could mean they are *by*, *for*, or *about* him. Like the book of Esther, the Song of Solomon never mentions the name "God," but it celebrates the institution of marriage that He created for Adam and Eve and all generations to follow.

The pleasure and satisfaction of marital love can even serve as a picture of God's own joy in His people.

Reading Plan: Song of Solomon 1–8

WHAT IS ISAIAH ALL ABOUT?

Like most prophets, Isaiah announced the bad news of punishment for sin. But he also described a coming Messiah who would be "wounded for our transgressions. . .bruised for our iniquities. . .and with his stripes we are healed" (53:5).

Called to the ministry through a stunning vision of God in heaven (chapter 6), Isaiah wrote a book that some call "the fifth Gospel" for its predictions of the birth, life, and death of Jesus Christ some seven hundred years later. These prophecies of redemption balance the depressing promises of God's discipline against Judah and Jerusalem, which were overrun by Babylonian armies about a century later.

Isaiah's prophecy ends with a long section (chapters 40–66) describing God's restoration of Israel, His promised salvation, and His eternal kingdom.

Early in His own ministry, Jesus said He fulfilled the prophecies of Isaiah: "The Lord hath anointed me to preach good tidings unto the meek; he hath sent me to bind up the brokenhearted, to proclaim liberty to the captives, and the opening of the prison to them that are bound; to proclaim the acceptable year of the Lord" (61:1–2). It's amazing how much God cares about us!

Reading Plan: Isaiah 1–4

HOW CAN I KNOW IF GOD IS CALLING ME TO MINISTRY?

*Also I heard the voice of the Lord, saying, Whom shall I send,
and who will go for us? Then said I, Here am I; send me.*

ISAIAH 6:8

If your heart has ever ached over the hurting and needy people in your neighborhood, throughout our nation, or around the world—if you've ever found yourself grieving over humanity's lostness, wondering how you can reach them with the message of salvation through Jesus Christ—then God may be calling you to some kind of service, just as He called the prophet Isaiah.

After purifying Isaiah, making him fit to speak the Lord's truth to His hardhearted people (see Isaiah 6:1–6), God asked, "Whom shall I send, and who will go for us?" (6:8). Isaiah eagerly volunteered.

God has something for you to do for His kingdom. He has given you gifts and enabled you to fulfill your calling. You just need to spend time in His presence, like the prophet Isaiah did, and ask what He wants you to do. Then listen to what He says and eagerly reply, "Here I am! Send me."

Reading Plan: Isaiah 5–7

WHY IS THE BOOK OF ISAIAH OFTEN CALLED THE "FIFTH GOSPEL"?

For unto us a child is born, unto us a son is given:
and the government shall be upon his shoulder: and his
name shall be called Wonderful, Counsellor, The mighty
God, The everlasting Father, The Prince of Peace.

ISAIAH 9:6

Although Isaiah lived around seven centuries before Jesus' birth, he wrote much about Him. Isaiah's book includes dozens of prophecies about Christ's birth, His work on earth, His death, and His resurrection. In fact, nearly one-third of this amazing book's chapters contain prophecies about Jesus. Here are some examples:

- He would miraculously be born to a virgin (7:14).
- He would start His work in a place called Galilee (9:1–2).
- He would be called "Wonderful," "Counselor," "Mighty God," "everlasting Father," and "Prince of Peace" (9:6–7).
- He would perform miracles of healing (35:5–6).
- A man (John the Baptist) would appear before His ministry began to prepare people for Him (40:3–4).
- He would be ridiculed and mistreated (50:3–6).
- He would suffer terribly (chapter 53).

As you read the prophecies about Jesus in Isaiah (and other Old Testament books), your faith can be strengthened and your heart warmed as you think about God's amazing act of love in bringing the Savior into the world.

Reading Plan: Isaiah 8–10

WHAT SHOULD I DO WITH MY FEAR?

Behold, God is my salvation; I will trust, and not
be afraid: for the LORD JEHOVAH is my strength and
my song; he also is become my salvation.

ISAIAH 12:2

Have you ever been absolutely consumed with fear, so stressed that you couldn't eat, sleep, or even think clearly?

Life has a way of frightening us. Marital problems, conflicts with our kids, issues at work, and health difficulties can all make us fearful, anxious, and tense.

In this fallen world, fear is a natural part of life. But Jesus promised that we can live an "abundant life" by learning how to handle our fears in a way that honors God.

In today's verse, the prophet Isaiah resolved to trust God and not be afraid—or at least not surrender to his fears. Centuries later, the apostle Paul echoed this sentiment when he wrote, "Do not be anxious about anything, but in every situation, by prayer and petition, with thanksgiving, present your requests to God. And the peace of God, which transcends all understanding, will guard your hearts and your minds in Christ Jesus" (Philippians 4:6–7 NIV).

When life gets scary, remember these two things: (1) God is in control, and (2) He has promised to comfort and give you peace when you take your fears to Him.

Reading Plan: Isaiah 11–14

IS ANYONE BEYOND HOPE OF SALVATION?

*And the L*ORD *shall smite Egypt: he shall smite and heal it: and they shall return even to the L*ORD*, and he shall be intreated of them, and shall heal them.*

ISAIAH 19:22

Isaiah 19 warned that God would bring terrible judgments upon Egypt. . .but also that He would mercifully heal many Egyptians when they finally called out to Him.

Egypt and Israel had been enemies on and off throughout their histories. But now, the Egyptians had become a proud, rebellious, idolatrous people who wanted nothing to do with the true God of Israel.

Still, God did not give up on them. One day, He promised, He would draw many Egyptians to Himself so that they could be saved. As it turned out, the church grew strongly in Egypt for more than six centuries after Jesus returned to heaven.

Egypt's story proves that even the worst of sinners—whether they're individuals or groups—are not beyond God's reach. We should pray that God would do whatever it takes to make lost people understand how desperately they need salvation. And when He does, we must be ready to speak the message.

Reading Plan: Isaiah 15–19

HOW SHOULD THE THOUGHT OF ETERNITY AFFECT MY LIFE ON EARTH?

And in that day did the Lord God of hosts call to weeping, and to mourning, and to baldness, and to girding with sackcloth: and behold joy and gladness, slaying oxen, and killing sheep, eating flesh, and drinking wine: let us eat and drink; for to morrow we shall die.

ISAIAH 22:12–13

You've probably seen the acronym *YOLO*, which means You Only Live Once. Our culture often views that expression as an encouragement to cram as much fun into our lives as possible—without a thought of what lies beyond this short earthly existence.

But the Bible teaches that this line of thinking is a diabolical lie. Yes, you only live your life on earth once. But after that comes a second life in eternity—with God in heaven or with Satan in a terrible place called hell. That's why the author of Hebrews warns, "People are destined to die once, and after that to face judgment" (9:27 NIV).

If you've placed your faith in Jesus Christ, your place in heaven is secure. But it's still important that you take regular stock of your life, turning away from anything the Bible forbids and toward the things that bring eternal rewards. If your self-examination makes you wonder if you're really part of God's family, why not settle that issue right now? He welcomes everyone with open arms.

Reading Plan: Isaiah 20–23

WHAT DOES THE BIBLE SAY ABOUT MY ETERNAL EXISTENCE?

He will swallow up death in victory; and the Lord GOD will wipe away tears from off all faces; and the rebuke of his people shall he take away from off all the earth: for the LORD hath spoken it.

ISAIAH 25:8

Have you ever been struggling through an especially difficult time— perhaps the death of a loved one, the loss of a job, or a devastating medical diagnosis—and a well-meaning friend tries to comfort you with a shallow platitude like "Just hang in there! Things will get better"?

You may have politely thanked your friend for this attempt at encouragement, but you probably walked away still wondering if your difficulties would ever end. But one of God's most encouraging promises is that one day, every earthly difficulty will be permanently erased. No more pain, death, or tears. . .only a joyful eternity in our heavenly Father's presence.

The apostle John echoed this amazing promise from today's verse when he wrote, "'He will wipe every tear from their eyes. There will be no more death' or mourning or crying or pain, for the old order of things has passed away" (Revelation 21:4 NIV).

On earth, it's hard to imagine a life without death, despair, or pain. But God has promised that to His people. This hope enables us to endure even our most difficult experiences in life.

Reading Plan: Isaiah 24–27

WHAT DOES THE BIBLE SAY ABOUT ALCOHOL?

Woe to the crown of pride, to the drunkards of Ephraim, whose glorious beauty is a fading flower, which are on the head of the fat valleys of them that are overcome with wine!

ISAIAH 28:1

This may surprise some Christians, but nowhere in the Bible is the consumption of alcohol forbidden. In fact, our Lord Jesus drank wine in moderation (see Matthew 11:19, Luke 7:34).

God doesn't have a problem with His people drinking. Drunkenness, however, is completely different—God repeatedly condemns it throughout His Word. In today's verse, He addresses drunkenness among the people of the northern kingdom of Israel (Ephraim).

Here are some more scriptures on the topic:

"Wine is a mocker and beer a brawler; whoever is led astray by them is not wise" (Proverbs 20:1 NIV).

"Who has woe? Who has sorrow? Who has strife? Who has complaints? Who has needless bruises? Who has bloodshot eyes? Those who linger over wine, who go to sample bowls of mixed wine" (Proverbs 23:29–30 NIV).

"Let us behave decently, as in the daytime, not in carousing and drunkenness" (Romans 13:13 NIV).

"Do not get drunk on wine, which leads to debauchery. Instead, be filled with the Spirit" (Ephesians 5:18 NIV).

Excessive drinking can ruin your professional life, your family, your health, and your testimony for Jesus. Be aware of the dangers even of permissible things.

Reading Plan: Isaiah 28–31

SHOULD I FEAR GOD'S JUDGMENT?

The sinners in Zion are afraid; fearfulness hath surprised the hypocrites. Who among us shall dwell with the devouring fire? who among us shall dwell with everlasting burnings?

ISAIAH 33:14

In Isaiah's day, the sinners and hypocrites in Jerusalem were afraid—and for good reason. Before, they had openly flaunted their unrighteousness, but now they knew God's judgment was coming.

In Isaiah 33:14–17, the prophet contrasted the sinful people with the people who did what was right in God's eyes. Here's what he wrote about the righteous:

Those who walk righteously and speak what is right, who reject gain from extortion and keep their hands from accepting bribes, who stop their ears against plots of murder and shut their eyes against contemplating evil—they are the ones who will dwell on the heights, whose refuge will be the mountain fortress. Their bread will be supplied, and water will not fail them.

VERSES 15–16 NIV

The ungodly were afraid, but God comforted His children with the promise of better things ahead. Nothing has changed. If Jesus has made you righteous, you needn't fear God's wrath. Instead, you can joyfully look forward to everything God has promised in the life to come.

As apostle John eloquently wrote, "There is no fear in love. But perfect love drives out fear, because fear has to do with punishment. The one who fears is not made perfect in love" (1 John 4:18 NIV).

Reading Plan: Isaiah 32–35

WHAT MIRACLE DID GOD PERFORM FOR KING HEZEKIAH AND JUDAH?

Then the angel of the LORD went forth, and smote in the camp of the Assyrians a hundred and fourscore and five thousand: and when they arose early in the morning, behold, they were all dead corpses.

ISAIAH 37:36

Hezekiah, Judah's great and godly king, knew his kingdom was in deep trouble. Sennacherib, the king of Assyria, had invaded Judah, capturing forty-six of its fortified cities (Isaiah 36:1), and now he had his eyes on Jerusalem. Hezekiah, hoping to bring peace between Judah and Assyria, sent gifts of silver and gold (2 Kings 18:13–16). But when that didn't work, Hezekiah did the only thing he could: pray (Isaiah 37:14–20).

The soldiers in Jerusalem wouldn't have posed much of a threat to the massive Assyrian army. But fortunately for Jerusalem, they didn't have to. God had promised King Hezekiah that the Assyrians wouldn't step foot in Jerusalem or shoot a single arrow into the city—and He kept His promise.

Whenever you're faced with an impossible situation, be like Hezekiah: turn to your all-powerful Father, who can do the impossible on your behalf. His answer may not be quite as dramatic, but He will bring you through.

Reading Plan: Isaiah 36–39

WHO IS GOD'S SERVANT IN ISAIAH 42?

*Behold my servant, whom I uphold; mine elect, in whom
my soul delighteth; I have put my spirit upon him: he
shall bring forth judgment to the Gentiles.*

ISAIAH 42:1

Jesus often spoke of the importance of serving others. In Matthew 20:25–28, He told His followers to be different from power-hungry authorities and to lead by becoming servants. He concluded this thought by instructing them to follow His example: "The Son of Man did not come to be served, but to serve, and to give his life as a ransom for many" (verse 28 NIV).

Centuries before Jesus' birth, the prophet Isaiah described the coming Messiah as the "servant" of the Lord (Isaiah 42:1)—and Jewish people from that time on knew whom Isaiah had written about. Later, the apostle Matthew wrote that Jesus had fulfilled this prophecy (see Matthew 12:17–21). There's no question that Isaiah's "Servant" was Jesus Christ.

Indeed, Jesus came to earth to serve God and humanity by suffering and dying on a cross then rising from the dead. He served us in the most profound way possible, and now He calls us to do the same. When we consider what He has done for us, our response should be, "Yes, Lord. I will serve You by serving others."

Reading Plan: Isaiah 40–42

HOW SHOULD I HANDLE GUILT?

*I, even I, am he that blotteth out thy transgressions
for mine own sake, and will not remember thy sins.*

ISAIAH 43:25

A big part of our fallen human condition is negative, destructive emotions—with guilt being one of the worst. We've all felt guilty over things we've done or failed to do. Guilt can be useful—when it's due to sin, we know we need to confess to God and stop sinning. But it can also be an anchor that holds us down and keeps us from living the abundant life Jesus promised His followers.

As a follower of Jesus Christ, you have the privilege of confessing your sins to God, knowing He will forgive you (see 1 John 1:9). You needn't dwell on your past mistakes and sins. And when you find yourself feeling guilt, remember today's scripture.

God didn't save you, forgive you, and set you on a new life path so that you could spend the rest of your days being eaten alive by guilt. So learn from your past mistakes and become a better man of God, not believing for a moment that God holds against you what He has forgotten.

Reading Plan: Isaiah 43–45

WHAT DOES GOD WANT US TO REMEMBER ABOUT HIM?

Remember this, and shew yourselves men: bring it again to mind, O ye transgressors. Remember the former things of old: for I am God, and there is none else; I am God, and there is none like me, Declaring the end from the beginning, and from ancient times the things that are not yet done, saying, My counsel shall stand, and I will do all my pleasure.

ISAIAH 46:8–10

When we see a Bible passage that begins with "Remember this," we should pay close attention. . .maybe even commit its words to memory in order to receive God's best for us.

In today's scripture, the Lord speaks through Isaiah, revealing two very important things about Himself: (1) "There is none like Me, declaring the end from the beginning," and (2) "My counsel shall stand, and I will do all my pleasure."

Our God knows the beginning and the end of every circumstance. But God isn't just a disinterested observer—He's in full control, working to ensure all His plans become reality.

If you want courage and empowerment to be the kind of man God wants you to be, then never forget this: He knows every detail of eternity past and eternity future, and He is in control of all things. That is part of His nature, and it gives us—the mere mortals that we are—full confidence in Him.

There truly is no one like Him!

Reading Plan: Isaiah 46–48

WAS JESUS FORCED TO SUFFER FOR US?

I gave my back to the smiters, and my cheeks to them that plucked off the hair: I hid not my face from shame and spitting. For the Lord GOD will help me; therefore shall I not be confounded: therefore have I set my face like a flint, and I know that I shall not be ashamed.

ISAIAH 50:6–7

Today's scripture lists some of the harsh indignities Jesus suffered in the hours before He was crucified. It mentions the beatings He endured (see Mark 15:15, Luke 22:63–65), how He was mocked and spat upon (Mark 15:19–20), and how the hair was yanked from His face.

Isaiah's prophecy graphically describes the torment Jesus would endure at the hands of men. But let's not miss these two important words: *I gave*.

Jesus came to earth to live as a human, to point people to the Father through His teaching and miracles, and finally to endure unspeakable torture before dying gruesomely on a wooden cross.

And He endured it all willingly.

Jesus endured His mistreatment not because the authorities forced Him to, but because His heart was set on freeing us from bondage and giving us everlasting life in heaven with Him. As He once said, "Greater love has no one than this: to lay down one's life for one's friends" (John 15:13 NIV).

> **Reading Plan: Isaiah 49–51**

WHY IS ISAIAH 53 SO IMPORTANT?

He is despised and rejected of men; a man of sorrows, and acquainted with grief: and we hid as it were our faces from him; he was despised, and we esteemed him not. . . . But he was wounded for our transgressions, he was bruised for our iniquities: the chastisement of our peace was upon him; and with his stripes we are healed.

ISAIAH 53:3, 5

The book of Isaiah contains many detailed predictions about the birth, life, and death of the coming Messiah, Jesus Christ. Isaiah 53 is a series of prophecies about the suffering Jesus endured for us when He died on the cross so that our sins could be forgiven.

Isaiah 53 describes Jesus as the suffering Servant who was rejected by His own people and endured unimaginable mental, spiritual, and physical agony—all for the benefit of a lost, hurting, and rebellious humanity. Isaiah 53 tells us that Jesus:

Suffered in our place (verse 4)

Bore the punishment for our sins (verse 5, 11–12)

Interceded on our behalf (verse 12).

Under the inspiration of the Holy Spirit, the Gospel writers and other New Testament authors quoted from Isaiah 53, explaining that Jesus fulfilled its prophecies. One of those writers was the apostle Peter, who wrote: "'He himself bore our sins' in his body on the cross, so that we might die to sins and live for righteousness; 'by his wounds you have been healed.' For 'you were like sheep going astray,' but now you have returned to the Shepherd and Overseer of your souls" (1 Peter 2:24–25 NIV).

Reading Plan: Isaiah 52–56

HOW DOES SIN SEPARATE US FROM GOD?

Behold, the LORD's hand is not shortened, that it cannot save;
neither his ear heavy, that it cannot hear: but your iniquities
have separated between you and your God, and your sins
have hid his face from you, that he will not hear.

ISAIAH 59:1–2

God's people wanted to know why He wasn't rescuing them from their troubles. The prophet Isaiah had an answer: God was more than able to hear them and act on their behalf, but their sins had separated them from their God.

The same thing can happen to us.

The apostle Paul wrote that nothing can separate us from God's love (see Romans 8:31–39). But our sins can still cause separation on several levels by robbing us of His blessings, His peace, His protection, and our close fellowship with Him. God doesn't want that, and neither should you.

Spiritual dry times will inevitably come, and they don't always result from our sin. However, when you start feeling distant from God—when your prayer seems to lack power and the blessings from above aren't flowing—seek His face and ask Him if you need to confess anything. He loves you (and always will), so He'll show you what needs to change.

Reading Plan: Isaiah 57–59

DAY 222

WHAT CAN I DO ABOUT THIS WORLD'S SPIRITUAL DARKNESS?

Arise, shine; for thy light is come, and the glory of the Lord is risen upon thee. For, behold, the darkness shall cover the earth, and gross darkness the people: but the Lord shall arise upon thee, and his glory shall be seen upon thee. And the Gentiles shall come to thy light, and kings to the brightness of thy rising.

ISAIAH 60:1–3

God spoke these words to Isaiah more than twenty-seven hundred years ago, but the words "the darkness shall cover the earth" could just as easily describe the modern world.

We Christian men need only to open our eyes to see what sinful people cannot—that this fallen, sinful, broken world is covered in spiritual darkness.

But here's the good news: you don't have to let this darkness overwhelm you. Instead, you can be a light in this world for the Light of the world, Jesus Christ, whom Isaiah described in today's scripture:

"You are the light of the world. A town built on a hill cannot be hidden. Neither do people light a lamp and put it under a bowl. Instead they put it on its stand, and it gives light to everyone in the house. In the same way, let your light shine before others, that they may see your good deeds and glorify your Father in heaven."

MATTHEW 5:14–16 NIV

It's dark out there. . .so let the light of Jesus shine from within you!

Reading Plan: Isaiah 60–63

230

WHAT KIND OF MAN DOES GOD BLESS?

For all those things hath mine hand made, and all those things have been, saith the Lord: but to this man will I look, even to him that is poor and of a contrite spirit, and trembleth at my word.

ISAIAH 66:2

According to the Bible, God loves to give His blessings—in this life and the next—to the man who is humble enough to acknowledge that he is a sinner in desperate need of the Lord's mercy. This kind of man gets God's attention.

Speaking through Isaiah, God said, "These are the ones I look on with favor: those who are humble and contrite in spirit, and who tremble at my word" (66:2 NIV). God blesses the humble and contrite in spirit because only they know how little they can do for themselves and how much they really need Him and His mercy.

The Bible repeatedly tells us that God wants to bless us with His presence. But God also demands—not requests or suggests—that our hearts remain humble and contrite before Him.

Do you want to see God's hand at work in your life and His presence with you at every moment? Then go to Him each day on your knees, asking Him to instill in you a humble, contrite heart—one that never forgets how much you need His favor and mercy.

Reading Plan: Isaiah 64–66

WHAT IS JEREMIAH ALL ABOUT?

Called to the ministry as a boy (1:6), Jeremiah prophesied bad news to Judah: "Lo, I will bring a nation upon you from far, O house of Israel, saith the Lord" (5:15). Jeremiah was mocked for his prophecies, occasionally beaten, and even imprisoned in a muddy well (chapter 38). The book of Jeremiah that we read is apparently an expanded, second version of a destroyed first draft, since King Jehoiakim, angry with Jeremiah for his dire prophecies, cut the original scroll with a penknife and "cast it into the fire that was on the hearth" (36:23). At God's command, Jeremiah produced a second scroll with additional material (36:32).

The eighteenth chapter of Jeremiah describes the prophet's visit to a potter's shop, where he realized that God could do with His people as the craftsman did with his clay: "O house of Israel, cannot I do with you as this potter? saith the Lord. Behold, as the clay is in the potter's hand, so are ye in mine hand, O house of Israel" (verse 6).

Ultimately, all of Jeremiah's predictions came true with the Babylonian invasion of chapter 52. Through this prophet, God gave Judah some forty years to repent. As Jesus' disciple Peter wrote many years later, God "is longsuffering to us-ward, not willing that any should perish, but that all should come to repentance" (2 Peter 3:9).

Reading Plan: Jeremiah 1–3

WHY IS FALSEHOOD SO DESTRUCTIVE?

A wonderful and horrible thing is committed in the land; the prophets prophesy falsely, and the priests bear rule by their means; and my people love to have it so: and what will ye do in the end thereof?

JEREMIAH 5:30–31

During Old Testament times, God charged His prophets with very difficult assignments. . .but none quite as difficult as Jeremiah's. God wanted Jeremiah to preach to a very stubborn, hard-hearted people who weren't going to accept his message.

Even worse, rival prophets were proclaiming what they knew the people wanted to hear—even though the messages came from their own thoughts and not from God.

It's hard to miss the similarities between Jeremiah's society and our world today. False truth, or "fake news," spreads mostly unchallenged through social media—and often through major news outlets. People, even professing Christians, seek information from sources that affirm their own opinions, regardless of biblical truth.

Jeremiah 5:31 ends with God asking Jeremiah this question: "What will ye do in the end?" In other words, *Will you remain committed to My truth, or will you compromise so that more people will like you?*

That's an important question for believers today. How we answer will determine our own speech and whom we will listen to.

Reading Plan: Jeremiah 4–6

IS BOASTING EVER APPROPRIATE?

*Thus saith the Lord, Let not the wise man glory in his wisdom,
neither let the mighty man glory in his might, let not the rich
man glory in his riches: But let him that glorieth glory in this,
that he understandeth and knoweth me, that I am the Lord
which exercise lovingkindness, judgment, and righteousness,
in the earth: for in these things I delight, saith the Lord.*

JEREMIAH 9:23–24

It's probably safe to say that no one likes being around people who boast a lot about their own accomplishments, possessions, or talents. Even hearing them drone on about their kids' achievements can get old after a while.

Think about how you feel after listening to "that guy"—the insufferable braggart—and remember that God feels the same way when we brag on our own accomplishments. By boasting about ourselves, we're communicating a mindset that our gifts and abilities result from our own efforts and not from God's blessing.

Indeed, God doesn't want His people carrying around an attitude, expending our energy on letting others know what great things we've done. Instead, He wants us to ensure that our words—especially those we speak about our gifts, blessings, and accomplishments—point to *Him* as our loving Benefactor. And as today's scripture instructs, we should begin with the fact that we know Him as our loving heavenly Father.

Reading Plan: Jeremiah 7–9

HOW DANGEROUS WAS JEREMIAH'S JOB?

*For even thy brethren, and the house of thy father, even they have
dealt treacherously with thee; yea, they have called a multitude after
thee: believe them not, though they speak fair words unto thee.*

JEREMIAH 12:6

Nobody enjoys hearing bad news, especially when it involves the end
result of their lifestyle. Jeremiah learned this from personal experience.

After King Josiah died, the people of Judah treated Jeremiah worse
and worse. Those from his own hometown—including some of his own
family—plotted to take his life (11:21; 12:6). A priest named Pashhur
had him beaten and placed in stocks for a day (20:1–2). Later, some evil
men arrested him and lowered him into a nearly empty well (38:1–6).

If you follow Jesus Christ, God promises to save you from eternal
judgment for your sin, grow you into the man He wants you to be, and
empower you through His Holy Spirit to live a life that pleases Him.

God doesn't, however, promise that it will always be easy or that
people will support your decision to live for the Lord and speak His truth.
That is why you must focus on God's promise to always be with you. He
will keep you as you remain true to your commitment to Him.

Reading Plan: Jeremiah 10–12

WHAT WAS THE "SIGN OF THE LINEN BELT"?

*For as the girdle cleaveth to the loins of a man, so have I caused
to cleave unto me the whole house of Israel and the whole house of
Judah, saith the LORD; that they might be unto me for a people, and for
a name, and for a praise, and for a glory: but they would not hear.*

JEREMIAH 13:11

Jesus once told His followers, "You are the salt of the earth. But if the
salt loses its saltiness, how can it be made salty again? It is no longer
good for anything" (Matthew 5:13 NIV).

Being "salt" means we influence the world around us. . .and glorify
our heavenly Father. So how do we remain "salty" Christians? Jeremiah
13:1–11 gives us some practical wisdom.

One day, God told Jeremiah to buy a linen belt, put it around himself,
then hide it in a hole in a rock near the Euphrates River. Later, God told
the prophet to retrieve the belt. When he did, he found that it was rotten
and worthless.

God revealed to Jeremiah that the belt represented the people of Judah
and Israel, who had once clung to Him as a belt clings to a man's waist.
Sadly, however, because they had stopped listening to Him and holding
on to Him, they had become as worthless as the rotten belt (verse 11).

We need to hold on to God, or, as Jesus said, "abide" in Him (John
15:4). Only by doing that can we truly be the salt of the earth.

Reading Plan: Jeremiah 13–15

HOW IS GOD LIKE A POTTER?

And the vessel that he made of clay was marred in
the hand of the potter: so he made it again another
vessel, as seemed good to the potter to make it.

JEREMIAH 18:4

Jeremiah 18:1–6 tells how God led the prophet to a potter's shop, where he watched the man mold a lump of clay into a pot. When the pot didn't turn out right, the potter started over—with the same lump of clay.

God's message was that even though He would destroy Judah and Jerusalem, He would one day reform the people He had molded, just like a potter reforms a lump of clay into a useable vessel.

A human potter possesses a unique set of skills and a lot of patience. So does our loving Father in heaven. He uses those skills to perfectly mold us into what He wants us to be. That is the message of Isaiah 64:8 (NIV): "Yet you, Lord, are our Father. We are the clay, you are the potter; we are all the work of your hand."

When God saved you, He figuratively (and almost literally) took a useless lump of clay and saved it for Himself. And then, "He who began a good work in you will carry it on to completion until the day of Christ Jesus" (Philippians 1:6 NIV).

God is the perfect Potter, so let Him shape you as He sees fit.

Reading Plan: Jeremiah 16–19

WHAT SHOULD I DO WHEN I'M HAVING A BAD DAY?

O LORD, thou hast deceived me, and I was deceived; thou art stronger than I, and hast prevailed: I am in derision daily, every one mocketh me. For since I spake, I cried out, I cried violence and spoil; because the word of the LORD was made a reproach unto me, and a derision, daily.

JEREMIAH 20:7–8

In Jeremiah 20, the great prophet of God was having a terrible day. Jeremiah was so discouraged that he told God he was thinking about giving up or changing his message.

But in the midst of his misery, Jeremiah apparently had a divine revelation. His words of complaint became words of praise and confidence in the Lord:

But the LORD is with me like a mighty warrior; so my persecutors will stumble and not prevail. They will fail and be thoroughly disgraced; their dishonor will never be forgotten. LORD Almighty, you who examine the righteous and probe the heart and mind, let me see your vengeance on them, for to you I have committed my cause.

JEREMIAH 20:11–12 NIV

God had given Jeremiah a very difficult assignment, but as Jeremiah refocused himself on God and his mission, he saw that God was bigger than his own misery and the people who opposed him.

When you're having a bad day, here's a question: will you let feelings of defeat drag you down, or will you keep your eyes on God's goodness and power and keep moving forward?

Reading Plan: Jeremiah 20–22

WHAT IS GOD'S WRATH?

*For thus saith the L*ORD *God of Israel unto me; Take
the wine cup of this fury at my hand, and cause all
the nations, to whom I send thee, to drink it.*

JEREMIAH 25:15

In many modern translations of today's scripture, the phrase "wine cup
of this fury" is translated, "wine of my wrath." In the Bible, the word
wrath means "anger" or "indignation."

We humans can feel wrath—and so can God. In the Old Testament,
God showed His wrath against sin, disobedience, idolatry, and unbelief.

While human wrath usually isn't justified (though the Bible has
examples of "righteous indignation"), God's wrath is always holy and
righteous. That's why the New Testament says, "Human anger does
not produce the righteousness that God desires" (James 1:20 NIV). God
commands us to "get rid of all bitterness, rage and anger, brawling and
slander, along with every form of malice" (Ephesians 4:31 NIV).

Christians today don't like to talk about God's wrath. But it's a part
of His character, just like love, longsuffering, holiness, and mercy. The
good news for us who have placed our faith in Jesus Christ is that we've
been justified through His blood—we no longer need to fear God's wrath
(Romans 5:9).

Reading Plan: Jeremiah 23–25

WHY DID GOD CALL NEBUCHADNEZZAR "MY SERVANT"?

*And now have I given all these lands into the hand of
Nebuchadnezzar the king of Babylon, my servant; and the
beasts of the field have I given him also to serve him.*

JEREMIAH 27:6

In Jeremiah 27:6, God referred to the evil, powerful Babylonian king Nebuchadnezzar as "my servant."

How ironic.

Nebuchadnezzar didn't follow God, love Him, or honor Him in any way. So when God called him "My servant," He meant He would use Nebuchadnezzar—the most powerful man in the world at the time—as a tool to bring judgment on Judah and Jerusalem.

Not only that, God told Jeremiah that Judah was to submit to the Babylonians, even though the false prophets preached resistance:

*"If, however, any nation or kingdom will not serve Nebuchadnezzar
king of Babylon or bow its neck under his yoke, I will punish that
nation with the sword, famine and plague, declares the Lord, until
I destroy it by his hand. So do not listen to your prophets, your
diviners, your interpreters of dreams, your mediums or your
sorcerers who tell you, 'You will not serve the king of Babylon.'"*

JEREMIAH 27:8–9 NIV

We can learn one very important truth from Nebuchadnezzar's story: God can and will use any means He chooses—including wicked leaders—to accomplish His purposes.

Reading Plan: Jeremiah 26–28

WHAT WAS GOD'S OPTIMISTIC MESSAGE FOR HIS EXILED PEOPLE?

For I know the thoughts that I think toward you, saith the Lord,
thoughts of peace, and not of evil, to give you an expected
end. Then shall ye call upon me, and ye shall go and pray unto
me, and I will hearken unto you. And ye shall seek me, and
find me, when ye shall search for me with all your heart.

JEREMIAH 29:11–13

The people of Judah probably weren't in the best frame of mind when Jeremiah relayed the above message. Not only were they in Babylonian exile, far away from their homeland, but they had learned that they would remain there several decades before being allowed to go home. They were probably very discouraged about the future.

Then, in their darkest hour, God promised the people that He hadn't—and wouldn't—forget them. He had great plans, He said, to give them a hopeful future. And that future included His promise to be there for His people and hear them when they called out to Him—an optimistic message for people who desperately needed to hear it.

God made the promises in today's passage for a specific time and place, but their truths still apply to us today. Even in our most difficult times, we can be assured of God's ultimate blessings. We may not see them immediately, but they will become reality in God's time and in His way.

Reading Plan: Jeremiah 29–30

WHY DID JEREMIAH BUY LAND IN JUDAH BEFORE THE BABYLONIAN INVASION?

And Jeremiah said, The word of the LORD came unto me, saying, Behold, Hanameel the son of Shallum thine uncle shall come unto thee saying, Buy thee my field that is in Anathoth: for the right of redemption is thine to buy it. . . . And I bought the field of Hanameel my uncle's son, that was in Anathoth, and weighed him the money, even seventeen shekels of silver.

JEREMIAH 32:6–7, 9

In the Old Testament, God often asked His prophets to do things that didn't make much earthly sense. Jeremiah 32:1–15 tells how God commanded Jeremiah to buy some property from a family member in Anathoth, his home village.

Jeremiah knew the Babylonians were going to brutally invade Jerusalem and the surrounding areas including Anathoth, but he bought the property anyway.

Humanly speaking, that doesn't sound very wise, does it?

But God had His reasons. Bible scholars believe that God wanted to use Jeremiah's purchase as a message of hope: The people of Judah had rebelled against God, and He had judged them harshly. But He would one day bring them back home and restore their nation.

Have you ever felt God prompting you to do something that didn't seem to make sense? When that happens, follow His lead—and then watch what He does with your decision.

Reading Plan: Jeremiah 31–32

WHAT HAPPENS WHEN WE CALL TO GOD?

*Thus saith the LORD the maker thereof, the LORD that formed it, to
establish it; the LORD is his name; Call unto me, and I will answer thee,
and show thee great and mighty things, which thou knowest not.*

JEREMIAH 33:2–3

When Jeremiah preached that the Babylonians would succeed in sacking
Jerusalem, King Zedekiah had him thrown into prison. There, Jeremiah
wrote chapter 33.

History confirms that Nebuchadnezzar's forces destroyed Jerusalem
and much of Judah. But it also confirms Jeremiah's message in today's
scripture—that God would one day restore Jerusalem. . .and His relationship with His beloved people.

God told Jeremiah, "Call unto me, and I will answer thee, and show
thee great and mighty things" (33:3). What a wonderful promise! And
this promise—which applies to all God's people—is found throughout the Bible, including Psalm 34:15 (NIV): "The eyes of the LORD are on
the righteous, and his ears are attentive to their cry."

Whether our trouble results from our own sin or the actions of others,
we can call upon God instead of people, confident He is faithful to respond
in a way that best demonstrates His deep and everlasting love.

Reading Plan: Jeremiah 33–35

CAN GOD'S WORD BE DESTROYED?

Then took Jeremiah another roll, and gave it to Baruch the scribe, the son of Neriah; who wrote therein from the mouth of Jeremiah all the words of the book which Jehoiakim king of Judah had burned in the fire: and there were added besides unto them many like words.

JEREMIAH 36:32

In Jeremiah 36, the Lord commanded Jeremiah to commit all His judgments against Judah to writing. As Jeremiah spoke the words, his scribe, Baruch, wrote them down. Then Baruch took the scroll to the temple and read it out loud for the people to hear.

Jeremiah's message for Judah was far from positive, and it frightened some of Judah's princes, who ran and told the evil king Jehoiakim about it. When Jehoiakim heard the prophet's words, he threw the scroll into a fire and ordered his men to arrest Jeremiah and Baruch.

Jehoiakim probably thought he'd destroyed God's message. But the Lord protected Jeremiah and Baruch, and together they wrote God's message on another scroll. This one included even harsher words of judgment—not just for Judah but for Jehoiakim himself.

God's Word may encounter opposition, but it will always endure, even when the most powerful people oppose it. That truth is shown in both Jeremiah 36 and Isaiah 40:8 (NIV), which says, "The grass withers and the flowers fall, but the word of our God endures forever."

Reading Plan: Jeremiah 36–38

HOW SHOULD I TAKE INPUT FROM OTHERS?

Moreover Johanan the son of Kareah, and all the captains of the forces that were in the fields, came to Gedaliah to Mizpah, and said unto him, Dost thou certainly know that Baalis the king of the Ammonites hath sent Ishmael the son of Nethaniah to slay thee? But Gedaliah the son of Ahikam believed them not.

JEREMIAH 40:13–14

After the Babylonians had destroyed Jerusalem and taken most of its people—except for the very poor—to Babylon, Nebuchadnezzar appointed a man named Gedaliah as governor over the city's small remnant. Residents of Judah who had fled when the Babylonians attacked—among whom were men named Johanan and Ishmael—started returning.

When Johanan learned of Ishmael's plot to kill Gedaliah, he tried to warn the governor. But instead of taking necessary actions to head off the threat, Gedaliah did nothing. The consequences of Gedaliah's failure to heed wise counsel are found in Jeremiah 41, which describes Ishmael's insurrection against Gedaliah.

Proverbs 15:22 (NIV) says, "Plans fail for lack of counsel, but with many advisers they succeed." By failing to seek wise, godly counsel when he learned of Ishmael's plans Gedaliah lost everything.

That's an extreme example, but the lesson for us is simple: when a Christian brother raises a concern with you, don't immediately dismiss his words. Pray to God to see if there's anything in them you need to consider. That concerned friend may save you a lot of grief.

Reading Plan: Jeremiah 39–41

CAN I TRUST IN HUMAN MEDIATORS?

Then Jeremiah the prophet said unto them, I have heard you; behold, I will pray unto the Lord your God according to your words; and it shall come to pass, that whatsoever thing the Lord shall answer you, I will declare it unto you; I will keep nothing back from you.

JEREMIAH 42:4

After seeing Jeremiah's dire warnings come true, those who remained in Jerusalem and Judah were probably quite frightened. Having seen many of their countrymen taken into captivity during the Babylonian invasion, they called out to Jeremiah in a panic. They knew he was a true prophet of God, and they hoped he could mediate between them and the Lord.

Sadly, the people of Judah weren't much different from people today. When disaster comes—whether it's a severe economic downturn or a life-threatening pandemic—people want solutions. But they tend to turn to human leaders to provide them, often finding nothing but disappointment.

The man of God, however, should be different. His hope should be 100 percent in the Lord, and he should instinctively follow the advice in Proverbs 3:5–6 (NIV): "Trust in the Lord with all your heart and lean not on your own understanding; in all your ways submit to him, and he will make your paths straight."

In difficult times, remember to look to God for solutions. You don't need to approach Him through any human mediator; He wants to hear directly from you when you pray in Jesus' name.

Reading Plan: Jeremiah 42–44

WHAT CAN I LEARN FROM BARUCH?

And seekest thou great things for thyself? seek them not: for,
behold, I will bring evil upon all flesh, saith the LORD: but thy life
will I give unto thee for a prey in all places whither thou goest.

JEREMIAH 45:5

Baruch was a man of God who served as Jeremiah's scribe, writing down God's message to the prophet. But he is last mentioned in Jeremiah 45, worrying about what God had in mind for him. "Woe to me!" he said. "The LORD has added sorrow to my pain; I am worn out with groaning and find no rest" (verse 3 NIV).

As God spoke a difficult message of judgment to the nation of Judah, Baruch took his eyes off the gravity of Judah's situation and focused on his own future.

We might look critically at Baruch, but let's be honest—most of us might say the same thing if we were in his situation.

God, speaking through Jeremiah, told Baruch not to focus on himself. He would survive the judgment on Judah (Jeremiah 45:4–5).

Christian men today would do well to receive this message. We've been saved and will escape God's final judgment on this world. Our eternal place in heaven is secure, so we can live joyfully and productively here and now, pursuing God's glory and focusing on the good of those around us.

Reading Plan: Jeremiah 45–47

WHAT CAN WE LEARN FROM THE MOABITES?

*For because thou hast trusted in thy works and in thy treasures,
thou shalt also be taken: and Chemosh shall go forth into captivity
with his priests and his princes together. And the spoiler shall
come upon every city, and no city shall escape: the valley also shall
perish, and the plain shall be destroyed, as the LORD hath spoken.*

JEREMIAH 48:7–8

In Jeremiah's day, the Moabites were a very wealthy people, mostly because important trade routes ran through their land. Sadly, however, their riches led to pride and self-reliance. They didn't believe they needed God—in fact, they worshipped the false deity Chemosh. This all set the Moabites up to suffer God's judgment.

As twenty-first century Christians, we could learn a lesson from the Moabites. We tend to place great value on self-reliance, admiring those independent, self-made types who don't seem to need anything or anyone to achieve greatness.

But all those accomplishments mean nothing without God at their center. In fact, they can actually lead a man down a road of destruction.

There's nothing wrong with working hard to build a strong financial future for yourself, your family, and others—the Bible teaches that hard work brings great blessings. But always be careful to make sure your trust is in God, not in your hard-earned riches. Getting this backwards eventually leads to disaster.

Reading Plan: Jeremiah 48–49

WHAT CAN I LEARN FROM THE FALL OF JUDAH?

My people hath been lost sheep: their shepherds have caused them to go astray, they have turned them away on the mountains: they have gone from mountain to hill, they have forgotten their restingplace.

JEREMIAH 50:6

The first five verses of Jeremiah 50 promised that Babylon would be destroyed and the wayward nations of Israel and Judah would be restored. Yes, God had used Babylon to bring judgment against His people, but Babylon would pay for its sins.

In verse 6, God said His people had followed corrupt leaders (shepherds) who had led them away from their "restingplace"—a loving God who wanted the best for His people—and caused them to go astray.

What a foolish decision!

Today, God calls us as Christians to keep Himself as our resting place—to rely on Him to give us peace and guidance, support us and protect us from evil and danger, heal our wounds, and fight our battles.

What a wonderful resting place our God is! We must consistently avoid the mistake of Israel and Judah by staying close to Him in every way.

Reading Plan: Jeremiah 50

HOW WORTHLESS ARE IDOLS?

Every founder is confounded by the graven image: for his molten image is falsehood, and there is no breath in them. They are vanity, the work of errors: in the time of their visitation they shall perish. The portion of Jacob is not like them; for he is the former of all things: and Israel is the rod of his inheritance: the LORD of hosts is his name.

JEREMIAH 51:17–19

In 1 Corinthians 10:14 (NIV), the apostle Paul instructed the Christians living in Corinth, "My dear friends, flee from idolatry." Today's verse tells you *why* you should make every effort to avoid idolatry—whether it's a graven image or any other worldly thing you might pursue more than God Himself for fulfillment.

When most people hear the word *idol*, their minds go to statues or other manmade items that people have worshipped. But we have our own idols today: material wealth, power, social status, sex, sports, and countless other things. And when men pursue those things over God, their actions are "vanity" and "the work of errors."

Today's scripture includes these words: "The portion of Jacob [the God of Israel] is not like them." In other words, the Lord is everything that worldly idols are not. He is infinitely more valuable than anything you can pursue to find peace and meaning. Only God Himself is eternal truth.

Earthly idols offer temporary satisfaction, but they will one day be destroyed. God, however, can be your everlasting pleasure. He will live on, blessing you, for eternity.

Reading Plan: Jeremiah 51–52

WHAT IS LAMENTATIONS ALL ABOUT?

Lamentations is basically a despairing poem about the destruction of Jerusalem. It was probably written around 586 BC, shortly after the fall of the city to the Babylonians.

After having warned the southern Jewish nation to obey God—only to be disregarded—the prophet Jeremiah witnessed the punishment he'd threatened. Judah's "enemies prosper; for the Lord hath afflicted her for the multitude of her transgressions," Jeremiah wrote; "her children are gone into captivity before the enemy" (1:5). The sight brought tears to Jeremiah's eyes ("Mine eye runneth down with water," 1:16) and provided his nickname, "the weeping prophet." Lamentations ends with a plaintive cry: "Thou hast utterly rejected us; thou art very wroth against us" (5:22).

This punishment was severe, and some of our own struggles might seem overwhelming and unfair. But as the book of Hebrews says, "No chastening for the present seemeth to be joyous, but grievous: nevertheless afterward it yieldeth the peaceable fruit of righteousness unto them which are exercised thereby" (12:11).

Reading Plan: Lamentations 1–2

WHAT IS LAMENTATIONS' MESSAGE OF HOPE?

It is of the LORD's mercies that we are not consumed,
because his compassions fail not. They are new every
morning: great is thy faithfulness. The LORD is my portion,
saith my soul; therefore will I hope in him.

LAMENTATIONS 3:22–24

After the Babylonians had destroyed the once-great city of Jerusalem, the prophet Jeremiah looked around at its smoldering rubble, his heart filled with crushing sorrow. He knew it didn't have to be this way—his own people's rebellion had brought the city to ruin.

Jeremiah had plenty to grieve over. Yet in the midst of these horrors, he was still able to thank God for His love, compassion, and faithfulness. Though his heart was shattered, the prophet still saw God for who He really is.

How would you respond if you were faced with a personal catastrophe—the loss of a loved one, financial disaster, divorce, or a troubling medical diagnosis? It's not easy to keep praising God during these difficult times. But it's the key to keeping yourself grounded and finding peace as your world falls apart.

You can do it. Just as Jeremiah did, start praising God for who He is and how good He is to you—for His amazing, never-ending love and mercy.

Reading Plan: Lamentations 3–5

WHAT IS EZEKIEL ALL ABOUT?

Ezekiel, an exiled Jewish priest in Babylon, became God's spokesman to his fellow exiles. He shared unusual (even bizarre) visions with the people, reminding them of the sin that led to their captivity but also offering hope of national restoration.

In one of the most memorable images of all scripture, Ezekiel's vision of a valley of dry bones indicated that God could bring back even His scattered, sinful people: "I prophesied as I was commanded: and. . .there was a noise, and behold a shaking, and the bones came together. . . . The sinews and the flesh came up upon them, and the skin covered them above. . . . And the breath came into them, and they lived, and stood up upon their feet, an exceeding great army" (37:7–8, 10). Ezekiel also proved that the greatest desire of God's heart is people's good: "I have no pleasure in the death of him that dieth, saith the Lord God: wherefore turn yourselves, and live ye" (18:32).

Though the events of Ezekiel happened long ago and, for many of us, far away, the prophet offered strong teaching on personal responsibility that applies to all people, everywhere: "The soul that sinneth, it shall die. But if a man be just, and do that which is lawful and right. . .he shall surely live" (18:4–5, 9).

Reading Plan: Ezekiel 1–3

HOW CAN MY ACTIONS "HURT" GOD?

And they that escape of you shall remember me among the nations whither they shall be carried captives, because I am broken with their whorish heart, which hath departed from me, and with their eyes, which go a whoring after their idols: and they shall lothe themselves for the evils which they have committed in all their abominations.

EZEKIEL 6:9

The Bible includes many examples of how the actions of God's people can anger Him. That was true in Old Testament days, and it's true today. God doesn't change!

But did you ever consider that the God who created and saved us can also feel emotional pain when we stop following Him? Today's scripture says that God's heart was broken—that He was hurt—when His beloved people turned their backs on Him and chose other things to love.

Genesis 1:27 tells us God created humans in His own image. That means several things, but it points to one motivation: God wanted a created being whom He could love and who could willingly love Him in return. But when that object of God's love chooses another, God feels heartbroken, similar to how a husband would feel if His wife left him for another man.

Nothing is better than a mutually loving relationship with your Creator. But God has given you a choice—to love Him or love other things. Is there really any question as to which we should pursue?

Reading Plan: Ezekiel 4–7

HOW CAN I BE WHOLEHEARTED TOWARD GOD?

And I will give them one heart, and I will put a new
spirit within you; and I will take the stony heart out of
their flesh, and will give them an heart of flesh.

EZEKIEL 11:19

Because of their continuing sin, God's people endured some difficult times. But Ezekiel 11 offered wonderful words of hope—one day, God would gather His people from exile and bring them back to their homeland. Then they would return to the one true God, burning up all the idols they had worshipped before. They would know His law and carefully obey it. They would be His people, and He would be their God (Ezekiel 11:16–20).

In today's scripture, the phrase "one heart"—translated as "undivided heart" in other Bible versions—pointed to a time when God's people would love Him wholeheartedly.

God still wants His people to love Him with an undivided heart, soul, and mind (see Matthew 22:37). That, as Jesus taught, is God's greatest commandment.

This commandment isn't easy to follow on our own. In fact, it's impossible! But when we turn to Jesus for salvation, He puts the Holy Spirit inside us, enabling us to love and follow God with an undivided heart.

Reading Plan: Ezekiel 8–11

WHAT ARE IDOLS?

*Therefore say unto the house of Israel, Thus saith the Lord
God; Repent, and turn yourselves from your idols; and
turn away your faces from all your abominations.*

EZEKIEL 14:6

As a modern Christian, you probably don't think much about idols. To most of us, idolatry was a problem in Old Testament times, when God's people kept turning away from Him and worshipping false deities. Today, few people in our culture worship literal false "gods" like those people did.

Sounds like we have this problem handled, right?

However, idolatry is as much of a threat for the man of God today as it was in Old Testament times. We may not worship statues or other inanimate objects, but that doesn't mean temptations toward idolatry don't exist. That's why the apostle John warned, "Dear children, keep yourselves from idols" (1 John 5:21 NIV).

That was sound counsel two thousand years ago, and it's sound counsel today.

What things are you tempted to worship? Money? Position? Social standing? These things aren't sinful in themselves. But if we fixate on them, believing they can bring the satisfaction and security we should find in God alone, then they become idols.

Be careful. Make sure you keep God alone as the object of your worship.

Reading Plan: Ezekiel 12–15

WHAT CAN KEEP ME HUMBLE?

Thus wast thou decked with gold and silver; and thy raiment was of fine linen, and silk, and broidered work; thou didst eat fine flour, and honey, and oil: and thou wast exceeding beautiful, and thou didst prosper into a kingdom. And thy renown went forth among the heathen for thy beauty: for it was perfect through my comeliness, which I had put upon thee, saith the Lord God.

EZEKIEL 16:13–14

God addressed the words above to a very gifted city: Jerusalem. In this scripture, He listed the many blessings He had poured out on His people; however, in the following twenty verses, He chided the people, pronouncing His judgment on the city because its residents had somehow forgotten that everything they had was a gift from the Lord. In the end, the people of Jerusalem lost everything—even their freedom.

This part of Jerusalem's story should remind us to heed the apostle Paul's words: "What do you have that you did not receive? And if you did receive it, why do you boast as though you did not?" (1 Corinthians 4:7 NIV).

Confidence isn't a bad thing—awareness of our abilities can help us in our work and ministries. But we must temper these otherwise helpful attitudes with the knowledge that all we have and all we are comes from the hand of our loving, generous Father in heaven.

Reading Plan: Ezekiel 16–17

DOES GOD HATE SINNERS?

Have I any pleasure at all that the wicked should die? saith the
Lord GOD: and not that he should return from his ways, and live?
EZEKIEL 18:23

Most of us probably think God is looking down on this lost, sinful world, ready to give up on humanity and execute His final judgment. But today's verse tells us otherwise.

As mere humans, we might not understand how God could save the vilest of sinners—or why He'd want to. But God has been doing just that from the start—*because* He wants to. He's a patient, loving God who doesn't want people to be eternally lost.

God is giving humans time to turn to Him so that they can live eternally. As the apostle Peter wrote: "The Lord is not slow in keeping his promise, as some understand slowness. Instead he is patient with you, not wanting anyone to perish, but everyone to come to repentance" (2 Peter 3:9 NIV).

When you think of some people as beyond God's reach, that's your human impatience showing. So let God be God, and pray that He would miraculously reach the unreachable. Never forget—He reached out to you. Pray that He will bring many others into His family.

Reading Plan: Ezekiel 18–20

WHAT IS INTERCESSORY PRAYER?

*And I sought for a man among them, that should make
up the hedge, and stand in the gap before me for the
land, that I should not destroy it: but I found none.*

EZEKIEL 22:30

The prophet Ezekiel had warned the people of Judah about God's judgment,
but tragically, no one would listen. He could find no man to "stand in
the gap" before Him on Judah's behalf.

Today, God still looks for men to stand in the gap in fervent prayer,
in obedience to the apostle Paul's command: "I urge, then, first of all,
that petitions, prayers, intercession and thanksgiving be made for all
people—for kings and all those in authority, that we may live peaceful
and quiet lives in all godliness and holiness" (1 Timothy 2:1–2 NIV).

For the Christian man, bad news about his community, state, nation,
or world gives him the opportunity to engage in intercessory prayer. In
this kind of prayer, someone stands in the gap before God, pleading
for His mercy and intervention on behalf of friends, family members,
government leadership. . .basically, anyone.

God has given you a tremendous responsibility and privilege: to be
a man of prayer, one who goes to Him and pleads fervently on behalf
of others.

What can you begin praying for today?

Reading Plan: Ezekiel 21–22

HOW SHOULD I MOURN?

Also the word of the LORD came unto me, saying, Son of man,
behold, I take away from thee the desire of thine eyes with a
stroke: yet neither shalt thou mourn nor weep, neither shall thy
tears run down. Forbear to cry, make no mourning for the dead.

EZEKIEL 24:15–17

In today's scripture, God gave Ezekiel a directive that looks insensitive at first glance—harsh, even. Ezekiel was about to experience a terrible loss, the death of his wife, but God instructed him to skip all the outward signs of grief and instead mourn quietly and privately.

God knew Ezekiel would be heartbroken when his wife died, so He almost certainly comforted him during this private time of praying and seeking His will.

It may be difficult to understand the purpose behind this command. But we can take one important lesson from this passage: When we serve God, tragedy might discourage us or steal our joy, and it's only natural that we mourn. But our heavenly Father will be with us through these seasons, strengthening us and encouraging us to press forward in what He's called us to do. And we should always remember that this temporary life, so full of disappointment and heartache, is just the practice ground for eternity. As the apostle Paul quoted the prophet Isaiah, " 'What no eye has seen, what no ear has heard, and what no human mind has conceived'—the things God has prepared for those who love him" (1 Corinthians 2:9; see also Isaiah 64:4 NIV).

> **Reading Plan: Ezekiel 23–24**

HOW SHOULD I VIEW LOST PEOPLE?

The word of the LORD came again unto me, saying, Now,
thou son of man, take up a lamentation for Tyrus.

EZEKIEL 27:1–2

In the prophet Ezekiel's day, Tyre was a booming Mediterranean coastal city, not to mention a leader in shipping and commerce. But as the story of powerful cities often go, Tyre became infected with pride and self-sufficiency (see Ezekiel 28). Now, God was about to judge it.

Ezekiel was not happy about Tyre's eventual fate, but neither was God. Our heavenly Father always wants people to turn to Him and live (see Ezekiel 18), but eventually, He must judge unrepentant sinners.

Have you ever hoped that God would drop the hammer on sinners—especially those whose sin hurts others? It's not wrong to want God to act on behalf of the mistreated, but you should also keep your heart soft toward the perpetrators.

We should grieve over injustice, but we should join Ezekiel—and God—in feeling sorrow for those who are lost and without direction.

Today, pray that God would soften your heart toward those who desperately need to hear His message of salvation. . .and give them the direction they so clearly need.

Reading Plan: Ezekiel 25–27

HOW SHOULD I RESPOND WHEN PEOPLE SPEAK WELL OF ME?

Son of man, say unto the prince of Tyrus, Thus saith the Lord God;
Because thine heart is lifted up, and thou hast said, I am a God,
I sit in the seat of God, in the midst of the seas; yet thou art a man,
and not God, though thou set thine heart as the heart of God. . .

EZEKIEL 28:2

The king of Tyre was a talented and wise leader who built the city into one of the richest, most beautiful cities in the world. But sadly, the king allowed his own accomplishments and the admiration of others to fill him with pride so extreme that he began to see himself as a god.

One of the biggest dangers of accomplishing great things—as a leader, businessman, or minister—is that people tend to heap on you. If you're not careful, these words can go to your head, causing you to think more highly of yourself than you should.

That happened to the king of Tyre. It can happen to any of us.

So when people say good things about you, say thanks. But humbly remind them—and yourself—that *God* deserves all credit for who you are and what you've accomplished.

Reading Plan: Ezekiel 28–30

HOW COSTLY IS PRIDE?

Therefore thus saith the Lord GOD; Because thou hast lifted up thyself in height, and he hath shot up his top among the thick boughs, and his heart is lifted up in his height; I have therefore delivered him into the hand of the mighty one of the heathen; he shall surely deal with him: I have driven him out for his wickedness.

EZEKIEL 31:10–11

Today's scripture is part of God's pronouncement of judgment on Egypt for its pride and arrogance. God was about to humble Pharaoh using "the hand of the mighty one of the heathen"—King Nebuchadnezzar of Babylon.

The lesson for us today is this: When we live in humility before God, He will protect us from our spiritual enemies. But when we live in pride, believing we can take care of ourselves without His help, the enemy has free reign.

Pride always has a heavy price. That's why the wise King Solomon wrote, "Pride goes before destruction, a haughty spirit before a fall" (Proverbs 16:18 NIV). Strong words indeed!

If you want to live under God's mighty hand of protection, remember that you alone can't defeat your spiritual enemies. Keep yourself humble, depending on your mighty heavenly Father.

Reading Plan: Ezekiel 31–32

HOW IMPORTANT IS PROPER MOTIVATION?

*And they come unto thee as the people cometh, and they
sit before thee as my people, and they hear thy words, but
they will not do them: for with their mouth they shew much
love, but their heart goeth after their covetousness.*

EZEKIEL 33:31

As a Christian man, you probably attend church services regularly. That's a good thing. You might also go to a weekly Bible study. That's also a plus. And you might even give generously to your church or another ministry. God approves!

There are many things we Christians do and say because we know God wants us to. But how often do we examine our real motives? How often do we look into our hearts to make sure we are truly motivated by our love for God and not by mere religious duty?

It's easy to play the part of a Christian man. But God looks first at your heart, so He sees when you are properly motivated and when you are not. That's why it's vitally important to engage in regular self-examination to ensure that you're not just doing the right things—but doing them out of a heart of true love for the Lord.

Reading Plan: Ezekiel 33–34

WHY DID GOD PROMISE HIS PEOPLE A "NEW HEART"?

A new heart also will I give you, and a new spirit will I put within you: and I will take away the stony heart out of your flesh, and I will give you an heart of flesh. And I will put my spirit within you, and cause you to walk in my statutes, and ye shall keep my judgments, and do them.

EZEKIEL 36:26–27

On December 3, 1967, at Groote Schuur Hospital in Cape Town, South Africa, surgeon Christiaan Barnard and his large team of physicians accomplished a medical miracle—the world's first human-to-human heart transplant.

As incredible as that was, God did something even more amazing when He saved you. The moment you humbled yourself before Him, He replaced your old, stony heart and gave you a new, soft one. This spiritual heart transplant changed you in every way—He actually made you a new person. That's why the apostle Paul wrote, "If anyone is in Christ, the new creation has come: The old has gone, the new is here!" (2 Corinthians 5:17 NIV).

Through the work of His Holy Spirit, God gave you a new, undivided heart that can hear Him, respond to what He says, and live in a way that pleases Him. This new heart will never fail, and it will never need to be replaced again.

> **Reading Plan: Ezekiel 35–36**

DOES GOD STILL DO MIRACLES?

And caused me to pass by them round about: and, behold,
there were very many in the open valley; and, lo, they were
very dry. And he said unto me, Son of man, can these bones
live? And I answered, O Lord Gᴏᴅ, thou knowest.

EZEKIEL 37:2–3

When God showed the prophet Ezekiel a vision of a valley filled with dry bones, He asked him a question that still has eternal importance for us today: "Can these bones live?"

Ezekiel knew God could do the impossible, and his vision ended with a miracle: flesh re-covered the dry bones, and they came to life.

Ezekiel's vision speaks to us today. Centuries later, during the early church age, the apostle Paul wrote, "But because of his great love for us, God, who is rich in mercy, made us alive with Christ even when we were dead in transgressions" (Ephesians 2:4–5 ɴɪᴠ).

Today, God shows each of us our own valleys filled with dry bones—the unbelieving people in our lives—and asks us, "Can these bones live?"

The answer, of course, is *Yes!* God can and does perform miracles today—namely, the miracle of bringing spiritually dead people to life. Our part in these miracles is to speak the words of life—the Gospel of Jesus Christ.

Reading Plan: Ezekiel 37–39

HOW CAN I BE PREPARED TO SHARE GOD'S LOVE?

And the man said unto me, Son of man, behold with thine eyes, and hear with thine ears, and set thine heart upon all that I shall shew thee; for to the intent that I might shew them unto thee art thou brought hither: declare all that thou seest to the house of Israel.

EZEKIEL 40:4

Have you ever been in a situation where you knew you needed to open your mouth and speak the Gospel message? But at the moment of truth, you froze up and said nothing? If so, you're not alone. Most Christian men have been there.

Moments like that are exactly why the apostle Peter wrote, "Always be prepared to give an answer to everyone who asks you to give the reason for the hope that you have" (1 Peter 3:15 NIV).

So how can you be prepared to speak up when God gives you the opportunity? Today's scripture provides a good clue. Before showing Ezekiel a vision of Jerusalem's rebuilt temple, an angel told the prophet to pay close attention to what he was about to hear and see—and then tell the Israelites everything he witnessed.

Obviously, Ezekiel wouldn't have been able to tell the people about something he hadn't paid proper attention to. In the same way, we Christian men need to pay attention to what God teaches us in our times of prayer and Bible reading. That way, we'll be better prepared when it's time to speak the news of Jesus.

Reading Plan: Ezekiel 40–42

HOW CAN I KNOW WHAT'S MOST IMPORTANT TO GOD?

And the LORD said unto me, Son of man, mark well, and behold with thine eyes, and hear with thine ears all that I say unto thee concerning all the ordinances of the house of the LORD, and all the laws thereof; and mark well the entering in of the house, with every going forth of the sanctuary.

EZEKIEL 44:5

Listen up, guys! In your high school days, you probably heard a coach or teacher utter those three words. And if they had their intended effect, you expected an important message to follow.

That's the response God wanted from the prophet Ezekiel in today's scripture.

God was about to give Ezekiel some detailed instructions about the Jewish priesthood for when the Jews returned to Jerusalem from the Babylonian Exile. That's why He told him, "Listen closely and give attention to everything I tell you" (44:5 NIV).

There may be times, especially during your Bible reading and prayer, when God seems to be saying, "Pay close attention. This is very important!"

And if God says it's important, you'd do well to listen closely!

When you follow your Bible reading with a time of prayer, make sure you don't just talk to God. Instead, pay close attention to what He may be saying about the words you've just read.

God has much to show and teach you through His Word. Pay close attention, and He'll help you grow in both your knowledge of Him and His expectations for your life.

Reading Plan: Ezekiel 43–44

HOW IMPORTANT IS HONESTY TO GOD?

Ye shall have just balances, and a just ephah, and a just bath.
The ephah and the bath shall be of one measure, that the bath
may contain the tenth part of an homer, and the ephah the
tenth part of an homer: the measure thereof shall be after the
homer. And the shekel shall be twenty gerahs: twenty shekels,
five and twenty shekels, fifteen shekels, shall be your maneh.

EZEKIEL 45:10–12

In the internet age, even most non-Christian businessmen understand that one shady deal or unhappy customer can quickly lead to failure, simply because people tend to take their complaints online.

Internet or no internet, honesty is always the best policy, and God wants it in the life of every Christian man.

The Bible makes a big deal about honesty in every part of our lives, including our business practices. Of course, honesty is all the more important for the man who follows Jesus. That's because God calls us to glorify and obey Him by being honest in every way.

How important is honesty to you? Do you always try your best to speak truthfully? Do you always make sure you don't waste your company's time at work? Do you always treat business clients fairly?

You demonstrate your love for God—and for your neighbor—when you practice integrity by treating people honestly.

Reading Plan: Ezekiel 45–46

HOW CAN I BE A SOURCE OF "LIVING WATER"?

*And he said unto me, Son of man, hast thou seen this? Then he brought
me, and caused me to return to the brink of the river. Now when I had
returned, behold, at the bank of the river were very many trees on the
one side and on the other. Then said he unto me, These waters issue out
toward the east country, and go down into the desert, and go into the
sea: which being brought forth into the sea, the waters shall be healed.*

EZEKIEL 47:6–8

A spring creek is a stream that originates underground and produces
enough cold, clean water to keep the stream flowing consistently. One
of the best-known spring creeks in North America—especially among
fly fishers—is the Henrys Fork River, a tributary of southeastern Idaho's
Snake River.

A spring creek is a solid illustration of what God wants us to be to
the world around us. It brings to mind Jesus' words: "Whoever believes
in me, as Scripture has said, rivers of living water will flow from within
them" (John 7:38 NIV).

God calls us to be a source of blessing and life-giving water to the
world around us. So don't keep it inside you. Let it flow into you from
above and then out to a thirsty, needy world.

Reading Plan: Ezekiel 47–48

WHAT IS DANIEL ALL ABOUT?

As a young man, Daniel—along with three others to be known as Shadrach, Meshach, and Abednego—were taken from their home in Jerusalem to serve the king of Babylon. Daniel's God-given ability to interpret dreams endeared him to King Nebuchadnezzar, whose vision of a huge statue, Daniel said, represented existing and future kingdoms. Shadrach, Meshach, and Abednego found trouble when they disobeyed an order to bow before a statue of Nebuchadnezzar; as punishment, they were thrown into a fiery furnace, where they were protected by an angelic being "like the Son of God" (3:25).

The next Babylonian king, Belshazzar, threw a drinking party using cups stolen from the temple in Jerusalem; he literally saw "the writing on the wall," which Daniel interpreted as the soon-to-come takeover of Babylon by the Medes. The Median king, Darius, kept Daniel as an adviser but was tricked into passing a law designed by other jealous officials to hurt Daniel, who ended up in a den of lions. Once again, God protected His people; Daniel spent a trouble-free night with the beasts and was replaced by the schemers, who were mauled by the hungry animals.

As an old Gospel song says, "Dare to be a Daniel." God will always take care of the people who "dare to stand alone. . .to have a purpose firm" for Him.

Reading Plan: Daniel 1–2

WHAT CAN WE LEARN FROM SHADRACH, MESHACH, AND ABEDNEGO?

*O Nebuchadnezzar. . . If it be so, our God whom we serve is
able to deliver us from the burning fiery furnace. . . . But if not,
be it known unto thee, O king, that we will not serve thy gods,
nor worship the golden image which thou hast set up.*

DANIEL 3:16–18

Shadrach, Meshach, and Abednego, three deeply committed Hebrew men of God during the Babylonian captivity, were faced with two terrible options: (1) worship King Nebuchadnezzar's golden idol, or (2) be tossed into a blazing hot furnace.

But because of their commitment to their God, these three didn't see their situation as a dilemma at all. For them, there really wasn't a choice. They weren't going to serve the king's gods or bow to his idol, period. And if that meant dying in a fiery furnace, so be it.

Has someone—perhaps a friend or your employer—ever asked you to do something you knew wouldn't please God?

Because you live in this fallen world, you may be forced to decide between honoring God or compromising your faith. Until you're in such a situation, you can't really say what you would do. But God has every intention of seeing you through even the most difficult and frightening of situations. "We do not belong to those who shrink back and are destroyed," the author of Hebrews wrote, "but to those who have faith and are saved" (10:39 NIV).

Reading Plan: Daniel 3–4

WHICH IS MORE IMPORTANT: THE WORLD'S LAWS OR GOD'S?

Now when Daniel knew that the writing was signed, he went into his house; and his windows being open in his chamber toward Jerusalem, he kneeled upon his knees three times a day, and prayed, and gave thanks before his God, as he did aforetime.

DANIEL 6:10

What would you do if the government passed a law forcing you to violate your conscience by disobeying God? (This once far-fetched idea is becoming more believable by the day.)

That's exactly the situation Daniel found himself in. King Darius had just issued a decree forbidding everyone from praying to or worshipping anyone but him—under the threat of being fed to a den full of hungry lions.

Powerless to change the law, Daniel did the only thing he could: he prayed. After learning of the decree, he went upstairs to his room three times every day and prayed to the God who could save him and keep him faithful.

Daniel was eventually thrown to the lions, but God spared him by closing the mouths of the ravenous beasts. Darius liked Daniel, so he was relieved to find him alive the next morning. Afterward, he decreed that the Persian people honor Daniel's God.

Plenty in today's culture can move a man of God to anger or even fear. That's not necessarily a bad thing, provided these emotions move him first to prayer, then to whatever action God calls for.

Reading Plan: Daniel 5–6

WHY DOES GOD HEAR OUR REQUESTS?

O my God, incline thine ear, and hear; open thine eyes, and behold our desolations, and the city which is called by thy name: for we do not present our supplications before thee for our righteousnesses, but for thy great mercies.

DANIEL 9:18

Becoming a father usually brings out a man's giving spirit. Whether or not his children deserve it, his desire to give remains. That's because he loves his kids, and the nature of love is to give—even when the recipient has done nothing to earn it.

The prophet Daniel understood that God is a loving, merciful Father who gives—but not because of any righteousness or merit on our part. That's why Daniel acknowledged that His people could come to Him requesting His favor. God loves like a Father, and He therefore gives to the unworthy. That's just His nature.

Recognizing this is the very definition of the type of humility God honors. It's knowing that we ourselves have nothing to offer God but our empty, outstretched hands as we wait to receive the undeserve blessings that our loving, generous heavenly Father deeply desires to give.

God is good to us because of who He is, not who we are. Consequently, our only response should be deep gratitude.

Reading Plan: Daniel 7–9

HOW CAN MY FAITH BE STRENGTHENED?

*Then there came again and touched me one like the appearance
of a man, and he strengthened me, and said, O man greatly
beloved, fear not: peace be unto thee, be strong, yea, be strong.
And when he had spoken unto me, I was strengthened, and
said, Let my lord speak; for thou hast strengthened me.*

DANIEL 10:18–19

Fathers who want to raise confident, courageous children must start by letting their children know they are genuinely loved.

That's true for children, and it was true for the prophet Daniel.

God encouraged and strengthened Daniel with the words "O man greatly beloved." And because he embraced his value in God's eyes, Daniel accomplished big things.

The apostle Paul echoed this truth when he wrote, "But because of his great love for us, God, who is rich in mercy, made us alive with Christ even when we were dead in transgressions—it is by grace you have been saved" (Ephesians 2:4–5 NIV).

As a Christian, you can think of yourself as *saved*, *redeemed*, *blessed*, *set apart*, and many other encouraging adjectives found throughout the scripture. Don't forget, however, that above all, you are *greatly beloved*.

Reading Plan: Daniel 10–12

WHAT IS HOSEA ALL ABOUT?

Sometime between 750 (approximately when Hosea began ministering) and 722 BC (when Assyria overran Israel), God gave Hosea a strange command: "Take unto thee a wife of whoredoms" (1:2). The marriage pictured God's relationship to Israel—an honorable, loving husband paired with an unfaithful wife. Hosea married an adulteress named Gomer and started a family with her. But when Gomer returned to her life of sin, Hosea—again picturing God's faithfulness—bought her back from the slave market.

Gomer ultimately had three children—perhaps Hosea's but maybe not—each given a prophetic name. Son Jezreel was named for a massacre, daughter Lo-ruhamah's name meant "not loved," and son Loammi's name meant "not my people." Those memorable names were part of Hosea's bad-news pronouncements to Israel.

But God is faithful, even when His people aren't—and He's always ready to forgive. "I will heal their backsliding," God said through His prophet. "I will love them freely" (14:4).

Reading Plan: Hosea 1–5

WHAT DOES HOSEA SAY ABOUT SPIRITUAL GROWTH?

*Sow to yourselves in righteousness, reap in mercy; break
up your fallow ground: for it is time to seek the Lord,
till he come and rain righteousness upon you.*

HOSEA 10:12

In Old Testament times, many Jews were familiar with farming practices. So in today's scripture, as the prophet Hosea gave his audience specific instructions on how they should prepare themselves to approach the God they had neglected for so long, he used agricultural word pictures.

While far fewer people today know much about farming, Hosea's message is still important. He simply taught that all believers should take time to earnestly seek God and ask Him to reveal to them any spiritual neglectfulness in their lives. That's what "break up your fallow ground" means.

There's not a man of God alive who doesn't need spiritual growth, and many of us know we need to make our hearts more receptive to God's plan for us. But here's the good news: God has promised to make that growth happen if you simply prepare your heart to receive His blessings, then seek Him in prayer and Bible reading.

Reading Plan: Hosea 6–10

HOW CAN I ALWAYS KNOW— AND DO—WHAT'S RIGHT?

Who is wise, and he shall understand these things? prudent, and
he shall know them? for the ways of the LORD are right, and the
just shall walk in them: but the transgressors shall fall therein.

HOSEA 14:9

It's been said that "common sense isn't so common today." And the same can be said of wisdom. In this social media age, people are drawn more often to witty aphorisms than to true words of wisdom.

Today's scripture says that true wisdom is knowing and obeying our Father in heaven. This is a good amplification of Solomon's words: "The fear of the LORD is the beginning of wisdom, and knowledge of the Holy One is understanding" (Proverbs 9:10 NIV).

Today, we can turn to many sources for worldly wisdom. But it's nearly always incomplete or wrong—and many people have sadly fallen into its trap.

That's why God's words to Hosea mean as much to us today as they did when they were written. God is our source of complete wisdom, so His ways are the best for us to follow. . .no matter what the world says.

Reading Plan: Hosea 11–14

WHAT IS JOEL ALL ABOUT?

Possibly just before the Babylonian invasion of Judah in 586 BC, a devastating locust swarm occurred. A prophet named Joel indicated this natural disaster would be nothing compared to the coming "great and very terrible" day of the Lord (2:11).

God was planning to judge His people for sin, but they still had time to repent. Unlike other prophets who condemned idolatry, injustice, or other specific sins of the Jewish people, Joel simply called for repentance without describing the sin committed. Obedience would bring both physical and spiritual renewal: "I will pour out my spirit upon all flesh," God said (2:28).

When the Holy Spirit came on Christian believers at Pentecost, the apostle Peter quoted the preceding verse from Joel to explain what had happened (Acts 2:17).

Though God judges sin, He always offers a way out—in our time, through Jesus. When we are in Him, there is no fear of a terrible future "day of the Lord."

Reading Plan: Joel 1–3

WHAT IS AMOS ALL ABOUT?

An average guy—a lowly shepherd, actually—took on the rich and powerful of Israelite society, condemning their idol worship, persecution of God's prophets, and cheating of the poor. Amos was from a place called Tekoa, near Bethlehem in Judah, but God called him to prophesy to the northern Jewish kingdom of Israel.

Though God had once rescued the people of Israel from slavery in Egypt, He was ready to send them into new bondage because of their sin. Amos saw visions that pictured Israel's plight: a plumb line, indicating the people were not measuring up to God's standards, and a basket of ripe fruit, showing the nation was ripe for God's judgment. Their external religious rituals weren't helping them at all with God, who wanted them to treat others with justice.

How are you treating the people around you? In God's eyes, that's an indicator of your true spiritual condition. (For a New Testament perspective, see James 2:14–18.)

Reading Plan: Amos 1–5

WHAT IS OBADIAH ALL ABOUT?

Edom was a nation descended from Esau—twin brother of Jacob, the patriarch of Israel. The baby boys had struggled in their mother's womb (Genesis 25:21–26), and their conflict had continued over the centuries. After Edom took part in the Babylonian ransacking of Jerusalem, Obadiah passed down God's judgment: "For thy violence against thy brother Jacob shame shall cover thee, and thou shalt be cut off for ever" (verse 10).

This briefest of all the Old Testament books is attributed to Obadiah (verse 1). It's unclear whether that is a person by that name or an unnamed prophet for whom "Obadiah" (meaning "servant of God") is a title.

Whatever the case, the little book of Obadiah shows God's faithfulness to His people. This prophecy is a fulfillment of God's promise from generations earlier: "I will bless them that bless thee, and curse him that curseth thee" (Genesis 12:3). As He fulfilled His promises to Israel, He will uphold His promises to you.

Reading Plan: Amos 6–9; Obadiah

WHAT IS JONAH ALL ABOUT?

God told His prophet Jonah to preach repentance in Nineveh, capital of the brutal Assyrian Empire. But Jonah disobeyed, sailing in the opposite direction—toward a rendezvous with literary immortality.

A storm rocked Jonah's ship, the pagan sailors reluctantly threw him overboard, and he spent three days in a giant fish's belly before deciding to obey God after all. When Jonah finally preached in Nineveh, the people repented—and God spared the city from the destruction He'd threatened. But then the prejudiced Jonah pouted: "I pray thee, O LORD, was not this my saying, when I was yet in my country? Therefore I fled before unto Tarshish: for I knew that thou art a gracious God, and merciful, slow to anger, and of great kindness, and repentest thee of the evil. Therefore now, O Lord, take, I beseech thee, my life from me; for it is better for me to die than to live" (4:2–3).

The book of Jonah ends with God proclaiming His concern even for vicious pagans. The fact is that God loves everyone—even the enemies of His chosen people. As Romans 5:8 says, "God commendeth his love toward us, in that, while we were yet sinners, Christ died for us."

Reading Plan: Jonah 1–4

WHAT IS MICAH ALL ABOUT?

A prophet named Micah, identified only as a "Morasthite," chastised both the northern and southern Jewish nations for pursuing false gods and cheating the poor. The two nations would be devastated by invaders (the Assyrians), but God would preserve "the remnant of Israel" (2:12).

Centuries before Jesus' birth, it was Micah who predicted the town where that would occur: "But thou, Bethlehem Ephratah, though thou be little among the thousands of Judah, yet out of thee shall he come forth unto me that is to be ruler in Israel" (5:2). And it was Micah who famously stated God's expectations of human beings: "He hath shewed thee, O man, what is good; and what doth the LORD require of thee, but to do justly, and to love mercy, and to walk humbly with thy God?" (6:8).

The book of Micah shows how God's judgment is tempered by mercy. "Who is a God like unto thee, that pardoneth iniquity, and passeth by the transgression of the remnant of his heritage? he retaineth not his anger for ever, because he delighteth in mercy" (7:18). When we fail, as all of us do, we can always return to God in confession, knowing that He delights in mercy.

Reading Plan: Micah 1–7

WHAT ARE NAHUM AND HABAKKUK ALL ABOUT?

As with the other minor prophets ("minor" simply meaning shorter than the "major" prophecies of Isaiah, Jeremiah, Ezekiel, and Daniel) Nahum and Habakkuk addressed particular situations pertaining to God's people.

Nahum cried out against Nineveh, capital of the brutal Assyrian Empire. God Himself would "make thee vile, and will set thee as a gazingstock" (3:6) for sins of idolatry and cruelty. Nahum's prophecy came true when the Babylonian Empire overran Nineveh in 612 BC.

Habakkuk complained that God allowed violence and injustice among His people. And the prophet was shocked to learn the Lord's plan for dealing with the problem: sending the "bitter and hasty" (1:6) Chaldeans to punish Judah. The Lord said He was only using the Chaldeans for His purposes and would in time punish them for their own sins.

Our world is much like Nahum and Habakkuk's—full of violence and injustice—but God is still in control. Whether we sense it or not, He's working out His own purposes. And it's not our job to question God's ways: "The Lord is in his holy temple," Habakkuk ultimately realized; "let all the earth keep silence before him" (2:20).

> Reading Plan: Nahum 1–3; Habakkuk 1–3

WHAT ARE ZEPHANIAH AND HAGGAI ALL ABOUT?

The book of Zephaniah begins with a jarring prophecy: "I will utterly consume all things from off the land," God declares (1:2). People, animals, birds, and fish will all perish, victims of God's wrath over Judah's idolatry. Other nearby nations would be punished, as well, in "the fire of [God's] jealousy" (3:8), but there was hope: In His mercy, God would one day restore a remnant of Israel that "shall not do iniquity, nor speak lies" (3:13).

Haggai, one of three "postexilic" prophets, encouraged former Babylonian captives to restore the demolished temple in Jerusalem. The new world power, Persia, had allowed the people to return to Jerusalem, but they had become distracted with building their own comfortable homes. Through Haggai, God told the people to rebuild the temple first in order to break a drought that affected the countryside.

Haggai seemed to hint at the end-times tribulation and second coming of Christ when he quoted God as saying, "I will shake the heavens, and the earth, and the sea, and the dry land; and I will shake all nations, and the desire of all nations shall come" (2:6–7). This world's trouble—and there's plenty of it—will be calmed and corrected when Jesus returns. Let's all be watching for that day.

Reading Plan: Zephaniah 1–3; Haggai 1–2

WHAT IS ZECHARIAH ALL ABOUT?

Like Haggai, another postexilic prophet, Zechariah urged the Jewish people to rebuild the temple in Jerusalem. He also gave several prophecies of the coming Messiah, including an end-times vision of a final battle over Jerusalem, when "the LORD [shall] go forth, and fight against those nations. . . . And his feet shall stand in that day upon the mount of Olives. . . . And the LORD shall be king over all the earth" (14:3–4, 9).

It was Zechariah who delivered the prophecy of the Messiah riding a donkey into Jerusalem (9:9), an event that was fulfilled to the letter in Jesus' "triumphal entry" (Matthew 21:1–11). Another prophecy of Zechariah, "They shall look upon me whom they have pierced" (12:10), refers to the Roman soldiers' spearing of Christ after the crucifixion (John 19:34).

Knowing that Zechariah's specific prophecies of the Messiah were fulfilled in Jesus, we can trust that his other, yet-to-be-fulfilled predictions—of the end times—will come true too. Zechariah served, as we do, a God who declares "the end from the beginning, and from ancient times the things that are not yet done, saying, My counsel shall stand, and I will do all my pleasure" (Isaiah 46:10).

Reading Plan: Zechariah 1–4

DAY 279

WHAT ARE JUSTICE, MERCY, AND COMPASSION?

Thus speaketh the LORD of hosts, saying, Execute true judgment, and shew mercy and compassions every man to his brother: and oppress not the widow, nor the fatherless, the stranger, nor the poor; and let none of you imagine evil against his brother in your heart.

ZECHARIAH 7:9–10

God wants His people to glorify Him by treating others with kindness and compassion. That is true in both the Old Testament and the New.

One day, Jesus told His disciples that His true followers (the sheep) would distinguish themselves from the false ones (the goats) by how they treated "the least of these." Here's His bottom line:

> *"The King will reply, 'Truly I tell you, whatever you did for one of the least of these brothers and sisters of mine, you did for me.' Then he will say to those on his left, 'Depart from me, you who are cursed, into the eternal fire prepared for the devil and his angels. For I was hungry and you gave me nothing to eat, I was thirsty and you gave me nothing to drink, I was a stranger and you did not invite me in, I needed clothes and you did not clothe me, I was sick and in prison and you did not look after me.'"*

MATTHEW 25:40–43 NIV

Your relationship with Jesus will always reveal itself through how you treat others. We offer true and practical worship when we treat people impartially—when we do good to widows, the fatherless, the homeless, the poor, the immigrants, and those forgotten by the world.

Reading Plan: Zechariah 5–9

CAN I TRUST GOD TO MEET MY NEEDS?

Ask ye of the LORD rain in the time of the latter rain;
so the LORD shall make bright clouds, and give them
showers of rain, to every one grass in the field.

ZECHARIAH 10:1

Have you ever been in such a financial predicament that you started wondering how you would pay the bills and still feed your family?

If so, you're far from the first. That's partly why Jesus told His followers, "Look at the birds of the air; they do not sow or reap or store away in barns, and yet your heavenly Father feeds them. Are you not much more valuable than they?" (Matthew 6:26 NIV).

Jesus' point is that God knows your needs and He wants to meet them.

You, however, have an advantage that birds don't: God has created you to relate with Him as a son relates to his father. That means you can ask Him for what you need, knowing He *wants* to provide.

When you're stressed, wondering how you're going to get by, lock your eyes on your heavenly Father, not on your circumstances. God provides for the billions of birds. You can count on Him to provide for you.

Reading Plan: Zechariah 10–14

WHAT IS MALACHI ALL ABOUT?

Prophesying a century after the return from exile, Malachi, whose name means "my messenger," chastised the Jews for offering "lame and sick" sacrifices to God (1:8); for divorcing their wives to marry pagan women (2:11, 14); and for failing to pay tithes for the temple (3:8). The Lord was angry with the attitude, "It is vain to serve God" (3:14), but He promised to bless the obedient: "Unto you that fear my name shall the Sun of righteousness arise with healing in his wings" (4:2).

The Jews had become careless in their attitudes toward God, still following some of the duties of the law of Moses, but without any true passion for the Lord. God doesn't want empty religious rituals, though—He wants people to worship Him "in spirit and in truth" (John 4:24).

This challenge of the post-exile Jews is a challenge we as Christians face today. May we never simply go through the motions of following Jesus. Let's be sure that, "Whether therefore ye eat, or drink, or whatsoever ye do, do all to the glory of God" (1 Corinthians 10:31).

Reading Plan: Malachi 1–4

WHAT IS MATTHEW ALL ABOUT?

The first of the four Gospels (meaning "good news"), the book of Matthew ties what follows in the New Testament to what came before in the Old. The book, written primarily to a Jewish audience, uses numerous Old Testament references to prove that Jesus is the promised Messiah the Jews have been anticipating for centuries.

Beginning with a genealogy that shows Jesus' ancestry through King David and the patriarch Abraham, Matthew then details the angelic announcement of Jesus' conception and the visit of the "wise men" with their gifts of gold, frankincense, and myrrh. Matthew introduces the character of John the Baptist, relative and forerunner of Jesus, and describes the calling of key disciples Peter, Andrew, James, and John. Jesus' teachings are emphasized, with long passages covering His Sermon on the Mount (chapters 5–7), including the Beatitudes ("Blessed are they. . .") and the Lord's Prayer ("Our Father, which art in heaven. . ."). As with all four Gospels, Matthew also details the death, burial, and resurrection of Jesus, and he is the only biographer of Jesus to mention several miracles—an earthquake, the breaking open of tombs, and the raising to life of dead saints—that occurred during that time (27:50–54).

The author of the book of Matthew is not stated, but he is traditionally believed to be Matthew, the tax collector chosen by Jesus to be a disciple (9:9). Matthew is also known as Levi (Mark 2:14). Though he collaborated with the Roman government in collecting taxes, he was a Jewish man who saw in Jesus the promised Messiah. As Messiah, Jesus is also King—and worthy of our worship.

Reading Plan: Matthew 1–4

WHAT IS THE GOLDEN RULE?

Therefore all things whatsoever ye would that men should do to you, do ye even so to them: for this is the law and the prophets.

MATTHEW 7:12

One day, a big crowd gathered around Jesus on the shore of the Sea of Galilee, and He started teaching them in a way they'd never heard before. The crowd listened closely as Jesus delivered what is called the Sermon on the Mount (see Matthew 5–7).

Near the end of His sermon, Jesus gave what is known as "the Golden Rule"—one of His best-known teachings. This rule instructs us to treat people the same way we would like to be treated.

Jesus knew how selfish and inconsiderate people can be, but He wanted all of His followers to treat each other with kindness, fairness, patience, forgiveness, and courtesy—just as God had already commanded.

How do you like to be treated? Do you want people to forgive you when you mess up? Do you want them to treat you generously? Do you want your friends to lend a hand when you're attempting a difficult task?

If so, do these things for others too. You'll be "golden."

Reading Plan: Matthew 5–7

WHY DID JESUS PERFORM MIRACLES?

*When the even was come, they brought unto him many that
were possessed with devils: and he cast out the spirits with
his word, and healed all that were sick: That it might be
fulfilled which was spoken by Esaias the prophet, saying,
Himself took our infirmities, and bare our sicknesses.*

MATTHEW 8:16–17

Most of chapters 8–9 of Matthew describe Jesus' miracles. In these two chapters alone, Jesus healed the sick and disabled, calmed a storm with just His words, cast evil spirits out of two men, and raised a young girl from the dead.

Many people who witnessed Jesus' amazing miracles followed Him, knowing there was something very special about this man.

Jesus gave the reason for performing these miracles: "That you may know and understand that the Father is in me, and I in the Father" (John 10:38 NIV). In other words, Jesus' miracles—in addition to fulfilling Old Testament prophecies about Himself (Isaiah 35:5–6)—proved that He truly was God in the flesh.

Today, we have the privilege of reading about Jesus' many miracles in the Gospels, the first four books in the New Testament. As we read, our faith can be strengthened as we consider the love and compassion God poured out on us when He sent His Son into the world.

Reading Plan: Matthew 8–9

HOW MUCH DOES GOD CARE FOR ME?

Are not two sparrows sold for a farthing? and one of them
shall not fall on the ground without your Father. But the
very hairs of your head are all numbered. Fear ye not
therefore, ye are of more value than many sparrows.

MATTHEW 10:29–31

In teaching His followers about God's amazing love and concern for His people, Jesus spoke of the sparrow—a bird that has very little value to anyone. Tens of thousands of sparrows likely die each day, yet very few people notice. But God does. Jesus said that not even a single sparrow falls to the ground without His knowledge.

Jesus used this example to illustrate God's concern over the smallest details in His creation—and by extension, the smallest details in the lives of His people, including you!

It's easy to think of God as distant and detached from our everyday lives. But nothing could be further from the truth. God knows even the smallest details in your life. If He knows the number of hairs on your head, He certainly recognizes your trouble and grief. God knows and He cares. . .and reminds you of that truth through His eternal Word.

Reading Plan: Matthew 10–11

HOW IMPORTANT TO GOD ARE MY WORDS?

But I say unto you, That every idle word that men shall speak, they shall give account thereof in the day of judgment. For by thy words thou shalt be justified, and by thy words thou shalt be condemned.

MATTHEW 12:36–37

Jesus' disciples often said some troubling and irresponsible things. For instance: James and John asked Jesus to call down thunder on people, and Peter tried to persuade Jesus to avoid the cross. Their words had the potential to cause serious problems—if it weren't for Jesus' presence.

In today's scripture, Jesus warned some Jewish religious leaders—who had spoken evil of Him and His ministry—that they would one day be either acquitted or condemned based on their words.

Our words have power to give life, encouragement, and freedom to others. But they can also condemn, discourage, and bind. Basic everyday statements can have eternal consequences. The stakes are high, so we can't afford to speak carelessly without considering if our words will benefit or hurt others.

Let's carefully weigh the words we speak today, so we don't need to worry about giving account of them before God. That day is coming, and sooner than we know.

Reading Plan: Matthew 12–13

WHAT IS THE MOST IMPORTANT QUESTION?

*When Jesus came into the coasts of Caesarea Philippi, he
asked his disciples, saying, Whom do men say that I the
Son of man am? And they said, Some say that thou art John
the Baptist: some, Elias; and others, Jeremias, or one of the
prophets. He saith unto them, But whom say ye that I am?*

MATTHEW 16:13–15

While traveling through the region of Caesarea Philippi, Jesus asked
His disciples what rumors had been circulating about His identity. The
Twelve eagerly volunteered what they knew—some believed He was
John the Baptist, while others said He was Elijah, Jeremiah, or one of
the other prophets returned to earth.

After listening to the disciples' answer, Jesus then asked the question
He'd been leading up to—the most important question in human history.

Who do *you* think I am?

Eleven of the disciples stayed silent, but Peter—true to his character—blurted out what the others may have been thinking: "You are
the Messiah, the Son of the living God" (16:16 NIV).

"Blessed are you, Simon son of Jonah," Jesus exclaimed, "for this
was not revealed to you by flesh and blood, but by my Father in heaven"
(verse 17 NIV).

Who do you think Jesus is? That's the most important question you'll
ever answer.

Reading Plan: Matthew 14–16

SHOULD I EVER STOP FORGIVING OTHERS?

Then came Peter to him, and said, Lord, how oft shall my brother sin against me, and I forgive him? till seven times? Jesus saith unto him, I say not unto thee, Until seven times: but, Until seventy times seven.

MATTHEW 18:21–22

Jesus emphasized the importance of forgiving those who hurt or offend us. He said, "If you forgive other people when they sin against you, your heavenly Father will also forgive you. But if you do not forgive others their sins, your Father will not forgive your sins" (Matthew 6:14–15 NIV).

One day, Peter asked Jesus, "Lord, how many times shall I forgive my brother or sister who sins against me? Up to seven times?" (Matthew 18:21 NIV).

Peter probably wanted to sound compassionate by suggesting forgiving someone seven times. But Jesus took Peter's suggestion and multiplied it by seventy. This doesn't mean we should stop forgiving at 490; the implication is that our forgiveness should be unlimited—just like God's.

Grudges hurt us spiritually, emotionally, mentally, and physically. They separate us from one another—and even from God.

That's no way to live!

So don't limit the number of times you forgive. Just love those who hurt you, trust God, and forgive in His strength.

Reading Plan: Matthew 17–19

WHAT IS "SERVANT LEADERSHIP"?

And he said unto her, What wilt thou? She saith unto him,
Grant that these my two sons may sit, the one on thy right
hand, and the other on the left, in thy kingdom.

MATTHEW 20:21

When Salome, the mother of James and John, approached Jesus, she did what many moms would do for their kids. Salome loved her children and, because she understood who Jesus was, wanted Him to grant them a special place in His kingdom.

It's hard to blame Salome for making such a request. The problem, however, was that Salome didn't get the point of Jesus' ministry on earth.

Jesus gently told Salome and her sons, "You will indeed drink from my cup, but to sit at my right or left is not for me to grant. These places belong to those for whom they have been prepared by my Father" (Matthew 20:23 NIV).

Jesus then used this incident to clarify some things about His mission—and what greatness in God's kingdom looks like. "Whoever wants to become great among you must be your servant," He said, "and whoever wants to be first must be your slave—just as the Son of Man did not come to be served, but to serve, and to give his life as a ransom for many" (Matthew 20:26–28 NIV).

You should desire to be great in God's kingdom—by following Jesus' example of servanthood.

Reading Plan: Matthew 20–21

WHAT DID JESUS HAVE AGAINST THE PHARISEES?

But all their works they do for to be seen of men: they make broad their phylacteries, and enlarge the borders of their garments, and love the uppermost rooms at feasts, and the chief seats in the synagogues, and greetings in the markets, and to be called of men, Rabbi, Rabbi.

MATTHEW 23:5–7

In the first seven verses of Matthew 23, Jesus explained exactly what He had against the Pharisees (as well as the teachers of the law of Moses). Yes, they knew the law, so the people should obey what they said. But Jesus also said, "Don't follow their example," because instead of practicing what they taught, they made religious demands that crushed people's spirits. Also, Jesus said these deeply religious men placed great importance on the approval of others.

Jesus told His disciples, "The greatest among you will be your servant. For those who exalt themselves will be humbled, and those who humble themselves will be exalted" (Matthew 23:11–12 NIV). Jesus' biggest problem with the Jewish religious leaders of His time was that they were far more concerned with looking religious and being treated with respect than they were with loving God and serving others.

It's easy to be a Pharisee, looking down on others while disregarding our own moral and spiritual failures. Their stories are captured in scripture for our benefit—let's see our own prideful tendencies in their behaviors, and consciously avoid them.

Reading Plan: Matthew 22–23

HOW DOES SERVING OTHERS RELATE TO OUR SALVATION?

And the King shall answer and say unto them, Verily I say unto you, Inasmuch as ye have done it unto one of the least of these my brethren, ye have done it unto me.

MATTHEW 25:40

At a glance, Matthew 25:31–46 seems to imply that doing good for others is required for salvation. That's a real head-scratcher for Christians who know that salvation is based on faith in Jesus alone.

But when we take a broader look at the biblical message of salvation, we see that Jesus' words here do not contradict the message of salvation by faith. The truth is simply this: those who have received salvation by faith—and therefore have God's Spirit living within them—will be motivated to serve others out of true love for God and others.

Good deeds won't make you a Christian, nor will they "earn" you God's eternal salvation. However, if you follow Jesus Christ, you'll find yourself *wanting* to serve others, knowing that you're serving God Himself in the process.

Have you been wondering what kind of service God has in mind for you? If so, ask Him to first give you the right motivation. Then request opportunities to serve others.

Reading Plan: Matthew 24–25

WHAT DID JESUS ENDURE BEFORE HIS ARREST?

And he went a little farther, and fell on his face, and prayed, saying, O my Father, if it be possible, let this cup pass from me: nevertheless not as I will, but as thou wilt.

MATTHEW 26:39

After Jesus served His disciples at His last Passover dinner, they all walked through the Kidron Valley to the Mount of Olives, a place near the eastern side of Jerusalem. When they arrived, Jesus took Peter, James, and John away from the other apostles, walked a short distance away, fell to His face, and began to pray the most agonizing prayer in the Bible.

Jesus—at once fully human and fully God—knew what was in store for Him. He knew He would face unimaginable physical agony as the Roman soldiers sadistically beat Him and then crucified Him on a wooden cross. And He knew He would be taking the sins of all humanity upon Himself in that moment.

Jesus' human side desperately wanted to find another way. In terrible mental pain, He prayed, "My Father, if it is not possible for this cup to be taken away unless I drink it, may your will be done" (Matthew 26:42 NIV).

From the beginning, Jesus knew that His ultimate mission on earth was to die a sacrificial death. And in His own moment of truth, Jesus chose to give Himself up as the perfect sacrifice for the sins of the entire world. What a Savior we serve!

Reading Plan: Matthew 26

WHAT SHOULD I DO WITH THE NEWS THAT JESUS IS ALIVE?

And the angel answered and said unto the women, Fear not ye: for
I know that ye seek Jesus, which was crucified. He is not here: for
he is risen, as he said. Come, see the place where the Lord lay.

MATTHEW 28:5–6

Very early on Sunday morning—the first day after the Sabbath—two faithful followers of Jesus arrived at His tomb to finalize the preparation of His body. As the two women neared the tomb, they fully expected to find Jesus' dead body.

Instead, they discovered an angel, who told them news that neither they nor any of Jesus' other followers expected, even though He had told them beforehand—God had raised Him from the dead! Immediately, the women ran to tell the other disciples this earth-shattering announcement.

Jesus is alive!

Each year, on a Sunday between March 22 and April 25, Christians around the world celebrate the resurrection of the Lord Jesus Christ. But we needn't limit our celebration to one day of the year. Instead, let's rejoice every day as we think about the risen Christ.

"He is risen," the angel announced to the women at the tomb. Now we can declare, "He is risen indeed!"

Now. . .go and tell someone the good news!

Reading Plan: Matthew 27–28

WHAT IS MARK ALL ABOUT?

The second of the four Gospels is believed by most to be the first one written. The author is not stated but traditionally believed to be John Mark, a missionary companion of Paul and Barnabas (Acts 12:25) and an associate of the apostle Peter (1 Peter 5:13). Many believe that an unnamed spectator at Jesus' arrest, mentioned in this Gospel, was Mark himself: "And there followed him a certain young man, having a linen cloth cast about his naked body; and the young men laid hold on him: and he left the linen cloth, and fled from them naked" (14:51–52).

The book of Mark is the briefest and most active of the four biographies of Jesus. Mark addresses a Gentile audience, portraying Jesus as a man of action, divinely capable of healing the sick, controlling nature, and battling the powers of Satan. Mark's theme of the suffering servant comes through in his narratives of Jesus' interaction with hostile doubters—the Jewish leaders, who wanted to kill Him (9:31); His neighbors, who took offense at Him (6:3); and even His own family members, who thought He was crazy (3:21). The abasement of Jesus pictures what His disciples should pursue: "Whosoever will be great among you, shall be your minister: and whosoever of you will be the chiefest, shall be servant of all. For even the Son of man came not to be ministered unto, but to minister, and to give his life a ransom for many" (10:43–45).

Mark teaches us that suffering and loss aren't necessarily bad things—in fact, for Christians, they're the pathway to real life (8:35).

Reading Plan: Mark 1–3

WHY DID JESUS NEED TO PRAY?

And when he had sent them away,
he departed into a mountain to pray.

MARK 6:46

Throughout the Gospels, Jesus prayed to His Father in heaven. For example, He prayed at His baptism (Luke 3:21), before choosing His twelve disciples (Luke 6:12), before Peter's confession (Luke 9:18), at His transfiguration (Luke 9:29), and before His arrest and crucifixion (John 17).

The Bible tells about many great men of prayer, but none were as great as Jesus. But why did Jesus—the Son of the living God—need to pray? As God in the flesh, didn't He have the authority to do anything He wished?

Jesus was fully God and fully man. He needed to sleep and eat, just like everyone else. But to prepare Himself for His mission, He needed help from His Father in heaven. That means He needed to pray—regularly. If the Son of God needed to pray, how much more must we!

Yes, Jesus prayed often. Even more amazingly, He continues to pray for each of us to this day and beyond (see Hebrews 7:25).

Reading Plan: Mark 4–6

CAN I BE HONEST WITH GOD ABOUT MY DOUBTS?

And straightway the father of the child cried out, and said with tears, Lord, I believe; help thou mine unbelief.

MARK 9:24

The words in today's scripture were spoken by a man who wanted Jesus to heal his demon-possessed son. He had no doubt heard of Jesus' ability to heal the sick, lame, and demon-possessed. But he still struggled with unbelief.

We might wonder how a man who had heard so much about Jesus could possibly doubt Him. But maybe we shouldn't assume he had a hard time believing Jesus could help people. Maybe he was doubting if Jesus would help *him*.

The thought of being this honest with God scares many of us. There are things we wish we could hide from Him—things we don't even want to admit to ourselves. But when we come to the end of ourselves and need God to do something great, this is just the kind of honesty He wants from us.

Do you sometimes doubt that God wants to do a miracle for you? If so, confess your doubt to Him. He can handle it, and He can open your heart and mind to His plans for you.

Reading Plan: Mark 7–9

HOW IMPORTANT IS FORGIVENESS?

*And when ye stand praying, forgive, if ye have
ought against any: that your Father also which
is in heaven may forgive you your trespasses.*

MARK 11:25

Have you ever been around someone who harbors anger and bitterness
over wrongs that were committed years ago? If so, you probably wanted
to get away as soon as possible.

God takes forgiveness very seriously. In fact, Jesus said, "If you forgive
other people when they sin against you, your heavenly Father will also
forgive you. But if you do not forgive others their sins, your Father will
not forgive your sins" (Matthew 6:14–15 NIV).

Jesus' parable of the unmerciful servant (Matthew 18:23–35) also
instructed His followers to forgive others the same way God has forgiven them.

If your prayers ever start feeling stale—as if they aren't reaching
God's ears—then try examining your own personal relationships with
others. Ask yourself if you're somehow harboring unforgiveness toward
someone. If you find any lingering grudges, forgive. . .from your heart.
That's absolutely essential for a healthy, two-way relationship with God.

Reading Plan: Mark 10–11

HOW CAN I LOVE MY NEIGHBOR AS MYSELF?

Thou shalt love the Lord thy God with all thy heart, and with all thy soul, and with all thy mind, and with all thy strength: this is the first commandment. And the second is like, namely this, Thou shalt love thy neighbour as thyself. There is none other commandment greater than these.

MARK 12:30–31

On day sixty-three of this book, you learned that the most important commandment in the Old Testament law was "Thou shalt love the Lord thy God with all thy heart, and with all thy soul, and with all thy mind, and with all thy strength." But Jesus didn't stop there. He went on to explain the second greatest commandment: "Love thy neighbor as thyself."

This commandment, found in Leviticus 19:18, is poignantly expressed in Romans 13:8 (NIV): "Let no debt remain outstanding, except the continuing debt to love one another, for whoever loves others has fulfilled the law."

Loving your neighbor as yourself isn't complicated at all. It simply means treating people with kindness, patience, and hospitality; showing respect and civility to those with whom you disagree; and going out of your way to meet people's needs—even people you don't even know.

Doing these things allows others to see Jesus in you. . .and prepares you to receive God's blessings.

Reading Plan: Mark 12–13

HOW CAN I MOVE BEYOND MY FAILURE?

*But Peter said unto him, Although all
shall be offended, yet will not I.*

MARK 14:29

Directly after His Passover meal with His disciples, Jesus told His disciples, "You will all fall away. . .for it is written: 'I will strike the shepherd, and the sheep will be scattered.' But after I have risen, I will go ahead of you into Galilee" (Mark 14:27–28 NIV).

Peter, though, wouldn't hear of it. "Even if all fall away," he protested, "I will not" (Mark 14:29 NIV).

Jesus knew Peter had good intentions, but He also knew that His disciple's temporary failure was part of God's plan. Jesus told Peter very pointedly that on this night, he would deny knowing his Lord—not once, not twice, but three times!

Although Peter had promised to follow Jesus no matter what, he failed miserably (see Mark 14:66–72). But Jesus didn't give up on him. After His resurrection, He met with Peter one morning and "reinstated" him (see John 21:15–23). And after Jesus returned to heaven, Peter became a pillar of the early church, fearlessly preaching the name of Jesus.

When you fail to live up to your own good intentions, don't quit. Go to God in humble confession, and He'll reinstate you, getting you back on the path He wants you to walk.

Reading Plan: Mark 14–16

WHAT IS LUKE ALL ABOUT?

This Gospel is addressed to a man named Theophilus (1:3), "to set forth in order a declaration of those things which are most surely believed among us" about Jesus Christ (1:1). It's unclear who Theophilus was, though some believe he may have been a Roman official—and Luke is the least Jewish and most universal of the four Gospels. The author is not stated but traditionally believed to be Luke, a Gentile physician (Colossians 4:14) and a missionary companion of the apostle Paul (2 Timothy 4:11).

Luke traces Jesus' genealogy beyond Abraham, the patriarch of the Jews, all the way back to Adam, "the son of God" (3:38), common ancestor of everyone. Luke also shows Jesus' compassion for all people, Jew or Gentile: Roman soldiers (7:1–10), widows (7:11–17), the "sinful" (7:36–50), the chronically ill (8:43–48), lepers (17:11–19), and many others—including a criminal condemned to die on a cross beside Jesus (23:40–43).

These accounts show that it doesn't matter who you are, where you come from, or what you've done—Jesus came "to seek and to save that which was lost" (Luke 19:10).

Reading Plan: Luke 1

WHAT IS THE "GOOD NEWS" OF LUKE 2?

And the angel said unto them, Fear not:
for, behold, I bring you good tidings of
great joy, which shall be to all people.

LUKE 2:10

If you've ever been outside, far from the city's activity, you know what quiet really sounds like. Aside from a few crickets and an occasional bird, silence rules the air.

That's what a group of shepherds felt as they tended their sheep near the town of Bethlehem one night. Suddenly, though, the night came alive when "an angel of the Lord appeared to them, and the glory of the Lord shone around them" (Luke 2:9 NIV).

The men were terrified, but the angel quickly calmed their fears by announcing, "I bring you good news that will cause great joy for all the people. Today in the town of David a Savior has been born to you; he is the Messiah, the Lord" (Luke 2:10–11 NIV). Then, a host of angels appeared on the scene, proclaiming, "Glory to God in the highest heaven, and on earth peace to those on whom his favor rests" (Luke 2:14 NIV).

The message of salvation is often called the "good news"—and for good reason! Jesus' arrival on earth brought the offer of salvation to the whole world.

You have good news that people desperately need to hear. Always be ready when God gives you a chance to share it.

Reading Plan: Luke 2–3

HOW DID JESUS OVERCOME THE DEVIL'S TEMPTATIONS?

And the devil said unto him, All this power will I give thee, and the glory of them: for that is delivered unto me; and to whomsoever I will I give it. If thou therefore wilt worship me, all shall be thine.

LUKE 4:6–7

From the time He arrived on earth, Jesus knew His ultimate mission—to live a perfectly sinless life, to teach and heal people, and to die a horrific death on the cross as payment for our sins. Everything He did and said was to bless people and glorify God.

The devil also knew why Jesus came to earth, so he offered three cleverly designed temptations to derail God's plan for His Son. These temptations were very real, but Jesus responded each time by quoting the Bible (see Matthew 4:4, 7, 10). His reaction illustrated two important truths: (1) He was committed to His heavenly Father's mission for Him, and (2) the Word of God enables *us* to fight temptation.

We can and should be grateful that Jesus overcame temptation and remained perfectly obedient to God. Because He kept His focus upon His earthly mission and prioritized His Father's will over His own, we get to enjoy an abundant and everlasting life—that's a benefit for whatever time we have on this earth, as well as the "forever" we'll spend with Him.

Reading Plan: Luke 4–5

HOW SHOULD I RESPOND TO THOSE WHO MISTREAT ME?

But I say unto you which hear, Love your enemies, do good to them which hate you, bless them that curse you, and pray for them which despitefully use you.

LUKE 6:27–28

Jesus' words in today's scripture go against everything we know about human nature. Do we love our enemies enough to do good to them? Do we bless and pray for those who take advantage of our kindness and speak evil of us?

That is what Jesus tells us to do. But He didn't just *tell* us to do those things—He *showed* us what this love really looks like.

The Bible teaches that we were all once God's enemies (Romans 5:10)—that we were alienated from Him and hostile toward Him (Colossians 1:21). But it also teaches that while we were still sinners, Jesus—God's only Son—died a horrible death so that we could be reconciled to Him (Romans 5:8).

By sending Jesus to die for us, God perfectly exemplified Jesus' command to love our enemies and do good to those who hate us.

It's not easy to love and bless those who don't reciprocate our kindness. But when we do what Jesus said, we give our enemies a much-needed glimpse of God's love. Maybe someday they'll choose to join us on His side.

Reading Plan: Luke 6–7

WHAT DOES IT MEAN TO FOLLOW JESUS?

Now the man out of whom the devils were departed besought
him that he might be with him: but Jesus sent him away, saying,
Return to thine own house, and shew how great things God hath
done unto thee. And he went his way, and published throughout
the whole city how great things Jesus had done unto him.

LUKE 8:38–39

Imagine how deeply grateful the man from Gadara—who had suffered many days and nights under the control of countless cruel demons—felt toward Jesus after he was healed.

The people in this man's home village were afraid of him. . .but Jesus wasn't. He asked the demons one question—"What is your name?" There was no bargaining—they knew exactly where they were headed that day. They left the man. . .simply because Jesus ordered them to.

The formerly wild, naked, demon-possessed man now sat at Jesus' feet, clothed, in his right mind and begging for permission to follow the Lord. He wanted to be with Jesus no matter where He went.

Your gratitude toward Jesus should manifest itself in your actions and words. But most of all, it will motivate you to obey Him no matter where He goes or what He asks you to do.

Reading Plan: Luke 8–9

WHAT IS THE LORD'S PRAYER?

And it came to pass, that, as he was praying in a certain place, when he ceased, one of his disciples said unto him, Lord, teach us to pray, as John also taught his disciples.

LUKE 11:1

During His earthly ministry, Jesus delivered many wonderful, life-changing teachings, including instruction on how to pray. This teaching is now called the "Lord's Prayer," and it goes like this:

"Our Father in heaven, hallowed be your name, your kingdom come, your will be done, on earth as it is in heaven. Give us today our daily bread. And forgive us our debts, as we also have forgiven our debtors. And lead us not into temptation, but deliver us from the evil one."

MATTHEW 6:9–13 NIV

Many people have memorized the Lord's Prayer (which is also found in Luke 11:2–4) and like to recite it word-for-word. There's nothing wrong with that, but Jesus didn't give this prayer just so we could read it back to God. Really, it's an example of how we should pray, kind of like a recipe for prayer. Start with praising God for who He is, then move on to asking God to do His will, to supply our earthly needs, to forgive our sins, and to keep us from temptation. It's a simple, easy-to-memorize outline that covers all the bases of our Christian lives.

Reading Plan: Luke 10–11

WHAT DOES GOD'S LOVE LOOK LIKE?

Fear not, little flock; for it is your Father's
good pleasure to give you the kingdom.

LUKE 12:32

When a man first learns that he and his wife are going to be parents, his love motivates him to give. That's because he wants more than anything to make sure his child has everything it needs to thrive—physically, emotionally, and spiritually.

In this way, earthly fathers reflect—no matter how imperfectly—our Father in heaven. The apostle John wrote that "God is love" (1 John 4:8), and Jesus Himself said that God loved sinful humanity so much that He gave His most precious gift: His one and only Son (John 3:16).

By its very nature, love has no choice but to give. Real love can't be hidden away in the heart; it must find expression through giving. And God, who is the perfect embodiment of love, doesn't just give. . .He gives joyfully and perfectly.

This perfect, giving love is what the apostle James referred to when he wrote, "Every good and perfect gift is from above, coming down from the Father of the heavenly lights, who does not change like shifting shadows" (James 1:17 NIV).

Our God has always been perfect in His holiness and love. And He always will be. We can take great confidence in this truth.

Reading Plan: Luke 12–13

WHAT CAN WE LEARN FROM THE PRODIGAL SON?

*And he arose, and came to his father. But when he was yet
a great way off, his father saw him, and had compassion,
and ran, and fell on his neck, and kissed him. And the son
said unto him, Father, I have sinned against heaven, and in
thy sight, and am no more worthy to be called thy son.*

LUKE 15:20–21

The parable of the prodigal son (Luke 15:11–32)—also known as the
parable of the lost son—is probably Jesus' best-known. In it, a young
man decided to leave the security and comfort of his father's home.
After collecting his inheritance early, he then moved away to a distant
land to enjoy some wild living.

Before long, the young man realized he was out of money. Even worse,
a severe famine was ravaging the land, so he wasn't able to earn enough
to buy food. Broke and hungry, the young man "came to his senses"
(Luke 15:17 NIV) and decided to return to his father, intending to ask if
he could work as a hired hand. Instead, his loving father forgave him
and welcomed him home as a son, not a servant.

Many men drift—or consciously walk—away from their Father's love.
When that happens, God lovingly waits for them to return. And when they
come to their senses, God is still waiting for them, eager to accept them
as beloved sons. Don't ever hesitate to return home.

Reading Plan: Luke 14–15

315

HOW DOES MY OWN GRATITUDE AFFECT ME?

And one of them, when he saw that he was healed, turned back,
and with a loud voice glorified God, and fell down on his face
at his feet, giving him thanks: and he was a Samaritan.

LUKE 17:15–16

Luke 17:11–19 tells the wonderful—but very sad—story of a time that Jesus healed ten men who had been afflicted with leprosy, a terrible skin disease.

"Jesus, Master, have pity on us!" they cried out. When they got Jesus' attention, He told them, "Go, show yourselves to the priests." Just like that, each man was healed (verses 13–14 NIV). That's the beautiful part of this account.

Now for the sad part.

Jesus healed ten men that day, but only one of them came back to express his gratitude. He ran to Jesus and threw himself at His feet, praising God as loudly as he could (verses 15–16). However, the other nine traveled on, seemingly unaware that God Himself had just gifted them with an authentic, life-altering miracle.

That one grateful man, now cleansed of a disfiguring disease that once rendered him an outcast, proved that true gratitude draws us closer to God.

Don't be like those ungrateful men. Emulate the one who came back. Run to spend time in Jesus' presence, telling Him how grateful you are for all His blessings.

Reading Plan: Luke 16–17

HOW CAN I BE JUSTIFIED BEFORE GOD?

*The Pharisee stood and prayed thus with himself, God,
I thank thee, that I am not as other men are, extortioners,
unjust, adulterers, or even as this publican. I fast twice
in the week, I give tithes of all that I possess.*

LUKE 18:11–12

During Jesus' time on earth, the Jews in Israel utterly hated tax collectors, also known as "publicans." Why? Because tax collectors worked for the Roman government—which the Jews despised—and often cheated the people by collecting more than what was owed. The publicans then pocketed the extra money.

In Jesus' parable of the pharisee and the tax collector, a religious leader and a publican went into the temple to pray. The tax collector, knowing he was a miserable sinner who had wronged so many people, begged God for mercy. The religious leader, however, thanked God that he wasn't as bad as the tax collector—or other sinners.

Here was Jesus' conclusion to the story: "I tell you that this [tax collector], rather than the [religious leader], went home justified before God. For all those who exalt themselves will be humbled, and those who humble themselves will be exalted" (Luke 18:14 NIV).

When we come to God, He wants us to come in humility, remembering two things: (1) we are all sinners in desperate need of His mercy, and (2) He is more than willing to provide that. He just wants us to ask in humility.

Reading Plan: Luke 18–19

HOW CAN I GIVE WHEN TIMES ARE TIGHT?

*And he said, Of a truth I say unto you, that this poor widow
hath cast in more than they all: for all these have of their
abundance cast in unto the offerings of God: but she of
her penury hath cast in all the living that she had.*

LUKE 21:3–4

One of the Bible's greatest themes is that God loves it when we give joyfully. God has called each of us to give generously and sacrificially—whether it's by taking the Gospel message to the world or giving to people in need.

In today's scripture, Jesus commended a poor widow who gave what little she had to the Lord. He even said that she gave more than the rich people who donated out of their abundance.

Sacrificial giving takes a special kind of faith. It requires us to trust God to meet our families' needs—especially when times are tight. Without that kind of faith, we'll hang on to what we have so that we can fulfill our obligations. But with that kind of faith, we give what little we have, knowing God will see our sacrifice and meet our needs in His unique way.

Reading Plan: Luke 20:1–22:38

WHAT MUST I UNDERSTAND ABOUT MYSELF?

*But the other answering rebuked him, saying, Dost not
thou fear God, seeing thou art in the same condemnation?
And we indeed justly; for we receive the due reward of
our deeds: but this man hath done nothing amiss.*

LUKE 23:40–41

In the most pivotal moment of human history, Jesus, the Son of the living God, hung on a wooden cross between two condemned criminals. One criminal mocked Jesus, but the other—painfully aware of the justice of his own punishment—spoke the words of today's scripture.

Then, as all three men hung in unimaginable agony, a true miracle happened: the self-admitted criminal, knowing his time was very short, said, "Jesus, remember me when you come into your kingdom" (verse 42 NIV). Jesus answered this penitent man, "Truly I tell you, today you will be with me in paradise" (verse 43 NIV).

There's universal truth in the second criminal's words. Every one of us deserves God's punishment. But here's the good news: when we recognize that we are unworthy of God's eternal kingdom—when we place our faith in the One who died like a common criminal then rose from the dead—we too will be with Him in that wonderful place called "paradise."

Reading Plan: Luke 22:39–24:53

WHAT IS JOHN ALL ABOUT?

While the books of Matthew, Mark, and Luke have many similarities (they're called the "synoptic Gospels," meaning they take a common view), the book of John stands alone. The fourth Gospel downplays Jesus' parables (none are recorded) and miracles (only seven are featured). Instead, this book provides more extensive treatments of Jesus' reasons for coming to earth ("I am come that they might have life, and that they might have it more abundantly," 10:10); His intimate relationship with God the Father ("I and my Father are one," 10:30); and His own feelings toward the job He had come to do ("Father, the hour is come; glorify thy Son, that thy Son also may glorify thee: as thou hast given him power over all flesh, that he should give eternal life to as many as thou hast given him," 17:1–2). John also gives special emphasis to Jesus' patient treatment of the disciples Thomas, who doubted the resurrection (20:24–29), and Peter, who had denied the Lord (21:15–23).

As with the other Gospels, the author is not stated. But it is traditionally believed to be John, the "disciple whom Jesus loved" (John 21:7), brother of James and son of Zebedee (Matthew 4:21). This Gospel writer was the only one to record Jesus' first miracle, of changing water to wine (John 2:1–12); the raising of Lazarus from the dead (11:1–44); and Jesus' interaction with Nicodemus, who heard the teaching "ye must be born again" (3:7). Ultimately, all of these things were written "that ye might believe that Jesus is the Christ, the Son of God; and that believing ye might have life through his name" (20:31).

Reading Plan: John 1–3

WHAT DOES "WORSHIP IN SPIRIT AND IN TRUTH" MEAN?

But the hour cometh, and now is, when the true worshippers shall worship the Father in spirit and in truth: for the Father seeketh such to worship him.

JOHN 4:23

John 4 recounts Jesus' encounter with a sinful Samaritan woman at a well near the town of Sychar. Because of the customary animosity between Jews and Samaritans, both Jesus and the woman recognized the strangeness of their conversation. But Jesus had some important reasons for speaking with her.

During their conversation, the woman acknowledged that the Jews worshipped God in Jerusalem while Samaritans worshipped at Mount Gerizim. Jesus knew that, of course, but He told her that from then on, people would worship "in spirit and in truth." Jesus was speaking of a time when the *place* of worship wouldn't matter—God the Holy Spirit would always be with His followers.

"In spirit and in truth" also means worshipping God with one's whole heart (focusing on the heavenly Father) and one's whole mind (focusing on the truth about God in His written Word).

Through the experience of true worship, we can enjoy authentic, heart-to-heart interactions with our Creator and heavenly Father. It's a powerful fellowship God has invited you to enjoy with Himself.

Reading Plan: John 4–5

HOW DID JESUS TEACH PHILIP ABOUT FAITH?

When Jesus then lifted up his eyes, and saw a great
company come unto him, he saith unto Philip, Whence
shall we buy bread, that these may eat? And this he said
to prove him: for he himself knew what he would do.

JOHN 6:5–6

Remember all those tests in high school or college? The idea behind these exams was to show you—and your instructor—what you really knew.

In today's scripture, Jesus—the Great Teacher Himself—tested one of His disciples, both to show him what he didn't yet understand and to teach him how faith really works.

Thousands of people had been following Jesus. On this particular day, it was almost dinnertime. Jesus knew there wasn't enough food—or money to buy it—for thousands of hungry followers. But He also knew what He was going to do and how. Before Jesus acted, however, He used this opportunity to teach his friend Philip an important truth about who his Provider really was. Philip's Provider, who came through miraculously, is also ours.

Do you sometimes know God wants you to do something, but find yourself asking, "How?" If so, you're probably going through a time of testing. Step forward in faith. It is in these places that God can teach you important truths about Himself.

Reading Plan: John 6–7

HOW CAN I KNOW GOD LISTENS TO ME?

*Now we know that God heareth not sinners: but if any man be
a worshipper of God, and doeth his will, him he heareth.*

JOHN 9:31

Have you ever wondered if God really listens to you? You may know the Bible promises that He listens and responds to His people's prayers. But do you ever doubt that this promise applies to *you*?

If so, look again at today's scripture, as well as the following biblical promises:

"As for me, I call to God, and the Lord saves me. Evening, morning and noon I cry out in distress, and he hears my voice" (Psalm 55:16–17 NIV)

The Lord is far from the wicked, but he hears the prayer of the righteous" (Proverbs 15:29 NIV).

"For the eyes of the Lord are on the righteous and his ears are attentive to their prayer" (1 Peter 3:12 NIV).

"This is the confidence we have in approaching God: that if we ask anything according to his will, he hears us. And if we know that he hears us—whatever we ask—we know that we have what we asked of him" (1 John 5:14–15 NIV).

Our God is the personification of perfect love. He listens to His people's prayers, simply because loving means listening. If you start believing He doesn't want to hear from you, ask yourself if you're where you need to be in your relationship with Him. After all, He's right where He's always been.

> **Reading Plan: John 8–9**

CAN I FEEL SECURE IN JESUS?

My sheep hear my voice, and I know them, and they follow
me: and I give unto them eternal life; and they shall never
perish, neither shall any man pluck them out of my hand.
My Father, which gave them me, is greater than all; and no
man is able to pluck them out of my Father's hand.

JOHN 10:27–29

John 10 contains many promises for Jesus' "sheep"—those who have been transformed by His work on the cross. However, none of them are so important and life-changing as the promise of eternal life. And this everlasting life is no illusion—Jesus also promises security in Himself.

Many a believer at some point has suffered through bouts of insecurity, wondering if it's possible to lose his place in God's eternal kingdom. But here, straight from our Savior's mouth, is the promise, "They shall never perish; no one will snatch them out of my hand" (John 10:28 NIV).

Don't ever worry that the devil will tempt you beyond what you can endure or that he will overpower God and take you away from His care. Rest assured, on the authority of Jesus Himself—if you truly belong to Him today, you'll belong to Him forever. Entry into His fold is simple: "If you declare with your mouth, 'Jesus is Lord,' and believe in your heart that God raised him from the dead, you will be saved" (Romans 10:9 NIV).

Reading Plan: John 10–11

HOW CAN I LOVE MY SIBLINGS IN CHRIST?

A new commandment I give unto you, That ye love one another; as I have loved you, that ye also love one another. By this shall all men know that ye are my disciples, if ye have love one to another.

JOHN 13:34–35

Love was such a big deal to Jesus during His earthly ministry that He labeled the commandment in Leviticus to love our neighbors as ourselves as one of the two greatest (Mark 12:31). And not long before He died, He instructed His followers to take their love to a new level.

God's command to love one another was hardly new, but Jesus' five words to His followers—"as I have loved you"—emphasized loving our fellow Christians by following His example of selfless, sacrificial love. If Jesus had simply said, "Love one another" and nothing more, that would have been an important commandment for us to obey. But He didn't stop there—He also set the perfect example of love for us to follow.

So love your brothers and sisters in Jesus Christ selflessly, sacrificially, unfailingly, and humbly. Give your time, your money, your energies, your entire life for the people He loves. You can't go wrong. Whatever we give up for Jesus and His followers will be paid back a hundred times (see Matthew 19:29).

Reading Plan: John 12–13

WHY PRAY IN JESUS' NAME?

And in that day ye shall ask me nothing. Verily, verily, I say unto you, Whatsoever ye shall ask the Father in my name, he will give it you. Hitherto have ye asked nothing in my name: ask, and ye shall receive, that your joy may be full.

JOHN 16:23–24

You've no doubt heard people end prayers by saying, "In Jesus' name, amen!" Today's scripture shows that this isn't just a nice-sounding platitude. These words mean something very important and powerful. They point to an amazing privilege Jesus Himself has given each of His followers.

When He came to earth, Jesus brought a message of change. From that time forward, the way people received God's forgiveness would change, as would the way they had fellowship with their Creator, the way they worshipped Him, and even the way they prayed.

Jesus said that when His followers prayed in His name, they would receive what they asked for. Because of Jesus' sacrificial death on the cross and His Resurrection three days later, everyone—including you—has full access to God the Father through Him.

When you pray, remember you are God's—and then make your requests in Jesus' powerful, wonderful name.

Reading Plan: John 14–16

WHAT DOES "SANCTIFIED" MEAN?

They are not of the world, even as I am not of the world.
Sanctify them through thy truth: thy word is truth.
JOHN 17:16–17

John 17 recounts Jesus' "High Priestly Prayer," which might be the most important prayer in the Bible. In it, Jesus prayed for Himself (verses 1–5), for His disciples (verses 6–19), and for all believers of all time (verses 20–26). As Jesus prayed for His disciples, He asked His Father, "Sanctify them through thy truth: thy word is truth" (John 17:17).

In the Bible, the word *sanctify* means to set apart for God's special purposes. Jesus had called His disciples and prepared them to be His special representatives after He returned to heaven. Jesus wanted them to speak, behave, and think like Him. So by praying "Thy word is truth," He was asking God to help them apply His Word (the scriptures) to their lives so that they could live out God's purpose—namely, taking His message of salvation to the world.

The apostle Paul taught, "It is God's will that you should be sanctified" (1 Thessalonians 4:3 NIV). In other words, God wants to set each believer aside for His purposes, preparing them through His Holy Spirit and His Word.

What a privilege to be used in such a way by God Himself!

Reading Plan: John 17–18

HOW DOES GOD EMPOWER ME TO TELL OTHERS ABOUT JESUS?

Then said Jesus to them again, Peace be unto you: as my Father hath sent me, even so send I you. And when he had said this, he breathed on them, and saith unto them, Receive ye the Holy Ghost.

JOHN 20:21–22

Jesus' twelve disciples—also called His "apostles"—had traveled three years with Him around the land of Israel, witnessing His astonishing miracles and hearing His life-changing teachings.

What the Twelve didn't fully understand, however, was that Jesus was preparing them to change the world with the eternal, life-giving message of God's love and forgiveness. That's why Jesus, on the night before He was crucified, prayed, "As thou hast sent me into the world, even so have I also sent them into the world" (John 17:18).

After He rose from the dead—but before He returned to His Father in heaven—Jesus told His eleven disciples, minus the betrayer Judas, that He was sending them into the world to preach the Gospel message. But before they went, they would receive much-needed empowerment through the Holy Spirit.

Jesus sent His disciples on a world-changing mission—and it's the same mission He sends you on today. That's a huge calling, and no matter how hard you try, you just can't do it under your own power. But with the Holy Spirit's empowerment, you are able to do anything and everything God calls you to do.

Reading Plan: John 19–21

WHAT IS ACTS ALL ABOUT?

Officially called "Acts of the Apostles," the book of Acts is a bridge between the story of Jesus in the Gospels and the life of the Christian church in the letters that follow. The book of Acts is traditionally attributed to Luke, the Gentile physician (Colossians 4:14).

Luke begins with Jesus' ascension into heaven after forty days of post-resurrection activity, "speaking of the things pertaining to the kingdom of God" (1:3). Ten days later, God sent the Holy Spirit on the festival day of Pentecost—and the church was born. Through the Spirit, the disciples were empowered to preach boldly about Jesus, and three thousand people became Christians that day. Jewish leaders, fearing the new movement called "this way" (9:2), began persecuting believers, who scattered to other areas and spread the Gospel through much of the known world. The ultimate persecutor, Saul, became a Christian himself after meeting the brightly shining, heavenly Jesus on the road to Damascus. Saul, later called Paul, ultimately joined Peter and other Christian leaders in preaching, working miracles, and strengthening the fledgling church.

The book of Acts also tells of the first Christian martyr, Stephen, stoned to death for blaming Jewish leaders for the death of Jesus (chapter 7). It depicts the Gospel's transition from a purely Jewish message to one for all people (9:15; 10:45) and the beginning of the Christian missionary movement (chapter 13).

Christians today are driven by the same force that Acts describes: "Ye shall receive power, after that the Holy Ghost is come upon you" (1:8).

Reading Plan: Acts 1–2

DAY 322

HOW SHOULD CHRISTIANS LOOK OUT FOR ONE ANOTHER?

And the multitude of them that believed were of one heart and of one soul: neither said any of them that ought of the things which he possessed was his own; but they had all things common.

ACTS 4:32

The first generation of Christians in Jerusalem set many impressive examples for modern believers. Today's scripture says they were all united in their love for Jesus and were committed to sharing their possessions among themselves.

What an example of love in action! Recognizing that God owned everything they had, they were able to let go of their money and assets for the good of others when necessary.

Their example should remind us to look for opportunities to share with the needy and love them with a "what's mine is yours" attitude. Fellowship with other believers is a wonderful privilege, and so is expressing our love for them by meeting their needs.

When you share with a heart of loving generosity, you both meet the needs of others and glorify God, thereby putting yourself in a position to receive His blessings. That's a big win for everyone involved.

Reading Plan: Acts 3–5

WHAT DOES IT MEAN TO BE FREED FROM SIN'S POWER?

*To whom our fathers would not obey, but thrust him from them,
and in their hearts turned back again into Egypt, saying unto Aaron,
Make us gods to go before us: for as for this Moses, which brought
us out of the land of Egypt, we wot not what is become of him.*

ACTS 7:39–40

Today's scripture includes some astonishing information about the Israelites who had, under Moses' God-ordained leadership, left Egyptian slavery. It says that they turned back to Egypt in their hearts, wanting Aaron to make gods to go before them.

Many Bible scholars believe the Israelites didn't literally want to go back to Egypt, where their lives had been extremely difficult. Instead, they wanted to resume the idolatrous practices of Egypt—practices God wanted them to leave behind as they began journeying toward the promised land.

God had miraculously freed the Israelites from slavery and idolatry, yet their hearts were inclined to return to spiritual bondage. Even today, many Christian men face this temptation.

The Bible teaches that all who don't know Jesus are enslaved to sin. However, just as God freed the Israelites from slavery, the apostle Paul wrote that "you have been set free from sin and have become slaves to righteousness" (Romans 6:18 NIV).

May we never go back to our own personal Egypt—in either heart or body.

Reading Plan: Acts 6–7

HOW CAN I BE PREPARED TO SHARE MY FAITH?

*And Philip ran thither to him, and heard him read the prophet
Esaias, and said, Understandest thou what thou readest? And
he said, How can I, except some man should guide me? And
he desired Philip that he would come up and sit with him.*

ACTS 8:30–31

Philip the evangelist was a man with a heart for telling people about
Jesus. He had prepared himself to tell others about the Lord whenever
God gave him the opportunity.

Acts 8:26–39 tells of Philip's encounter with an unnamed Ethiopian
man who had been worshipping God in Jerusalem. Philip heard the
man reading a messianic prophecy from Isaiah. The Ethiopian didn't
understand what he was reading, but Philip did. So Philip sat with him
and "began with that very passage of Scripture and told him the good
news about Jesus" (verse 35 NIV).

No missed opportunity there!

Phillip exemplified Peter's command to "always be prepared to give
an answer to everyone who asks you to give the reason for the hope that
you have" (1 Peter 3:15 NIV). As Christian men, we should follow this
example every day.

Ask God today for opportunities to tell others about Jesus. And ask
Him to prepare you through His Word and Spirit to answer questions they
may have. Maybe, like the Ethiopian eunuch, they'll come to believe "that
Jesus Christ is the Son of God" (Acts 8:37).

Reading Plan: Acts 8–9

WHAT NAMES DID JESUS CALL HIS FOLLOWERS?

*And when he had found him, he brought him unto Antioch.
And it came to pass, that a whole year they assembled
themselves with the church, and taught much people. And
the disciples were called Christians first in Antioch.*

ACTS 11:26

Today's scripture tells us that followers of Jesus were first called "Christians" in the city of Antioch. Later, Herod Agrippa II told the apostle Paul, "Almost thou persuadest me to be a Christian" (Acts 26:28). The word *Christian*—which literally means "follower of Christ"—caught on, and it's been used ever since.

Jesus Himself used many names—each having an important meaning—to describe His followers. Here are some great examples:

- "The light of the world" (Matthew 5:14 niv)
- "Children of your Father in heaven" (Matthew 5:45 niv)
- "People of the kingdom" (Matthew 13:38 niv)
- "Blessed by my Father" (Matthew 25:34 niv)
- "Children of the Most High" (Luke 6:35 niv)
- "Children of the resurrection" (Luke 20:36 niv)
- "My disciples" (John 8:31 niv)
- "Friends" (John 15:15 niv)
- "My brothers" (John 20:17 NIV)

Whenever Jesus spoke, His words had tremendous meaning. Reread the list above and then consider how Jesus sees you—and how deeply God loves and values you.

Reading Plan: Acts 10–12

HOW SHOULD WE CELEBRATE GOD'S WORK?

And thence sailed to Antioch, from whence they had been recommended to the grace of God for the work which they fulfilled. And when they were come, and had gathered the church together, they rehearsed all that God had done with them, and how he had opened the door of faith unto the Gentiles. And there they abode long time with the disciples.

ACTS 14:26–28

A city called Antioch of Syria had become a headquarters of sorts for the early church. Here, a group of "prophets and teachers" (Acts 13:1 NIV) were worshipping God and praying when the Holy Spirit told them, "Set apart for me Barnabas and Saul for the work to which I have called them" (13:2 NIV).

After that, they laid hands on Barnabas and Saul (soon to be called Paul) and sent them out to tell people in far-away places about Jesus.

In about AD 47, Paul dedicated his life as a traveling preacher for Jesus. The book of Acts describes Paul's three different journeys, and today's reading tells of the first trip.

When Paul and Barnabas returned to Antioch, they called together the entire church and reported all the marvelous things God had done through them.

When God uses you to accomplish something great for His kingdom, how do you respond? Don't be shy—share it with your brothers and sisters in Jesus Christ!

Reading Plan: Acts 13–14

HOW DID PAUL AND SILAS RESPOND TO PERSECUTION?

And when they had laid many stripes upon them, they cast them into prison, charging the jailor to keep them safely: who, having received such a charge, thrust them into the inner prison, and made their feet fast in the stocks. And at midnight Paul and Silas prayed, and sang praises unto God: and the prisoners heard them.

ACTS 16:23–25

When the apostle Paul cast a demon from a slave girl in Philippi, her owners were upset that they could no longer collect income from her fortune-telling. They raised a ruckus, and Paul and Silas were beaten and jailed.

The next part of the story shows what can happen when a Christian man looks beyond his own suffering and focuses on glorifying God.

Instead of complaining about their situation, Paul and Silas—still in the stocks—prayed and sang songs of praise while the other prisoners listened. And after God miraculously released them by sending a powerful earthquake, they led their prison guard to faith in Jesus.

God indeed brought something wonderful out of a terrible situation!

By responding to mistreatment with praise and gratitude, you glorify God and place yourself in a prime position for Him to do something great through you.

Reading Plan: Acts 15–17

WHAT CAN WE LEARN FROM APOLLOS?

*And a certain Jew named Apollos, born at Alexandria, an
eloquent man, and mighty in the scriptures, came to Ephesus.
This man was instructed in the way of the Lord; and being
fervent in the spirit, he spake and taught diligently the
things of the Lord, knowing only the baptism of John.*

ACTS 18:24–25

Priscilla and Aquila were a married couple who were good friends of the apostle Paul. After meeting the great apostle in Corinth, they shared in his tentmaking work over the years. The couple eventually moved to Ephesus, where they mentored a preacher named Apollos, a Jewish Christian from Alexandria.

Apollos was a polished speaker who eloquently and powerfully preached the scriptures. "He was a learned man, with a thorough knowledge of the Scriptures," Luke wrote in the book of Acts. "He had been instructed in the way of the Lord, and he spoke with great fervor and taught about Jesus accurately" (18:24–25 NIV). However, Priscilla and Aquila realized something was missing—Apollos hadn't heard the complete Gospel message, so they took him aside to help him fill in the blanks. After that, he was able to preach even more effectively.

Apollos' passion and knowledge of the scriptures was commendable. Even better, he had the humility to receive the wisdom and learning that made him a great minister of the Gospel. Let's commit ourselves to receiving instruction and correction, when necessary. A little humility will go a long way in what we will accomplish for God.

Reading Plan: Acts 18–19

WHAT DOES IT MEAN TO BE JESUS' AMBASSADOR?

And he said, The God of our fathers hath chosen thee, that thou shouldest know his will, and see that Just One, and shouldest hear the voice of his mouth. For thou shalt be his witness unto all men of what thou hast seen and heard.

ACTS 22:14–15

After Paul's dramatic encounter with Jesus (see Acts 9:1–19), a Christian man named Ananias had a message for Paul—which he repeated before a crowd in today's scripture. Ananias's message was simple: God had chosen Paul as Christ's ambassador, meaning he would be a powerful witness to everyone regarding what he'd seen, heard, and learned.

Later, Paul wrote that all believers—us included—are called to represent Jesus to the world. In 2 Corinthians 5:20 (NIV), he said, "We are therefore Christ's ambassadors, as though God were making his appeal through us. We implore you on Christ's behalf: Be reconciled to God."

That conciliatory message is the good news of the Gospel—the story of Jesus' life, teachings, death, and resurrection—which humbly believed and accepted saves our souls. As Paul put it, "If, while we were God's enemies, we were reconciled to him through the death of his Son, how much more, having been reconciled shall we be saved through his life!" (Romans 5:10 NIV). Once we accept that message and gain new life, we are automatically enlisted as ambassadors for our Lord.

It's both a profound calling and a great privilege for any man of God.

Reading Plan: Acts 20–22

HOW DOES GOD ENCOURAGE US IN DIFFICULT TIMES?

And the night following the Lord stood by him, and said, Be of good cheer, Paul: for as thou hast testified of me in Jerusalem, so must thou bear witness also at Rome.

ACTS 23:11

After inadvertently insulting the high priest Ananias, the apostle Paul found himself in deep trouble with the Jewish religious leaders in Jerusalem. Even though Paul apologized—telling them, "It is written: 'Do not speak evil about the ruler of your people'" (Acts 23:5 NIV)—some of them began planning to kill him.

That night, Paul probably wondered if his fruitful ministry was coming to an end. He looked forward to his reward in heaven, but he also wanted to stick around longer to tell more people about Jesus. Jesus, however, assured Paul, "Take courage! As you have testified about me in Jerusalem, so you must also testify in Rome" (Acts 23:11 NIV). In other words, Paul wasn't finished sharing Jesus.

God wants to encourage us in our hard times too. Sometimes He'll use a scripture passage, at other times the words of a fellow believer, and yet other times a sermon at church or on the radio. He will strengthen you in whatever way He knows will work best for you.

Reading Plan: Acts 23–25

HOW DID PAUL WITNESS TO THE KING?

Whereupon, O king Agrippa, I was not disobedient unto the heavenly vision: but shewed first unto them of Damascus, and at Jerusalem, and throughout all the coasts of Judaea, and then to the Gentiles, that they should repent and turn to God, and do works meet for repentance.

ACTS 26:19–20

In the Bible's greatest testimonial of a changed life, the apostle Paul stood before the Roman king Herod Agrippa II and described his conversion to Jesus. He spoke of his early life as a Pharisee and an opponent of the Christian faith. But then he explained how Jesus Himself appeared to him, appointing him as a witness to the Gentiles. He told Agrippa that he was simply obeying God when he proclaimed Jesus' saving power.

Paul's words were powerful, and Herod was at once skeptical and impressed. "Almost thou persuadest me to be a Christian," he said (Acts 26:28).

Do you have a heart to reach people with the good news of salvation through Jesus, even though you aren't sure what to say? Then follow Paul's example, talking about who you were before you knew Jesus, how He saved you, and what He's done in and through you.

There may never be a more powerful and effective way to reach people for Jesus than simply describing your own changed life.

Reading Plan: Acts 26–28

WHAT IS ROMANS ALL ABOUT?

Some call Romans a "theology textbook" for its thorough explanation of the Christian life. Written by the apostle Paul (1:1), with the secretarial assistance of Tertius (16:22), Romans was addressed to a congregation Paul had never met. The great missionary was hoping to see the Roman Christians personally while traveling westward to Spain (15:23–24), though it's unclear if he ever actually reached Spain or was executed in Rome after the end of the book of Acts.

Romans begins by describing God's righteous anger against human sin (chapters 1–2), noting that everyone falls short of God's standard (3:23). But God Himself provided the only way to overcome that sin, "the righteousness of God which is by faith of Jesus Christ unto all and upon all them that believe" (3:22).

Being justified (made right) through faith in Jesus, we can now consider ourselves "to be dead indeed unto sin, but alive unto God through Jesus Christ our Lord" (6:11). God's Spirit will "quicken" (give life to, 8:11) all who believe in Jesus, allowing us to "present [our] bodies a living sacrifice, holy, acceptable unto God" (12:1). It is possible, with God's help, to "be not overcome of evil, but [to] overcome evil with good" (12:21).

The end result of all this divine work is, in Paul's own words, "we have peace with God through our Lord Jesus Christ" (5:1).

Reading Plan: Romans 1–3

WHAT IS SUBSTITUTIONARY ATONEMENT?

And not only so, but we also joy in God through our Lord Jesus Christ, by whom we have now received the atonement.

ROMANS 5:11

The word *atonement*—which refers to the settlement of differences between God and people through animal sacrifices—appears dozens of times in the Old Testament. The New Testament, however, teaches "substitutionary atonement"—a theological term referring to a sacrifice made on someone's behalf in order to reconcile that person with God.

The Bible teaches that before we could be forgiven, someone had to pay a price. Blood had to be shed (Hebrews 9:22). In Old Testament times, people's sins were paid for through animal sacrifice. But Jesus ended all that by shedding His own blood, dying on the cross in our place "while we were still sinners" (see Romans 5:6–11 NIV).

As sinful human beings, we are fully responsible for the separation between ourselves and God. But God, in His amazing love and grace, sent Jesus to shed His blood as an atonement for our sin, thereby making a way for us to be at peace with Him again.

Today, take a moment to thank God that Jesus, the sinless Lamb, died in your place so that you could spend eternity with Him in heaven.

Reading Plan: Romans 4–7

HOW DEPENDABLE IS GOD?

*For the scripture saith, Whosoever believeth
on him shall not be ashamed.*

ROMANS 10:11

In modern psychology, those who have a difficult time depending on another person are said to have "trust issues." Sometimes, these personal issues result from an undependable father figure.

While some earthly fathers aren't nearly as dependable as they should be, we never have to worry about our Father in heaven. He is the one Father who always keeps His promises, and He's always there for us when we call out to Him.

Jesus, who knew our heavenly Father better than anyone, said this: "Which of you, if your son asks for bread, will give him a stone? Or if he asks for a fish, will give him a snake? If you, then, though you are evil, know how to give good gifts to your children, how much more will your Father in heaven give good gifts to those who ask him!" (Matthew 7:9–11 NIV).

When you come to God in faith for something—whether it's your salvation or some other need—you can trust Him to generously give what you ask for. When you place that kind of trust in your heavenly Father, he'll never let you down. He's the perfect picture of dependability.

Reading Plan: Romans 8–10

HOW DOES GOD WANT ME TO LIVE AND THINK?

And be not conformed to this world: but be ye transformed
by the renewing of your mind, that ye may prove what is
that good, and acceptable, and perfect, will of God.

ROMANS 12:2

If you are a Bible-believing, Jesus-following Christian, people will say you are different—whether they mean it as a compliment or mockery. When you have God's Spirit inside you, your thoughts, words, and actions should be noticeably different from those of unbelievers.

In today's scripture, Paul encouraged Christians to avoid thinking the way non-believers do. Instead, we should allow the Spirit of God to "transform" and "renew" our thinking. As we do that, we'll understand how God wants us to live.

It's no secret that our thoughts will eventually affect our behavior. If we consistently think about worldly things, we'll act in worldly ways. However, if we focus our thoughts on the things of God, we'll live the way God wants us to live. That's why it's so important that we welcome the Holy Spirit into our conscious minds, allowing Him to imprint the truth of God's Word onto our entire being.

Reading Plan: Romans 11–13

WHAT DOES "EDIFYING" MEAN?

*Let us therefore follow after the things which make for
peace, and things wherewith one may edify another. For
meat destroy not the work of God. All things indeed are pure;
but it is evil for that man who eateth with offence.*

ROMANS 14:19–20

Jesus, as well as the writers of the New Testament, had much to say about how we Christians are to relate to one another. We should love, pray for, encourage, and give to one another. In short, we are to "edify" one another.

One dictionary defines the word *edify* as "to instruct or improve someone morally or intellectually." The term in the King James Version comes from a Greek word that means "the building of a house." Some more modern Bible versions use phrases like "build up."

Interestingly, these words appear only in Paul's letters—about twenty times—so he obviously thought it important that believers prioritize the "building up" of fellow Christians. And since Paul wrote under the inspiration of God's Holy Spirit, we can conclude that edifying our fellow Christians is important to the Lord too.

How can we edify others? By saying and doing things that encourage them to grow in their daily walk with Jesus. Let's use our words always to lift up and challenge our fellow Christians to greater spiritual heights. May we never discourage them.

Reading Plan: Romans 14–16

WHAT IS 1 CORINTHIANS ALL ABOUT?

The apostle Paul had helped found the church in Corinth (Acts 18) but then moved on to other mission fields. While in Ephesus, he learned of serious problems in the Corinthian congregation and wrote a long letter to address those issues.

For those arguing over who should lead the church, Paul urged "that ye be perfectly joined together in the same mind and in the same judgment" (1:10). Regarding a man involved in an immoral relationship with his stepmother, Paul commanded, "Put away from among yourselves that wicked person" (5:13). For those church members filing lawsuits against others, Paul warned, "Know ye not that the unrighteous shall not inherit the kingdom of God?" (6:9). The apostle also taught on marriage, Christian liberty, the Lord's Supper, spiritual gifts, and the resurrection of the dead. In the famous thirteenth chapter of 1 Corinthians, Paul described the "more excellent way" (12:31): that of charity, or love.

Church problems are nothing new—and neither is the way to correct them. Personal purity, self-discipline, and love for others are vital to any congregation's success.

Reading Plan: 1 Corinthians 1–6

WHERE DO TEMPTATIONS COME FROM?

*There hath no temptation taken you but such as is common
to man: but God is faithful, who will not suffer you to be
tempted above that ye are able; but will with the temptation
also make a way to escape, that ye may be able to bear it.*

1 CORINTHIANS 10:13

Many young believers come into the faith thinking they will no longer be tempted to sin. But when they find that temptations don't just "go away," some become discouraged or disillusioned.

Temptation will always be a part of our lives on earth. It existed at humanity's beginning, and it's still around today. According to scripture, temptation comes from three sources: the devil (remember, Adam and Eve sinned when they gave in to Satan's temptation; also, the devil tempted Jesus Himself, though unsuccessfully); the world (see 2 Peter 1:4, Galatians 1:4, and 1 John 2:15); and our own evil, fallen natures (see Romans 7:18, Galatians 5:19–21, and James 1:14–15).

We can't escape the fact that every human on earth will be tempted to sin. But as today's verse promises, God will provide a way for us to overcome these temptations. Believe that promise, and walk in it each day!

Reading Plan: 1 Corinthians 7–10

WHAT DOES GODLY (AGAPE) LOVE LOOK LIKE?

And now abideth faith, hope, charity, these three;
but the greatest of these is charity.
1 CORINTHIANS 13:13

The apostle Paul wrote to the Christians in Corinth about the many spiritual gifts God had given to individuals—and how they all worked together to strengthen and grow the church. However, he ended chapter 12 of 1 Corinthians with these words: "Now eagerly desire the greater gifts. And yet I will show you the most excellent way" (verse 31 NIV).

Chapter 13 opens by telling the Corinthian Christians that engaging all their spiritual gifts wouldn't mean anything if they weren't motivated by *agape* love—an unconditional love that resembles the love God pours out on His people.

This godly love is very different our usual perception of the word *love*. Here is what Paul wrote about it:

Love is patient, love is kind. It does not envy, it does not boast,
it is not proud. It does not dishonor others, it is not self-seeking,
it is not easily angered, it keeps no record of wrongs. Love does
not delight in evil but rejoices with the truth. It always protects,
always trusts, always hopes, always perseveres.
1 CORINTHIANS 13:4–7 NIV

This is real love, the kind God pours out on His children every day. Now, He wants us to show the same kind of love to everyone He's placed in our lives. Is that a natural thing? Not at all—it's supernatural. Ask God to love like this *through* you.

Reading Plan: 1 Corinthians 11–13

WHY IS JESUS' RESURRECTION SO IMPORTANT?

And if Christ be not risen, then is our preaching vain,
and your faith is also vain. . . . And if Christ be not
raised, your faith is vain; ye are yet in your sins.

1 CORINTHIANS 15:14, 17

Each Easter Sunday morning, Christians greet one another with a hearty "He is Risen!" This is answered with an enthusiastic, "He is risen indeed!"

Jesus' death on the cross is central for the Christian faith, for at that moment, He single-handedly paid for our sins with His once-and-for-all sacrifice. But in 1 Corinthians 15:14–17, the apostle Paul plainly stated that if Jesus' *resurrection* hadn't happened three days later, the Christian faith would be worthless.

Paul told his readers that the Resurrection—which was foretold by the Old Testament prophets and Jesus Himself—incontrovertibly proved that Jesus is the Son of God who has conquered sin and death forever. He also wrote that Jesus' Resurrection is central to our renewed relationship with the Father: Jesus "was delivered over to death for our sins and was raised to life for our justification" (Romans 4:25 NIV).

So when you thank God for Jesus' death on the cross, don't forget to thank Him for the Resurrection. Because Jesus lives, you know you can live with Him forever!

Reading Plan: 1 Corinthians 14–16

WHAT IS 2 CORINTHIANS ALL ABOUT?

The Corinthian believers had apparently addressed some of the problems that the apostle Paul's first letter mentioned—though there were still troublemakers who questioned his authority. He was forced to "speak foolishly" (11:21), boasting of hardships he'd faced serving Jesus: "in labours more abundant, in stripes above measure, in prisons more frequent, in deaths oft" (11:23). Paul even suffered a "thorn in the flesh" (12:7), which God refused to take away, telling him instead, "My grace is sufficient for thee: for my strength is made perfect in weakness" (12:9). Paul never identified his "thorn in the flesh," though some speculate it may have been bad eyesight, moral temptations, or even physical unattractiveness.

Paul wrote 2 Corinthians with the assistance of a young man named Timothy (1:1), who would later receive two "pastoral epistles" from Paul. Whether in the church, the home, or society at large, Christians should respect authority—that of God Himself, of His pastors and Bible teachers, and of government officials, who are in place by God's will (Daniel 2:21). May we always do so, living the "quiet and peaceable life" Paul described to Timothy (1 Timothy 2:2).

The apostle's parting warning to the cantankerous Christians of Corinth was this: "Examine yourselves, whether ye be in the faith; prove your own selves" (13:5).

Reading Plan: 2 Corinthians 1–5

WHAT DOES "UNEQUALLY YOKED" MEAN?

Be ye not unequally yoked together with unbelievers: for what fellowship hath righteousness with unrighteousness? and what communion hath light with darkness? And what concord hath Christ with Belial? or what part hath he that believeth with an infidel?

2 CORINTHIANS 6:14–15

If you attended Christian youth groups as a kid, you probably heard adult leaders warning you not to be "unequally yoked" with non-Christians. They almost always meant you shouldn't date or eventually marry those who didn't share your faith in Jesus.

But Paul's admonition can apply to many areas of our lives, such as our friendships and business associations.

Paul wasn't telling Christian men to hide away in a monastery, sequestered from the "unsaved" world—in fact, he wrote that we should only separate ourselves from professing Christians who live immoral lives, not from unbelievers—otherwise, "you would have to leave this world" (1 Corinthians 5:10 NIV). However, the apostle recognized the wisdom of keeping ourselves from relationships that could influence us to think, speak, and behave in ways that don't please God and that keep us from growing in our faith.

Remember, "The righteous choose their friends carefully, but the way of the wicked leads them astray" (Proverbs 12:26 NIV).

Reading Plan: 2 Corinthians 6–9

WHY IS THE DOCTRINE OF THE TRINITY IMPORTANT?

The grace of the Lord Jesus Christ, and the love of God,
and the communion of the Holy Ghost, be with you all. Amen.

2 CORINTHIANS 13:14

In today's scripture, the apostle Paul blesses the Christians living in Corinth. In this blessing, he alludes to all three persons of what we now call "the Trinity"—God the Father, God the Son (Jesus), and God the Holy Spirit.

Even though the word *Trinity* does not appear in the Bible, the scriptures reveal the Lord as a "triune" God, meaning He exists as three distinct persons.

We see these three persons in action at Jesus' baptism (see Matthew 3:13–17). When Jesus, the Son of God, came out of the water, the Holy Spirit descended upon Him and God the Father declared, "This is my Son, whom I love; with him I am well pleased" (verse 17 NIV).

The doctrine of the Trinity is important because it defines God's true nature. Not only that, these three persons work in perfect harmony to save, transform, and grow you into the man God wants you to become.

Reading Plan: 2 Corinthians 10–13

WHAT IS GALATIANS ALL ABOUT?

Galatians is one of the apostle Paul's earliest letters, dating to around AD 49. Writing to several regional churches, he could only "marvel" (1:6) that Galatian Christians had turned from their freedom in Jesus back to the rules of Old Testament Judaism. Some people had tried to compel Christians "to live as do the Jews" (2:14), an error even the apostle Peter made (2:11–13). But Paul argued strongly "that no man is justified by the law in the sight of God. . .for, The just shall live by faith" (3:11).

The Galatians were "foolish" and "bewitched" for wandering from their freedom in Christ (3:1). The great apostle urged them to allow God's Spirit to work in their lives, producing "fruit. . .love, joy, peace, longsuffering, gentleness, goodness, faith, meekness, temperance" (5:22–23). Against such things, Paul said, "there is no law."

Old Testament rules don't control our lives as Christians—but God's Spirit must: "Walk in the Spirit, and ye shall not fulfil the lust of the flesh" (5:16).

Reading Plan: Galatians 1–6

WHAT IS EPHESIANS ALL ABOUT?

Dating to about AD 62, toward the end of the apostle Paul's life, Ephesians teaches that Christians are all members of Jesus' "body," the church.

Paul had started the church in Ephesus (Acts 19) and now explained in detail the church members' relationship to Jesus—so that they might "grow up into him in all things, which is the head, even Christ" (4:15). Through Jesus, God reconciled both Jews and Gentiles to Himself (2:11–18). This new life should result in pure, honest living in the church and in the home (chapters 4–6).

Ephesians helps to explain the tension between grace and works in the Christian life. Our salvation is purely a gift of God: "By grace are ye saved through faith; and that not of yourselves: it is the gift of God: not of works, lest any man should boast" (2:8–9). But having received this gift, we have an obligation to work—fight even—for our growth in grace: "Put on the whole armour of God, that ye may be able to stand against the wiles of the devil" (6:11).

Once in Jesus, and members of His body, we are "builded together for an habitation of God through the Spirit" (2:22). What could be a higher calling?

Reading Plan: Ephesians 1–6

WHAT IS PHILIPPIANS ALL ABOUT?

Philippians has been called a "friendship letter" between the apostle Paul and a beloved church. It was written around the early AD 60s by Paul, along with his younger ministry associate, Timothy.

With sixteen references to "joy" and "rejoicing," Philippians is one of the apostle Paul's most upbeat letters—even though he wrote it in "bonds" (1:13), anticipating his own death: "for to me to live is Christ, and to die is gain" (1:21). Paul thanked the church at Philippi for its support (1:5) and encouraged its people to "rejoice in the Lord alway: and again I say, Rejoice" (4:4).

These reminders were needful, as a pair of women in the church, Euodias and Syntyche, were apparently at odds. Paul pleaded that they "be of the same mind in the Lord" (4:2).

These women, and all of us, should "be careful [anxious] for nothing; but in every thing by prayer and supplication with thanksgiving let your requests be made known unto God" (4:6). When we do this, living in the joy of the Lord, "the peace of God, which passeth all understanding, shall keep [our] hearts and minds through Christ Jesus" (4:7).

Reading Plan: Philippians 1–4

WHAT IS COLOSSIANS ALL ABOUT?

Written in the early AD 60s, with the assistance of Timothy, Paul's letter to the Colossians teaches that Jesus Christ is supreme—over everyone and everything.

False teaching ("enticing words," 2:4) had infiltrated the church at Colosse, apparently causing some people to add unnecessary and unhelpful elements to their Christian faith. Paul sent this letter to remind Christians of the superiority of Jesus over Jewish rules and regulations (2:16), angels (2:18), and anything else. Jesus is "the image of the invisible God, the firstborn of every creature" (1:15). Because of these truths, every Christian believer should set their "affection on things above, not on things on the earth" (3:2). "Beware lest any man spoil you through philosophy and vain deceit, after the tradition of men," Paul wrote, "and not after Christ" (2:8).

Our world also offers many "enticing words" that stray from the plain teaching of salvation by grace, through faith in Jesus Christ. Let us, like the Colossians, beware of any idea that disagrees with the "faith which was once delivered unto the saints" (Jude 3).

Reading Plan: Colossians 1–4

WHAT ARE 1 AND 2 THESSALONIANS ALL ABOUT?

Among the apostle Paul's earliest letters, these epistles to believers in the Greek city of Thessalonica emphasized the return of Jesus.

In 1 Thessalonians, Paul taught on the second coming, apparently an issue of some concern to the church. The apostle described how Jesus would return but didn't say exactly when. The important thing, in his words, was "that ye would walk worthy of God, who hath called you unto his kingdom and glory" (2:12).

Shortly after writing 1 Thessalonians, Paul dictated a follow-up. Apparently, a letter falsely claiming to be from him had left the Thessalonians "shaken in mind. . .troubled" (2:2) at the thought that Jesus had already returned. Paul assured them that the event was still future—and urged everyone to live positive and productive lives until the second coming. "If any would not work," Paul commands those who have dropped out in anticipation of Jesus' return, "neither should he eat" (3:10).

As with all of the Christian life, balance is key: We should always look forward to Jesus' return, but we should also be busy doing good while we're here on earth.

Reading Plan: 1 Thessalonians 1–5; 2 Thessalonians 1–3

WHAT IS 1 TIMOTHY ALL ABOUT?

This letter to Paul's protégé Timothy is the first of three "pastoral epistles" and contains the aging apostle's insights for a new generation of church leaders. Timothy had often worked alongside Paul but was now pastoring in Ephesus (1:3). Paul warned him against legalism and false teaching (chapter 1), listed the qualifications for pastors and deacons (chapter 3), and described the behavior of a "good minister of Jesus Christ" (4:6) in the final three chapters.

The ministry, according to Paul, is an honorable profession: "This is a true saying, if a man desire the office of a bishop, he desireth a good work" (3:1). And, Paul added, ministers should be paid well: "Let the elders that rule well be counted worthy of double honour. . . . The labourer is worthy of his reward" (5:17–18).

Though many of us are not professional ministers, Paul's teaching "that thou mayest know how thou oughtest to behave thyself in the house of God" (3:15) can speak to every follower of Jesus.

Reading Plan: 1 Timothy 1–6

WHAT ARE 2 TIMOTHY AND TITUS ALL ABOUT?

These letters comprise the apostle Paul's other pastoral epistles.

Second Timothy may be the last known letter of Paul. Addressed to "my dearly beloved son" (1:2), it warns the young pastor against false teaching and urges him to live a life of purity before his congregation. Timothy should expect trouble ("All that will live godly in Christ Jesus shall suffer persecution," 3:12), but God will be faithful ("The Lord shall deliver me from every evil work, and will preserve me unto his heavenly kingdom," 4:18). Paul begs Timothy to join him as quickly as possible, as "the time of my departure is at hand" (4:6).

Titus was sent to the Mediterranean island of Crete, where the recipient had been placed by Paul to "set in order the things that are wanting, and ordain elders" (1:5) for a fledgling church. Known for their poor behavior ("The Cretians are always liars, evil beasts, slow bellies," 1:12), the people of Crete needed the kind of church leader who holds fast to "the faithful word as he hath been taught, that he may be able by sound doctrine both to exhort and to convince the gainsayers" (1:9).

Paul held his church leaders to a high standard. But it's a standard every Christian must meet. What's good for the pastor is good for everyone else.

Reading Plan: 2 Timothy 1–4; Titus 1–3

WHAT ARE PHILEMON AND HEBREWS ALL ABOUT?

We know that the apostle Paul wrote the letter to Philemon; he's been suggested, along with familiar names such as Luke, Barnabas, and Apollos, as the author of the unattributed letter to the Hebrews.

Philemon, a "fellowlabourer" (verse 1) of Paul, was a man who "refreshed" (verse 7) other Christians with his love and generosity. But the apostle wrote with a request—that Philemon forgive and take back a runaway slave, who apparently accepted Christ under Paul's teaching: "my son Onesimus, whom I have begotten in my bonds" (verse 10).

Hebrews, meanwhile, was written to Jewish Christians—hence the name "Hebrews." The long letter emphasizes the superiority of Christianity to Old Testament Judaism. Jesus is "so much better" (1:4) than angels, Moses, and the previous animal sacrifices. "For if the blood of bulls and of goats, and the ashes of an heifer sprinkling the unclean, sanctifieth to the purifying of the flesh," Hebrews asks, "how much more shall the blood of Christ, who through the eternal Spirit offered himself without spot to God, purge your conscience from dead works to serve the living God?" (9:13–14). Jewish Christians, some of whom were apparently wavering in their commitment to Jesus, were reminded that Christ "is the mediator of a better covenant, which was established upon better promises" (8:6)—a once-for-all sacrifice on the cross that provides "eternal redemption for us" (9:12).

Reading Plan: Philemon; Hebrews 1–6

DO I NEED TO GO TO CHURCH?

*Not forsaking the assembling of ourselves together, as
the manner of some is; but exhorting one another: and
so much the more, as ye see the day approaching.*

HEBREWS 10:25

You've probably heard a fellow Christian say, "I don't need to go to church to be a Christian!" Maybe you've even thought that yourself. But it's not sound thinking—certainly not what the Bible teaches.

God has designed the Christian faith so that it requires fellowship. We are to hold each other accountable, encourage each other, and pray for each other. No one should try to live as a "Lone Ranger" Christian. That just doesn't work.

Consider this: the phrase "one another" appears dozens of times in the New Testament. In the book of Romans alone, Christians are enjoined to be devoted to one another, to live in harmony with one another, to love one another, to accept one another, and to greet one another.

It's probably safe to say that no one can obey all of these "one anothers" without meeting together regularly. That means, among other things, attending a Bible-teaching church.

There are many things you should never neglect, and one of them is meeting together regularly with your brothers and sisters in Christ.

Reading Plan: Hebrews 7–10

WHY DOES GOD ALLOW TOUGH TIMES?

*If ye endure chastening, God dealeth with you as with
sons; for what son is he whom the father chasteneth
not? But if ye be without chastisement, whereof all are
partakers, then are ye bastards, and not sons.*

HEBREWS 12:7–8

When you experience life's difficulties, you might be tempted to believe God is punishing you for some sin you've overlooked. Eventually, that line of reasoning can lead you to wonder *Why me?*

But instead of flooding your mind with such questions when hardship strikes, try focusing on this biblical truth: God is your loving, perfect heavenly Father who wants to teach you more about Himself and how He wants you to live and think.

Jesus promised that His followers would go through tough times. Sometimes, God allows (or even causes) them as a means of correction when we stray—there are many scriptural examples of this, such as the Israelites, King David, and King Solomon. But today's verse says God often uses hardship to discipline, teach, and correct—not to punish us. These measures show the extent of His love—not His anger—toward us.

Reading Plan: Hebrews 11–13

WHAT IS JAMES ALL ABOUT?

James, written around AD 60, was likely penned by a brother of Jesus (1:1; see also Matthew 13:55; Mark 6:3). Its message is that real Christian faith is shown by one's good works.

Though the apostle Paul clearly taught that salvation is by faith alone and not by any works we do (see Romans 3:28), James clarifies that good works will *follow* true faith: "What doth it profit, my brethren, though a man say he hath faith, and have not works?" (2:14). James encouraged Christians, in everyday life, to view trials as opportunities for spiritual growth, to control their tongues, to make peace, to avoid favoritism, and to help the needy. The bottom line? "Therefore to him that knoweth to do good, and doeth it not, to him it is sin" (4:17).

And for anyone who thinks it's enough just to believe in God, James says, "The devils also believe, and tremble" (2:19). Life-changing faith in Jesus is the key.

If you want practical wisdom for living the Christian life, you'll find it all through the book of James.

Reading Plan: James 1–5

WHAT IS 1 PETER ALL ABOUT?

In brief, suffering for the sake of Jesus is noble and good.

The apostle Peter wrote this letter (1:1), with the assistance of Silvanus (or Silas, 5:12), probably around AD 65. It had been some three decades since the death, burial, resurrection, and ascension of Jesus, and the early church was growing. But the Roman Empire had begun persecuting Christians—and Peter assured them that God was still in control: "Beloved, think it not strange concerning the fiery trial which is to try you, as though some strange thing happened unto you" (4:12).

What is the proper response to such suffering? "Rejoice, inasmuch as ye are partakers of Christ's sufferings; that, when his glory shall be revealed, ye may be glad also with exceeding joy" (4:13). Peter could speak with authority on this subject, even apart from the divine inspiration the Holy Spirit gave him. . .he had suffered much for the name of Jesus over the years.

Life may be hard, but God is always good. And for Christians, there's a much better day ahead.

Reading Plan: 1 Peter 1–5

WHAT IS 2 PETER ALL ABOUT?

The letter of 2 Peter was written in the late AD 60s, shortly before Peter's execution. (One tradition says he was crucified, but at his request, upside-down since he didn't feel worthy of dying like his Lord.)

Peter wrote this letter knowing his death was near: "Shortly I must put off this my tabernacle, even as our Lord Jesus Christ hath shewed me" (1:14). So he wanted to warn his readers about false teachers. The Christian qualities of faith, virtue, knowledge, self-control, patience, god-liness, and love (1:5–8), coupled with a reliance on scripture (1:19–21), would help believers avoid the false teachings of those who "privily shall bring in damnable heresies, even denying the Lord that bought them" (2:1).

Peter's experience with Jesus confirmed what he had to say: "We have not followed cunningly devised fables, when we made known unto you the power and coming of our Lord Jesus Christ, but were eyewitnesses of his majesty" (1:16). He didn't want anyone to be "led away with the error of the wicked, [and] fall from your own stedfastness" (3:17). This is a warning applicable to Christians of the twenty-first century, as much as the first.

Reading Plan: 2 Peter 1–3

WHAT IS 1 JOHN ALL ABOUT?

First John tackles a strange heresy that claimed Jesus had been on earth only in spirit, not in body: "Every spirit that confesseth not that Jesus Christ is come in the flesh is not of God: and this is that spirit of antichrist" (4:3). Though the author is not stated, church tradition attributes this letter to the apostle John, who apparently lived to an advanced age. The letter is thought to have been written around AD 92.

John wrote that he knew Jesus personally, as one "which we have looked upon, and our hands have handled" (1:1), and that deep personal knowledge leads to a saving belief in Jesus. Saving belief leads to obedience, but even when we sin, we know that God "is faithful and just to forgive us our sins" when we confess (1:9).

First John includes none of the usual features of a Bible letter—greetings, identification of the author, and the like. But it's a very warm, compassionate letter, written "that ye may *know* that ye have eternal life" (5:13, emphasis added). That's a promise that should encourage every follower of Jesus.

Reading Plan: 1 John 1–5

WHAT ARE 2 JOHN, 3 JOHN, AND JUDE ALL ABOUT?

Addressed to "the elect lady and her children" (2 John 1), perhaps an actual family or, figuratively, a church, 2 John tackles the heretical idea that Jesus had not been physically present on earth. The letter may be a reaction to the "gnostics," who taught that Jesus was spirit only and that He just appeared to suffer and die on the cross. This teaching, of "a deceiver and an antichrist" (verse 7), should be avoided at all costs—to the point of barring one's door against those who believe it (verse 10).

Third John, written to a believer named Gaius, praises those (like Gaius and another Christian named Demetrius) who lead in "charity before the church" (verse 6). But 3 John also has harsh words for Christians like Diotrephes, "who loveth to have the preeminence" (verse 9) and refuse to show kindness and hospitality to traveling evangelists.

Jude, likely written by a half brother of Jesus, tackles the same problems Peter did in his second letter: false teachers who were leading the early church astray. "Murmurers" and "complainers" who were "walking after their own lusts" (verse 16) were apparently using the grace of God as a cover for their sinful lifestyles—and encouraging Christian believers to do the same. True believers, Jude says, reflect God's love, show compassion, and work to pull sinners "out of the fire" (verse 23).

Reading Plan: 2 John; 3 John; Jude

WHAT IS REVELATION ALL ABOUT?

Written by God's "servant John" (1:1), presumably Jesus' beloved disciple, Revelation describes how God will ultimately judge evil and reward His saints.

Jesus Himself arranges for John to receive a "revelation" of "things which must shortly come to pass" (1:1). First, Jesus gives John words of challenge and/or encouragement for seven churches—good, bad, and in-between. Then the vision turns to God's throne room, where a Lamb, looking "as it had been slain" (5:6), breaks seven seals from a scroll, unleashing war, famine, and other disasters on earth. A dragon and two beasts, allied against God, arise to demand worship from the people who had been killed in the earlier catastrophes. The satanic forces and their human followers incur seven "vials of the wrath of God" (16:1), which bring plagues, darkness, and huge hailstones on earth. "Babylon the great," the evil, arrogant world system, is destroyed (18:2) just before an angel from heaven seizes Satan, "that old serpent" (20:2), and imprisons him for a thousand years. After a brief release to instigate worldwide war, Satan is thrown into "the lake of fire and brimstone," to be "tormented day and night for ever and ever" (20:10). God unveils "a new heaven and a new earth" (21:1), where He will "wipe away all tears" (21:4) from His people's eyes.

An old Southern gospel song says, "I've read the back of the Book and we win!" God has given us a preview of how this world ends—and the new-and-improved world we'll enjoy forever. The curse of sin gone, we'll live in perfect fellowship with the Lord Himself, reigning with Him "for ever and ever" (22:5). This should put any bad day into perspective!

Reading Plan: Revelation 1–3

WHAT MAKES GOD WORTHY OF PRAISE?

*Thou art worthy, O Lord, to receive glory and honour
and power: for thou hast created all things, and for
thy pleasure they are and were created.*

REVELATION 4:11

In Revelation 4, John related his spectacular vision of God's throne in heaven. John must have been awestruck by this vision, which included four angelic creatures continuously crying out day and night:

*Holy, holy, holy
Lord God Almighty,'
which was, and is, and is to come.*
(Revelation 4:8)

And verse 11 gives these amazing words of praise for our almighty, all-loving Creator:

*Thou art worthy, O Lord,
to receive glory and honour and power:
for thou hast created all things,
and for thy pleasure
they are and were created.*

Faced with the God whose power created all things—and whose love brings people close to Himself through His Son's death and resurrection—the twenty-four elders in this vision could not help but shout.

God, the all-powerful Creator and loving heavenly Father, is more than worthy of your praise and adoration. That is your ultimate purpose.

Reading Plan: Revelation 4–6

WHAT WILL HEAVEN BE LIKE?

They shall hunger no more, neither thirst any more; neither shall the sun light on them, nor any heat. For the Lamb which is in the midst of the throne shall feed them, and shall lead them unto living fountains of waters: and God shall wipe away all tears from their eyes.

REVELATION 7:16–17

If you've come this far in the Bible, you already know that suffering in this world is just part of the deal for us Christian men.

But today's scripture offers hope for those who suffer heartache, loss, failure, sickness, or disappointment. One day, Jesus will wipe away every tear from our eyes and welcome us into heaven. On that day, the only tears we'll shed will be tears of joy. We'll never hunger or thirst for anything, for Jesus our Lord will be our all.

Suffering, pain, and death result from sin's curse. But all that will change:

> *No longer will there be any curse. The throne of God and of the Lamb will be in the city, and his servants will serve him. They will see his face, and his name will be on their foreheads. There will be no more night. They will not need the light of a lamp or the light of the sun, for the Lord God will give them light. And they will reign for ever and ever.*
> REVELATION 22:3–5 NIV

Reading Plan: Revelation 7–10

WHAT BECOMES OF THE DEVIL?

And I heard a loud voice saying in heaven, Now is come
salvation, and strength, and the kingdom of our God, and the
power of his Christ: for the accuser of our brethren is cast
down, which accused them before our God day and night.

REVELATION 12:10

The Bible refers to the devil as "Satan" fifty-two times, but he also has other names: the tempter, the evil one, the father of lies, the ruler of the kingdom of the air, and many more. Today's scripture calls the devil "the accuser of the brethren," meaning that to this day he comes before God to declare our guilt for our sins.

The thought that the very embodiment of evil brings his accusations against us to God is quite disturbing, but the Bible tells us that his recriminations will come to nothing in the end.

By dying on the cross for us, Jesus allowed us to triumph over Satan "by the blood of the Lamb" (Revelation 12:11 NIV). In other words, the devil's accusations are meaningless because Jesus paid the full price for our sins. Now, even though the devil's allegations may be factually accurate, we "have redemption through his blood, the forgiveness of sins, in accordance with the riches of God's grace" (Ephesians 1:7 NIV).

And Satan? Ultimately, God will toss him "into the lake of burning sulfur, where the beast and the false prophet had been thrown. They will be tormented day and night for ever and ever" (Revelation 20:10 NIV).

Reading Plan: Revelation 11–13

CAN I TRUST GOD'S JUDGMENTS?

And I heard another out of the altar say, Even so,
Lord God Almighty, true and righteous are thy judgments.

REVELATION 16:7

Those of us in the West tend to be very democratic in our thinking—sometimes overly so. For example, when polls show that a big majority holds a certain position, people tend to take that position as absolute truth.

But majority belief doesn't make something true. Opinions can be—and very often are—wrong. But what about God's opinions? Well, since the word *opinion* is defined as a judgment formed about something that isn't necessarily based on facts, God doesn't hold "opinions." Instead, He bases His judgments on His perfect knowledge and His sense of what is right and just.

The apostle Paul pointed to this truth when he wrote, "Let God be true, and every human being a liar" (Romans 3:4 NIV).

You can't always trust the judgments of fallen humanity, even when it involves something most people believe. People can be wrong—sometimes in overwhelming numbers. Nobody, no matter how well-educated, possesses perfect knowledge of all things. But God does. His judgments are 100 percent true, 100 percent of the time.

Reading Plan: Revelation 14–16

WHAT IS THE MARRIAGE SUPPER OF THE LAMB?

And he saith unto me, Write, Blessed are they which are called unto the marriage supper of the Lamb. And he saith unto me, These are the true sayings of God.

REVELATION 19:9

Most all of us have been invited to at least one wedding. Usually, the invitation begins something like this: "Jim and Stacey request the honor of your presence. . ."

Did you know that you, as a follower of Jesus Christ, have been invited to a wedding celebration? Not only that, you've been chosen as one of the guests of honor!

The Bible refers to Jesus as our "Bridegroom" and His church (which includes all believers) as the "Bride." As a follower of Jesus Christ, you've been betrothed to Him, and the "marriage" will be completed when He gathers you and the rest of His church for a wonderful and blessed wedding supper of the Lamb.

If you know Jesus Christ as your Lord and Savior, you are one of the "blessed," having been assured of an eternity in God's heavenly kingdom. Even more, you've been invited to the most amazing party in history.

As God's angel stated, "These are the true sayings of God." You can count on this invitation.

Reading Plan: Revelation 17–19

WHEN WILL JESUS RETURN?

He which testifieth these things saith, Surely I
come quickly. Amen. Even so, come, Lord Jesus.

REVELATION 22:20

Revelation includes some frightening, deeply disturbing images of events that will happen on earth before Jesus returns. But then it delivers a great message at the end: we win!

The book's final three chapters teach that the devil and his followers will be tossed into a fiery lake of burning sulfur, where they will be tormented forever (Revelation 20:10). Next, God will establish a new heaven and a new earth to replace the old ones (21:1). There, "no more death or mourning or crying or pain" will exist, "for the old order of things has passed away" (21:4 NIV). Revelation 22:12 also contains the wonderful promise that Jesus will return to earth to reward those who faithfully follow Him.

Indeed, the Bible promises that Jesus will return to earth one day in an event called His "Second Coming." But before Jesus was arrested and crucified, He told His followers, "About that day or hour no one knows" (Matthew 24:36 NIV). We can't say when Jesus will return. So we should always be ready, doing all we can to prepare others as well.

Reading Plan: Revelation 20–22

SCRIPTURE INDEX

GENESIS

1:1. . . . . Day 1
1:6 –7. Day 1
1:9. . . . . Day 1
1:11. . . . . Day 1
1:14 –15. . . . . Day 1
2:7. . . . . Day 1
3:1. . . . . Day 1
3:15. . . . . Day 2
4:6–7. . . . . Day 2
6:5. . . . . Day 2
6:9. . . . . Day 3
8:20. . . . . Day 3
12:1, 4. Day 4
12:2. . . . . Day 5
12:3. . . . . Days 4, 273
15:2–3 . . . . Day 5
21:1–2 . . . . Day 6
21:6. . . . . Day 6
22:2. . . . . Day 7
22:16–18 . . . . Day 7
25:33–34 . . . . Day 8
29:25. . . . . Day 9
30:22–24 . . . . Day 10
32:10. . . . . Days 8, 12
32:25–26 . . . . Day 11
35:10. Day 12
39:3–4 . . . . Day 13
41:15–16 . . . . Day 14
42:21. Day 15
42:22. Day 15
45:4–5 . . . . Day 16
46:3–4 . . . . Day 17
50:20–21 . . . . Day 18

EXODUS

2:24. . . . . Day 19
4:10. . . . . Day 20
7:1–2 . . . . Day 21
12:13. . . . . Days 19, 22
13:21–22 . . . . Day 33
14:8. . . . . Day 23

14:13. Day 23
17:3. . . . . Day 24
17:4. . . . . Day 24
20:8. . . . . Day 29
20:12–17 . . . . Day 25
20:14. . . . . Day 173
20:17. . . . . Day 123
22:21. Day 26
25:8. . . . . Day 27
28:1. . . . . Day 28
31:12–13 . . . . Day 29
32:19–20 . . . . Day 30
34:29. Day 31
36:5–6 . . . . Day 32
40:38. Day 33

LEVITICUS

7:11–12 . . . . Day 35
7:27. . . . . Day 34
8:1–3 . . . . Day 36
11:44. . . . . Days 34, 37
11:46 –47 . . . . Day 37
13:1–2 . . . . Day 38
15:31. Day 39
16:34. Day 40
17:11. Day 34
19:17–18 . . . . Day 41
19:18. . . . . Days 26, 68
22:19–20 . . . . Day 42
25:14. Day 43
26:3–4 . . . . Day 44

NUMBERS

4:49. . . . . Day 46
6:1–2 . . . . Day 47
7:1. . . . . Day 48
7:89. . . . . Day 48
10:29, 32. . . . . Day 49
10:35. Day 50
11:15. Day 50
11:17. Day 50

14:3 . . . . Day 51
14:18 . . . . Day 45
16:3 . . . . Day 52
16:31–32 . . . . Day 52
17:5 . . . . Day 53
17:8 . . . . Day 53
20:12 . . . . Day 72
21:5 . . . . Day 54
21:8–9 . . . . Day 54
22:28 . . . . Day 55
22:34 . . . . Day 55
23:19 . . . . Day 57
26:10–11 . . . . Day 56
30:1–2 . . . . Day 57
32:23 . . . . Day 58
33:1–2 . . . . Day 59
35:10–11 . . . . Day 60

DEUTERONOMY

4:9 . . . . Day 62
6:3 . . . . Day 61
6:4 . . . . Day 61
6:4–5 . . . . Day 63
6:5 . . . . Day 61
6:15 . . . . Day 61
10:12–13 . . . . Day 64
12:12 . . . . Day 65
15:11 . . . . Day 66
18:17–18 . . . . Day 67
22:1 . . . . Day 68
24:1 . . . . Day 69
28:1–2 . . . . Day 70
28:15 . . . . Day 70
30:19–20 . . . . Day 71
34:4 . . . . Day 72
34:5–6 . . . . Day 61

JOSHUA

1:9 . . . . Day 74
3:7 . . . . Day 74
4:14 . . . . Day 74
7:19 . . . . Day 75
9:14 . . . . Day 73
9:15 . . . . Day 76
13:1 . . . . Day 77

14:6–7 . . . . Day 78
14:14 . . . . Day 78
18:3 . . . . Day 79
21:43, 45 . . . . Day 80
24:15 . . . . Day 81
24:23 . . . . Day 73
24:31 . . . . Day 81

JUDGES

1:21 . . . . Day 82
2:2-3 . . . . Day 82
2:18 . . . . Day 87
4:8–9 . . . . Day 83
7:2 . . . . Day 84
9:56–57 . . . . Day 85
11:1 . . . . Day 86
11:30–31 . . . . Day 86
14:19 . . . . Day 87
17:5–6 . . . . Day 88
17:6 . . . . Day 82
21:25 . . . . Days 82, 89

RUTH

1:16 . . . . Day 90

1 SAMUEL

4:3 . . . . Day 92
7:3 . . . . Day 93
12:23 . . . . Day 94
13:14 . . . . Day 95
16:7 . . . . Day 96
17:45 . . . . Day 97
18:1 . . . . Day 98
19:2 . . . . Day 98
23:7 . . . . Day 99
25:30–31 . . . . Day 100
25:32–33 . . . . Day 100
26:10–11 . . . . Day 101
26:23 . . . . Day 91
30:8 . . . . Day 102

2 SAMUEL

3:27, 30 . . . . Day 104
5:9–10 . . . . Day 105
7:16 . . . . Day 103

9:7. Day 106
11:2–3 . . . . Day 107
12:7. . . . . Day 103
13:21–22 . . . . Day 108
15:14. . . . . Day 109
18:32–33 . . . . Day 110
19:2–4 . . . . Day 111
22:2–4 . . . . Day 112
23:1. . . . . Day 143
24:1. . . . . Day 141
24:10. . . . . Day 113

1 KINGS

3:11–12 . . . . Day 115
3:12. . . . . Day 196
7:1. Day 116
8:57–58 . . . . Day 117
11:9–10 . . . . Day 118
11:11. . . . . Day 118
13:8–9 . . . . Day 119
15:1–3 . . . . Day 120
17:1. . . . . Day 121
19:14. . . . . Day 122
19:18. . . . . Day 122
21:2–3 . . . . Day 123
22:13–14 . . . . Day 124

2 KINGS

4:2–3 . . . . Day 126
6:15. . . . . Day 127
6:16. . . . . Day 127
6:17. . . . . Day 127
10:16–17 . . . . Day 128
10:30. . . . . Day 128
10:31. . . . . Day 128
12:6–7 . . . . Day 129
14:3. . . . . Day 130
14:11–12 . . . . Day 130
17:6. . . . . Day 125
17:15. . . . . Day 131
17:18. . . . . Day 131
18:5. . . . . Day 153
18:11–12 . . . . Day 132
20:1. . . . . Day 133
20:5. . . . . Day 133

22:1–2 . . . . Day 134
24:8–9 . . . . Day 135
24:14. . . . . Day 125
25:4. . . . . Day 125

1 CHRONICLES

5:20. . . . . Day 137
10:13–14 . . . . Day 138
12:32. . . . . Day 139
17:23. . . . . Day 140
21:1–2 . . . . Day 141
22:11-13. . . . . Day 142
25:1. . . . . Day 143
28:9. . . . . Day 144

2 CHRONICLES

6:3–4 . . . . Day 146
8:11–12 . . . . Day 147
10:6–7 . . . . Day 148
10:11. . . . . Day 148
14:2. . . . . Day 149
15:2. . . . . Day 149
16:10. . . . . Day 149
20:12. . . . . Day 150
24:2. . . . . Day 151
24:17–18 . . . . Day 151
26:4–5 . . . . Day 152
26:21. . . . . Day 152
29:11. . . . . Day 153
33:11–12 . . . . Day 154
33:13. . . . . Day 154
36:12. . . . . Days 135, 155
36:15–16 . . . . Day 155

EZRA

4:2. Day 157
4:3. Day 157
7:6. Day 158
7:10. . . . . Day 158
9:1. Day 159
9:3. Day 159

NEHEMIAH

1:1. Day 160
1:11. . . . . Day 160

6:15–16 . . . . Day 161
6:16. . . . . Days 160, 161
6:17. . . . . Day 161
8:10. . . . . Day 162
10:29. . . . . Day 163
13:25–26 . . . . Day 164

ESTHER

1:7. . . . . Day 165
4:15–16 . . . . Day 166
7:2. . . . . Day 167
7:3–4 . . . . Day 167

JOB

1:1. . . . . Days 168, 169, 197
2:9. . . . . Day 168
6:9–10 . . . . Day 169
12:7–8 . . . . Day 170
16:1–3 . . . . Day 171
22:5. . . . . Day 168
24:24–25 . . . . Day 172
31:1. . . . . Day 173
32:2–3 . . . . Day 174
38:1–3 . . . . Day 175
38:4. . . . . Day 175
42:2. . . . . Day 168

PSALMS

3:1–4 . . . . Day 109
15:2, 4. . . . . Day 76
16:10. . . . . Day 177
18:2. . . . . Day 112
18:29. . . . . Day 167
19:14. . . . . Day 178
32:1–2 . . . . Day 179
32:3–4 . . . . Day 179
32:5. . . . . Day 179
34:15. . . . . Day 235
37:4. . . . . Day 93
37:7–8 . . . . Day 180
42:5. . . . . Day 181
46:1. . . . . Day 60
51:1. . . . . Day 182
51:3–4 . . . . Day 182
55:16–17 . . . . Day 315

57:1. . . . . Day 183
69:1–2 . . . . Day 184
73:25–26 . . . . Day 185
82:2–4 . . . . Day 186
86:6–7 . . . . Day 187
90:8. . . . . Day 58
91:4–5 . . . . Day 183
92:4. . . . . Day 188
103:11–12 . . . . Day 189
107:8–9 . . . . Day 190
118:8–9 . . . . Day 191
119:10–11 . . . . Day 192
119:71. . . . . Day 133
127:1. . . . . Days 146, 193
139:2. . . . . Day 178
139:23–24 . . . . Day 194
144:1–2 . . . . Day 195
150:6. . . . . Day 176

PROVERBS

1:7. . . . . Day 196
3:5–6 . . . . Days 33, 93, 238
4:7. . . . . Day 196
4:23. . . . . Day 178
9:10. . . . . Day 270
9:10–11 . . . . Day 197
11:24–25 . . . . Day 198
12:26. . . . . Day 342
14:12. . . . . Day 89
15:22. . . . . Day 237
15:29. . . . . Day 315
16:18. . . . . Days 130, 255
18:7. . . . . Day 199
20:1. . . . . Day 213
22:1. . . . . Day 200
22:17. . . . . Day 196
23:29–30 . . . . Day 213
24:17–18 . . . . Day 201
29:7. . . . . Day 202

ECCLESIASTES

1:1. . . . . Day 203
1:2. . . . . Day 203
1:12. . . . . Day 203
1:16. . . . . Day 203
12:13. . . . . Days 203, 204

SONG OF SOLOMON

1:15. . . . . Day 205
1:16. . . . . Day 205

ISAIAH

1:17. . . . . Day 202
6:8. Day 207
9:6. Day 208
12:2. . . . . Day 209
19:22. . . . . Day 210
22:12–13 . . . . Day 211
25:8. . . . . Day 212
28:1. . . . . Day 213
33:14. . . . . Day 214
33:15–16 . . . . Day 214
37:36. . . . . Day 215
38:17. . . . . Day 133
40:8. . . . . Day 236
42:1. . . . . Day 216
43:25. . . . . Day 217
46:8–10 . . . . Day 218
46:10. . . . . Day 278
50:6–7 . . . . Day 219
53:3, 5. . . . . Day 220
53:5. . . . . Day 206
59:1–2 . . . . Day 221
60:1–3 . . . . Day 222
61:1–2 . . . . Day 206
64:8. . . . . Day 229
66:2. . . . . Day 223

JEREMIAH

5:15. . . . . Day 224
5:30–31 . . . . Day 225
9:23–24 . . . . Day 226
12:6. . . . . Day 227
13:11. . . . . Day 228
17:9. . . . . Day 113
18:4. . . . . Day 229
18:6. . . . . Day 224
20:7–8 . . . . Day 230
20:11–12 . . . . Day 230
25:15. . . . . Day 231
27:6. . . . . Day 232
27:8–9 . . . . Day 232

29:11–13 . . . . Day 233
32:6–7, 9 . . . . Day 234
33:2–3 . . . . Day 235
36:23. . . . . Day 224
36:32. . . . . Day 236
40:13–14 . . . . Day 237
42:4. . . . . Day 238
45:3. . . . . Day 239
45:5. . . . . Day 239
48:7–8 . . . . Day 240
50:6. . . . . Day 241
51:17–19 . . . . Day 242

LAMENTATIONS

1:5. Day 243
1:16. . . . . Day 243
3:22–24 . . . . Day 244
5:22. . . . . Day 243

EZEKIEL

6:9. Day 246
11:19. . . . . Day 247
14:6. . . . . Day 248
16:13–14 . . . . Day 249
18:4–5, 9 . . . . Day 245
18:23. . . . . Day 250
18:32. . . . . Day 245
22:30. . . . . Day 251
24:15–17 . . . . Day 252
27:1–2 . . . . Day 253
28:2. . . . . Day 254
31:10–11 . . . . Day 255
33:31. . . . . Day 256
36:26–27 . . . . Day 257
37:2–3 . . . . Day 258
37:7–8, 10 . . . . Day 245
40:4. . . . . Day 259
44:5. . . . . Day 260
45:10–12 . . . . Day 261
47:6–8 . . . . Day 262

DANIEL

3:16–18 . . . . Day 264
3:25. . . . . Day 263
6:10. . . . . Day 265

9:18. Day 266
10:18–19 . . . . Day 267

HOSEA

1:2. Day 268
10:12. . . . . Day 269
14:4. . . . . Day 268
14:9. . . . . Day 270

JOEL

2:11. . . . . Day 271
2:28. . . . . Day 271

OBADIAH

10 . . . . Day 273

JONAH

4:2–3 . . . . Day 274

MICAH

2:12. . . . . Day 275
5:2. Day 275
6:8. . . . . Days 186, 202, 275
7:18. . . . . Day 275

NAHUM

3:6. Day 276

HABAKKUK

1:6. Day 276
2:20. . . . . Day 276

ZEPHANIAH

1:2. Day 277
3:8. Day 277
3:13. . . . . Day 277

HAGGAI

2:6–7 . . . . Day 277

ZECHARIAH

7:9 –10 . . . . Day 279
10:1. . . . . Day 280
12:10. . . . . Day 278
14:3–4, 9 . . . . Day 278

MALACHI

1:8. Day 281
3:10. . . . . Day 198
3:14. . . . . Day 281
4:2. Day 281

MATTHEW

3:17. . . . . Day 343
5:6. Day 190
5:13. . . . . Day 228
5:14. . . . . Day 325
5:14–16 . . . . Day 222
5:36–37 . . . . Day 57
5:44–45 . . . . Day 100
5:45. . . . . Day 325
6:9–13 . . . . Day 305
6:14–15 . . . . Day 297
6:26. . . . . Day 280
7:9–11 . . . . Day 334
7:12. . . . . Days 26, 41, 283
8:16–17 . . . . Day 284
10:29–31 . . . . Day 285
12:36–37 . . . . Day 286
13:38. . . . . Day 325
16:13–15 . . . . Day 287
16:16. . . . . Day 287
16:17. . . . . Day 287
18:21–22 . . . . Day 288
19:6. . . . . Day 69
19:7. . . . . Day 69
20:21. . . . . Day 289
20:23. . . . . Day 289
20:26–28 . . . . Day 289
20:28. . . . . Day 216
22:36. . . . . Day 63
22:37–38 . . . . Day 63
23:5–7 . . . . Day 290
23:11–12 . . . . Day 290
24:36. . . . . Day 365
25:34. . . . . Day 325
25:40. . . . . Days 186, 202, 291
25:40–43 . . . . Day 279
26:39. . . . . Day 292
26:42. . . . . Day 292
28:5–6 . . . . Day 293

MARK

2:27. Day 29
6:46. . . . . Day 295
9:24. . . . . Days 185, 296
10:43–45 . . . . Day 294
11:25. . . . . Day 297
12:30–31 . . . . Day 298
14:27–28 . . . . Day 299
14:29. . . . . Day 299
14:51–52 . . . . Day 294

LUKE

1:1. Day 300
1:3. Day 300
2:9. Day 301
2:10–11 . . . . Day 301
2:14. . . . . Day 301
3:38. . . . . Day 300
4:6–7 . . . . Day 302
6:27–28 . . . . Day 303
6:35. . . . . Day 325
8:38–39 . . . . Day 304
11:1. . . . . Day 305
12:32. . . . . Day 306
15:17. . . . . Day 307
15:20–21 . . . . Day 307
17:13–14 . . . . Day 308
17:15–16 . . . . Day 308
18:11–12 . . . . Day 309
18:14. . . . . Day 309
19:10. . . . . Day 300
20:36. . . . . Day 325
21:3–4 . . . . Day 310
22:42. . . . . Day 85
23:40–41 . . . . Day 311
23:42. . . . . Day 311
23:43. . . . . Day 311

JOHN

3:7. . . . . Day 312
3:14–15 . . . . Day 54
4:23. . . . . Day 313
4:24. . . . . Day 281
6:5–6 . . . . Day 314
7:38. . . . . Day 262

8:31. . . . . Day 325
9:31. . . . . Day 315
10:10. . . . . Day 312
10:27–29 . . . . Day 316
10:28. . . . . Day 316
10:30. . . . . Day 312
10:38. . . . . Day 284
13:34–35 . . . . Day 317
14:10. . . . . Day 67
14:15. . . . . Day 63
15:4. . . . . Day 228
15:7. . . . . Day 93
15:13. . . . . Days 166, 219
15:15. . . . . Day 325
16:23–24 . . . . Day 318
16:33. . . . . Day 169
17:1–2 . . . . Day 312
17:16–17 . . . . Day 319
17:18. . . . . Day 320
20:17. . . . . Day 325
20:21–22 . . . . Day 320
20:31. . . . . Day 312
21:7. . . . . Day 312

ACTS

1:3. . . . . Day 321
1:8. . . . . Day 321
2:24. . . . . Day 177
4:32. . . . . Day 322
7:39–40 . . . . Day 323
8:30–31 . . . . Day 324
8:37. . . . . Day 324
9:2. . . . . Day 321
10:34. . . . . Day 186
11:26. . . . . Day 325
13:1. . . . . Day 326
13:2. . . . . Day 326
14:26–28 . . . . Day 326
16:23–25 . . . . Day 327
18:24–25 . . . . Day 328
22:14–15 . . . . Day 329

23:5. . . . . Day 330
23:11. . . . . Day 330
26:19–20 . . . . Day 331
26:28. . . . . Days 325, 331
4:25. . . . . Day 340

ROMANS

3:4. . . . . Day 363
3:22. . . . . Day 332
5:1. . . . . Day 332
5:8. . . . . Day 274
5:9. Day 22
5:10. . . . . Day 329
5:11. . . . . Day 333
6:11. . . . . Day 332
6:18. . . . . Day 323
6:23. . . . . Day 131
8:11. . . . . Day 332
8:28. . . . . Day 16
10:9. . . . . Day 316
10:11. . . . . Day 334
12:1. . . . . Days 3, 332
12:2. . . . . Day 335
12:19. . . . . Day 104
12:21. . . . . Day 332
13:1. . . . . Day 101
13:8. . . . . Day 298
13:13. . . . . Day 213
14:19–20 . . . . Day 336

1 CORINTHIANS

1:10. . . . . Day 337
2:9. . . . . Day 252
4:7. . . . . Day 249
5:10. . . . . Day 342
5:13. . . . . Day 337
6:9. . . . . Day 337
6:19–20 . . . . Day 27
10:13. . . . . Days 141, 338
10:14. . . . . Day 242
10:31. . . . . Day 281
12:31. . . . . Days 337, 339
13:4–7 . . . . Day 339
13:13. . . . . Day 339
15:14, 17. . . . . Day 340

2 CORINTHIANS

4:18. . . . . Day 127
5:17. . . . . Day 257
5:20. . . . . Day 329
5:21. . . . . Day 42
6:14–15 . . . . Day 342
9:7. . . . . Day 198
11:21. . . . . Day 341
11:23. . . . . Day 341
12:7. . . . . Day 341
12:9. . . . . Day 341
13:5. . . . . Day 341
13:14. . . . . Day 343

GALATIANS

1:6. . . . . Day 344
2:14. . . . . Day 344
3:1. . . . . Day 344
3:11. . . . . Day 344
5:14. . . . . Day 25
5:16. . . . . Day 344
5:22–23 . . . . Day 344
6:1. . . . . Day 164
6:7. Day 9
6:7–8 . . . . Day 44

EPHESIANS

1:7. . . . . Day 362
2:4–5 . . . . Days 258, 267
2:5. Day 53
2:8–9 . . . . Day 345
2:10. . . . . Days 28, 153
2:22. . . . . Day 345
3:20. . . . . Day 79
4:15. . . . . Day 345
4:29. . . . . Day 199
4:31. . . . . Day 231
5:18. . . . . Day 213
6:10–20 . . . . Day 195
6:11. . . . . Day 345

PHILIPPIANS

1:3–5 . . . . Day 106
1:6. . . . . Day 229
1:13. . . . . Day 346

1:21. . . . . Day 346
2:3–4 . . . . Days 85, 152
4:2. . . . . Day 346
4:4. . . . . Days 65, 346
4:6. . . . . Day 346
4:6–7 . . . . Day 209
4:7. . . . . Day 346

COLOSSIANS

1:15. Day 347
2:4. . . . . Day 347
2:8. . . . . Day 347
2:16–17 . . . . Day 29
3:2. . . . . Day 347

1 THESSALONIANS

2:11–12 . . . . Day 47
2:12. Day 348
4:3. . . . . Day 319
5:16–18 . . . . Day 111
5:24. Day 80

2 THESSALONIANS

2:2. . . . . Day 348
3:10. Day 348

1 TIMOTHY

2:1–2 . . . . Day 251
3:1. . . . . Day 349
3:15. Day 349
4:6. . . . . Day 349
5:17–18 . . . . Day 349

2 TIMOTHY

1:2. . . . . Day 350
2:13. Day 10
3:12. Day 350
4:6. . . . . Day 350
4:18. Day 350

TITUS

1:5. . . . . Day 350
1:9. . . . . Day 350
1:12. Day 350

PHILEMON

1 . . . . Day 351
7 . . . . Day 351
10 . . . . Day 351

HEBREWS

1:4. . . . . Day 351
3:3. . . . . Day 67
4:16. Day 187
6:18. Day 60
8:6. . . . . Day 351
9:12. Day 351
9:13–14 . . . . Day 351
9:15. Day 40
9:22. . . . . Days 22, 42
9:27. Day 211
10:25. . . . . Day 352
10:39. . . . . Day 264
11:8. Day 4
12:2. Day 89
12:7–8 . . . . Day 353
12:11. . . . . Day 243
13:5. Day 117
13:14. . . . . Day 59
13:15. . . . . Day 35

JAMES

1:5. . . . . Days 115, 196
1:13. Day 141
1:17. Day 306
1:20. Day 231
2:14. Day 354
2:17. Day 202
2:19. Day 354
4:10. Day 135
4:17. Day 354

1 PETER

2:5. . . . . Day 36
2:9. . . . . Day 36
2:12. Day 161
2:24–25 . . . . Day 220
3:12. . . . . Days 137, 315
3:15. . . . . Days 49, 259, 324
4:12. Day 355

4:13. Day 355	20:10. . . . . Day 362
5:7. Day 181	21:1. . . . . Day 359
	21:4. . . . . Days 212, 359, 365

2 PETER

1:14. . . . . Day 356	22:3–5 . . . . Day 361
1:16. . . . . Day 356	22:5. . . . . Day 359
2:1. . . . . Day 356	22:20. . . . . Day 365
3:9. . . . . Days 224, 250	
3:17. . . . . Day 356	

1 JOHN

1:1. Day 357
1:9. . . . . Days 182, 357
4:3. Day 357
4:8. Day 306
4:18. . . . . Day 214
5:13. . . . . Day 357
5:14. . . . . Day 187
5:14–15 . . . . Days 140, 315
5:21. . . . . Day 248

2 JOHN

1 . . . . Day 358
7 . . . . Day 358

3 JOHN

6 . . . . Day 358
9 . . . . Day 358

JUDE

3 . . . . Day 347
16 . . . . Day 358
23 . . . . Day 358

REVELATION

1:1. Day 359
4:8. Day 360
4:11. . . . . Day 360
5:6. Day 359
7:16–17 . . . . Day 361
12:10. . . . . Day 362
12:11. . . . . Day 362
16:1. . . . . Day 359
16:7. . . . . Day 363
19:9. . . . . Day 364
20:2. . . . . Day 359